Levinas and the Night of Being

Levinas and the Night of Being

A Guide to *Totality and Infinity*

Raoul Moati

Translated by Daniel Wyche

FORDHAM UNIVERSITY PRESS

New York 2017

This book was first published in French as *Événements
nocturnes: Essai sur "Totalité et infini,"* by Raoul Moati
© Éditions Hermann, 2012.

This book's publication was supported by a subvention
from the University of Chicago's Visiting Committee to
the Division of Humanities.

Library of Congress Cataloging-in-Publication Data is
available online at http://catalog.loc.gov.

Printed in the United States of America
19 18 17   5 4 3 2 1
First edition

CONTENTS

Perhaps the only thing as difficult as translating the work of Emmanuel Levinas is translating a book about Levinas. It goes without saying that Levinas's prose, choice of technical terms, and so on are very much his own. Indeed, over the course of this translation project, more than one of my conversations with Raoul Moati would end with a sentence of the form, "Yes, it is very strange in French too." Despite those difficulties, one of the greatest strengths of Moati's reading of *Totality and Infinity* here is his markedly deep insight into, and therefore faithfulness to, Levinas's own style and its necessity to the latter's overall project. But it is in turn for that reason that the greatest challenges that arose for me in translating Moati's *Événements nocturnes: Essai sur "Totalité et infini"* (2012) were ultimately raised by Levinas's text.

Alphonso Lingis, in his translation of *Totality and Infinity*, made an admirable attempt to remain faithful to Levinas's voice, and in so doing he has set the standard for English translations of most of the technical vocabulary and important turns of phrase. But despite those efforts, Levinas's style can still sound odd even to English ears that are used to it and remains all the more difficult for those who are not. It is here that I've faced the most daunting task of this project: navigating between a drive toward lucid and properly English prose and the necessity of remaining faithful not just to the content of the original but to the carefully chosen technical terms that populate these texts, however strange or unintuitive they may seem at first. My goal then has been to make Moati's text as fruitful and rewarding as possible to those who choose to take it up, by rendering it in a way that retains both his voice and that of Levinas but minimizes unnecessary obscurity by translating, rather than transliterating, the grammar, style, and vocabulary into English without betraying any technical necessity. If I have even begun to approach such a balance, then I consider my work here a success.

We have had to make several important choices about how to represent a number of technical terms, including when and when not to depart from

Lingis's standardizations. Such terms are thus noted when they occur for the first time, and the French is included in brackets when it is clear that it will help with a distinction that would not be apparent in English. It is worth highlighting some of the more important instances here, and it should be kept in mind that all these choices were made after long and in-depth discussion with Moati.

First, in the original, each of the two crucial French terms for "the Other" and "other," *autrui* and *autre*, appear in both capitalized and lowercase versions, depending on an entire range of criteria particular to Levinas's thought. This distinction doesn't exist in English, and so Lingis addressed this problem by rendering *autrui* as "Other," and *autre* as "other," with the approval of Levinas himself. As he says in an early note on this point, "With the author's permission, we are translating 'autrui' (the personal Other, the you) by 'Other,' and 'autre' by 'other.' In doing so, we regrettably sacrifice the possibility of reproducing the author's use of capital or small letters with both these terms in the French text."[1] After a great deal of discussion, we have chosen to rigorously follow Lingis's now standard rendering, insofar as it does not contradict Moati's explicit goal of demonstrating that *autrui* (Other) is the concretization of *autre* (other). For Moati's discussion of concretization in general, see "Nocturnal Phenomenology," the third section of chapter 1, as well as the beginning of chapter 2.

We have also decided to follow Lingis in the use of "dwelling" for the term *demeure*, the place that the subject inhabits, the place where he or she lives or resides in the full sense explicated by Levinas and here by Moati. This choice has the added bonus of allowing an implicit emphasis on the continuity of this concept with the verb form *demeurer*, to "dwell or reside," but also to "remain, to stay," and so on. For the sake of making the distinction between the two concepts clear, the English "home" has been reserved for the French *maison*.

Le moi appears as "the I" in Lingis, but I have departed from his usage, and this term is translated here "the self" and "the separated self," when it appears as *le moi separé*.

The numerous variations on the term *être* also provided some difficulty in attempts to distinguish them in English, although all instances of the word *être* itself are rendered here simply as "being." The term *étant* proved more of a challenge, but we have followed Lingis in rendering *étant* as "existent" in all cases. Part of the difficulty there, however, comes from Levinas's, and thus Moati's, use of the term *éxistant*, which we have simply transliterated as "existant," with an *a* rather than an *e*, as it appears in the French. In all cases in which "existent" and "existant" appear near each other in the text, the original French (*étant* and *éxistant*) appear in brackets, and we have included Lingis's own note on this point, for reference.[2] Finally, we have distinguished *existence* from *l'éxister*, by transliterating the former as simply "existence," and rendering *l'éxister* with "existing," or sometimes "to exist," depending on context.

Along with these issues of technical vocabulary, it should be noted that many of the sources that Moati refers to in this text are not as yet translated into English. Moati has made ample, and excellent, use of the three extant volumes of the newly published *Oeuvres complètes*, in which many of Levinas's early writings are collected for the first time. In particular, Moati draws heavily on three pieces, "Pouvoirs et origines," "Parole et silence," and "L'écrit et l'oral," all found in *Parole et silence*, volume 2 of the *Oeuvres complètes*. All original translations from these texts are my own, as noted at their respective first appearances in this book.

Finally, over the course of this translation project, Raoul Moati has chosen to rewrite certain passages of his own work, *Événements Nocturnes*, for this English version. Readers comparing the texts will easily spot certain sentences, and even entire paragraphs, that depart completely from the original French. Any such case is the result of a total rewrite on Moati's part, integrated into the text according to his instruction.

I thank Raoul Moati for the privilege of working on this project, Arnold Davidson for making Levinas clear where he had been obscure, my family for their support over the course of this work, and finally the members, past and present, of the Contemporary European Philosophy Workshop at the University of Chicago.

Daniel Wyche
Chicago, 2015

Jocelyn Benoist

There is no doubt that Raoul Moati's *Levinas and the Night of Being* represents a turning point in Levinasian exegesis. This is first and foremost, and in a way that is perhaps obvious, because Moati departs from the teleological illusion of reading Levinas's early work against the backdrop of the late material—as if the "truth" of the former somehow lies hidden within the latter. Against this tendency, Moati rather simply takes up *Totality and Infinity* and reads it for itself. There is nothing arbitrary about that choice, however, and Moati's work is not, for all that, simply a monograph on *Totality and Infinity*. Rather, if the text is studied for itself and, as it were, rendered more autonomous in relation to the rest of the Levinasian corpus (notably in its final developments), it is because Moati recognizes the irreducible originality of a project from which we may garner certain insights that are to some extent lost with *Otherwise Than Being*. For my part, I will not come down either way on this point, the full evaluation of which would require a more detailed analysis of *Otherwise Than Being* than either this book or I myself am capable of here.

That being said, however, it is clear to me that Moati is quite correct about the interest and richness particular to the project of *Totality and Infinity*, and he delimits his hypothesis and arguments in terms that are, if novel, quite convincing. Indeed, the great originality of his intervention consists in the systematic and precise elucidation of the ontological character of Levinas's project in *Totality and Infinity*. In fact, from a certain perspective, it can be said that Moati takes the traditional reading, which insists that the structure and content of *Totality and Infinity* is dependent on that of *Being and Time*, very much at its word. In that reading, it is taken for granted that the former text constitutes an ongoing critique of *Being and Time*, and that one must, step by step, refer the phenomenological analyses of Levinas to their counterparts in Heidegger, which they directly oppose.

This latter point is certainly true. However, we will never actually be able draw out its full implications if we continue to believe that Levinas treads the same ground as Heidegger—in treating the same kinds of phenomena or related alternatives—in providing an "ontology." And yet Moati shows very clearly that the situation is at once much more complex and much simpler than all that: In reality, Levinas does not merely withdraw to a certain extent from Heidegger's terrain (the field of phenomena) but rather departs from the latter's project altogether. *Totality and Infinity* is indeed a critique of ontology in the sense in which Heidegger was able to envision one—this much has been well understood. It is also, however, an ontological text: that is, a book that designates the real conditions of all ontology in a way that has, generally speaking, never before been seen.

In this sense, what we have is a kind of reparative critique. Levinas takes up the Heideggerian venture just at its point of impossibility and liberates the singular, authentic space—a space overlooked by Heidegger—wherein such a project may be rendered comprehensible. Here then is a Levinas at once much more and much less Heideggerian, a Levinas that only comes into focus through the lens of Moati's presentation: much more, on the one hand, because the project of *Totality and Infinity* can thus be understood only as the critical repetition and destruction (that is, the interrogation of the conditions of possibility) of that of *Being and Time*; much less, on the other hand, because in contrast to the standard reading, the analyses of *Totality and Infinity* cannot leave intact *any* of those of *Being and Time*.

Thus the former inevitably comes to disrupt the latter on its own terms, by revealing the insufficiency of its principles. In this way, beyond the naïve opposition between ontology and ethics, established as a kind of cliché by a certain post-Levinasian vulgate, we must provide another sense of ontology, inextricably linked in its content to another ontology altogether: an ontology that is ethical through and through.

This is the path that Raoul Moati attempts to tread here, and the voyage without return (although also without nostalgia) on which he leads us is certainly worth the effort. This is because, following the hermeneutic principle he lays out, numerous aspects of the text—hitherto ignored, pure and simple—become, if not "visible," intelligible.

And so we begin to see that what makes *Totality and Infinity* an undertaking concurrent with *Being and Time* is that the former at once retraces and, in so doing, definitively requalifies the project of the latter. This is because at the center of Levinas's inquiry, just as that of Heidegger, it is the *world* that is at stake, in the sense of what we mean when we say that we are "in the world." At the same time, the necessary conditions for such a being-in-the-world are quite different in each case. The Levinasian analysis foregrounds the fact that "the world" as such does not appear. This is, of course, not to be taken in the simple sense of the nonappearance of something hidden but rather that the world itself does not fall within that category of things of which one can say that they "do or do not appear." "The world" begins beyond phenomena and their existential solipsism, in the space in which these latter are spoken, and therefore offered to us by an other (*d'un Autre à Un*).

What will not work then, in the early Heidegger at least, is the prejudicial understanding of discourse as comprehension—as if, in this notion, ontology had already been acquired—which conceals teaching as the truth of ontology. Raoul Moati devotes many formidable pages here to just that teaching, such that the space of the ongoing renewal of learning is at once the space of ontology. The Other (*Autrui*) constantly teaches us the world; indeed, this process, this dynamic, is integral to the notion of "world" itself.

For this reason, *alterity* is the very condition of onto-logic, with the latter understood as a discourse wherein it is only things that have a sense; indeed, it is only in this way that there is anything like a world in which things can be what they are. Here we depart from the domain of appearances (should they appear to a single individual or many people) for the space of that which produces itself in the fecundity and succession of generations, in order to understand this plurality, this "many," itself. Such is the real—and nonphenomenological—locus of being and the Levinasian principle of "ontology"—as revealed in *Totality and Infinity*, at least.

It seems to me that this reading, as strong as it is novel, frees *Totality and Infinity* from the obstacle of what I would call its "phenomenological recuperation." It is tempting, finally, in a laudable concern for systemization within the phenomenological field, to read Levinas—above all, the Levinas of *Totality and Infinity*, which certainly lends itself to it much more than the later work—as a kind of extreme or inverted phenomenologist, a phenomenologist who has in some sense already exceeded the limit. However, in the full-frontal attack on the Derridean reading of Levinas with which he ends this book—a reading whose influence on so-called Continental philosophy is well known—Moati offers us a glimpse of something rather different. Far from returning to that form of phenomenology whose primary function has been the thematization of presence and the meditation on absence, Levinas simply frees up another, completely nonphenomenological, sense of the term "presence."

Here, it is not in the failure of the intentionality of knowledge that ethical significance is to be found, any more than it is in the impossibility of the appearance of the Other. This is because, in a certain sense, the Other does indeed appear: It is not a lacuna or an absence in phenomena. And yet in another sense the Other does not at all appear, because, logically, it does not belong to the class of things that appear. It does not "exceed" phenomena, any more than it "saturates" them, because, quite simply, it is something other than a phenomenon. And yet at the same time, without this nonphenomenon, no phenomena could have a sense, because no phenomena could then be spoken.

Thus, following Levinas, this book is driven by a gap in a rather different, and nonteleological, sense of presence. The question can thus no longer be one of whether or not consciousness, in its solitary sovereignty, has or has not "obtained" presence, because the particular kind of presence that concerns Levinas is already there and thus cannot actually be "missed"[1] in any meaningful way. Nor can we be said to "have it" (*l'avoir*) either, as such a claim, and these terms in general, make no sense here. The infinite is *there*. How, despite all our efforts, philosophical or otherwise, can we ignore it? The answer lies, as we will see, in something called "society."

PREFACE: THE NOCTURNAL FACE OF BEING

I was in one of those forests where the sun has no access, but
where the stars penetrate by night. The place could only exist
because the inquisition of the State had overlooked it.

—RENÉ CHAR, "PENUMBRA"

Although René Descartes discovered the idea of the infinite during his *Metaphysical Meditations*, the full significance of the concept and its most extreme consequences remain unappreciated. Indeed, to fully unfold the idea of the infinite is, in fact, to free being itself (*l'être lui-même*) from its reduction to absolute knowledge—and from the ontological understanding that is articulated by the existence of the human existent (*étant humain*)—in ultimate events that are essentially nocturnal. And yet the inscription of the idea of the infinite within the order of a thought that such an idea actually transcends is clearly insufficient for such a liberation as, in its own regime, the idea of the infinite cannot be so reduced. It remains for us, then, to extract the ethical kernel from this discovery. The event that concretely consummates the production of the idea of the infinite in us is human sociality.

The history of Western states and the reign of objective reason continue to hinder the production of those events through which the experience of being (*être*) may become absolute. The centralization of generalized conflict as that which exclusively delimits the face of the real persists within an understanding that reduces ontology to the totality of knowledge. Here the ethical does not even begin to appear, not even in its potentiality, and it has no more substance than the opinions of the naïve. Human peace has no chance of realizing itself as long as objective reason and fundamental ontology continue to have the last word on being.

I attempt to show here that the eschatology of messianic peace is not the complement of ontology; the former does not add something to the latter but rather superposes itself on it as the herald of the production within being of those ultimate events contained within the idea of the infinite. The goal of the present work, then, is to take the ontological project pursued by Emmanuel Levinas in *Totality and Infinity* seriously, even if Levinas himself does not maintain that project in this particular form in the texts that follow. Indeed, he will later come to describe the appeal to ontology in

Totality and Infinity as a kind of provisional theoretical form in the service of avoiding the pitfall of psychologism.[1]

The question thus arises whether my goals in the present work consequently run the risk of misrepresenting or distorting Levinas's explicit intentions regarding the orientation of his oeuvre. Certainly those who consider *Otherwise Than Being* the sole approach to Levinasian philosophy will think so. However, despite all that, this ontological reading of *Totality and Infinity* is firmly grounded in a scrupulous attention to Levinas's text. Moreover, it is my belief that the general and overall coherence of the book remain unintelligible if we do not take seriously the ontological project that guides it. The task before us, then, in light of this claim, is to prove it.

It has certainly been insisted, and rightly so, that Levinas did indeed adopt a metaphysical approach in his opposition to fundamental ontology. For my part, I would like to situate Levinas's confrontation with Heidegger in the former's discovery of the properly ontological productivity of metaphysics. The advent of metaphysics coincides with the production of ultimate events of being, just as irreducible to the totalizing function of knowledge as they are to fundamental ontology. I endeavor to show, contra the retrospective interpretation of Levinas himself, that the ontological inscription of the text cannot be reduced to an ill-suited appeal to an inadequate lexicon.[2] The fundamental question is one of knowing whether it is possible to liberate being from the totalization of fundamental ontology. Levinas's response in *Totality and Infinity* is clearly positive. The later works, however, are far more ambiguous on this point, as they reinvoke the very same totalizing "diurnal," sense of being from which *Totality and Infinity*, as eschatology, attempts to liberate ontology.

Following Levinas, the present work attempts to deduce an essentially nocturnal productivity of being, one that has been overlooked by the ontology of truth, in order to introduce a new reading with unexpected consequences: on the one hand, for the question of the relationship between Levinas and ontology, and, on the other hand, and as a result of this approach, far more radical consequences for the continuing challenge represented by the ontological question after Heidegger. Must we go beyond ontology or expose a transcendence hitherto unnoticed within the fully developed work of being and without which the ontological question loses all intelligibility? This question serves as the guiding thread of these investigations.

Preliminary versions of this work have appeared in the context of a cycle of conferences held at the Husserl Archives at the École Normale Superior de Paris (Ulm), as well as the Collège des études Juives et de philosophie contemporaine. The complete project appeared for the first time in its definitive form in the context of a talk titled "Événements Nocturnes," presented in a series of conferences at the École des sciences philosophiques des Facultés Universitaires Saint-Louis (Bruxelles), at the kind invitation of Laurent Van Eynde and Raphaël Gély. For the many stimulating conversations around my work, I also thank Augustin Dumont and all of the interlocutors whose questions and comments have fostered the development of what would become this book. Above all, I thank Jocelyn Benoist, who, by his philosophical generosity and unparalleled friendship, made possible the increasingly subtle and detailed investigations developed here. The present work is marked by both his confidence and our invaluable conversations.

I also thank Danielle Cohen-Levinas for her unfailing support and interest in my project. I further thank Rodolphe Calin for having put me on the path of "nocturnal events" through conversations that have proven decisive in the elaboration of this project, as well as Alexander Schnell, David Brézis, and Judith Sadock. I also extend many thanks to all of those who by their inestimable intelligence and friendship have accompanied me in the evolution of this work, and to whom I would like to render homage through the book itself—perhaps the most fitting way possible: Laurent Villevieille, Thibaut Gress, Ronan de Calan, Raphaël Ehrsam, Lorenzo Altieri, and David Zerbib. Finally, I thank my students at the Université de Paris 1, Pantheon-Sorbonne, and I dedicate this book to my parents, Monette and Jacky, as well as Néjia.

LEVINAS AND THE NIGHT OF BEING

CHAPTER I

Messianic Eschatology, or The Production of Ultimate Events of Being

To see clearly is to see darkly.

—PAUL VALÉRY, *Variety*

Ontology and Eschatology

"Everyone will readily agree that it is of the highest importance to know whether we are not duped by morality."[1] This sentence, which opens the preface of *Totality and Infinity*, is doubtless among the most famous of Levinas's 1961 masterpiece. The question, however, is one of understanding just what such a claim could mean in the context of a work explicitly devoted to the elevation of ethics to the rank of first philosophy. To begin by associating morality with dupery is no small or unimportant paradox for a text that aims to take up such a challenge. To be duped by morality is to believe in the moral in a world fundamentally dominated by war as the ultimate principle of reality. It is, against every demand for coherence, to find moral intentions in a reality that is ontologically allergic to morality, where the antagonisms between human beings constitute the exclusive form of the real.

That our reality is exclusively constituted by relations of confrontation signifies the incompatibility of morality and effective action of any kind. The moral perspective conceals from view any clear identification of reality

I

with the permanence of war. But war is no accidental or transitory state, it is rather the ultimate structure of reality. Further, war does not merely affect reality in a most visible and spectacular way, as "the most patent fact," but indeed "as the very patency, or the truth, of the real" (21). When war is declared, it reveals itself to human beings as "the pure experience of pure being" (21). In the moment that war breaks out, the truth of the real, which diluted words and the illusions of morality ceaselessly hide from view, itself erupts into broad daylight: "In war reality rends the words and images that dissimulate it, to obtrude in its nudity and in its harshness" (21).

In a reality dominated by war as the exclusive horizon of the experience of being, where war is no accident, but rather forges the ultimate structure of the real, morality can no longer merely designate some bloodless phenomenon, a term drained of all meaning. The universal ordeal of war "refutes morality" (24), and in a reality governed by war, politics as "the art of foreseeing war and winning it by every means" (21) completely overrides the moral. However, the replacement of the moral by the political does not simply amount to the disappearance of morality but rather its enlistment in the cause of war. The universal significance of morality is lost immediately once our recourse to it is justified in terms of its long-term strategic efficacy in a given situation of conflict: to obtain victory over the adversary, that singular goal that guides human beings in a reality that stands beneath the banner of war. The universal reach of the moral dissolves in the moment that it is placed under the stewardship of the political as the exclusive practical principle of human phenomena. Here its universality then finds itself repurposed for "the functions of prudence" (22), which refers, in the Aristotelian tradition, to those situations in which practical intelligence is dominated by politics, perverted by ruse and calculation.

By its reduction to a supporting role within the political, and under the weight of this substitution, morality thus witnesses the complete demise of the unconditionality of its eternal principles. Human conflicts do not occur merely as a series of events to which the moral could stand in opposition, because reality understood as the permanent state of war signifies precisely the suspension of the ability of morality to oppose itself to war. Indeed, the universality of war does not rest content with merely contravening the moral, rather it renders the moral "derisory." As Levinas says, "War is not only one of the ordeals—the greatest—of which morality lives; it renders morality derisory" (21).

War thus appears beyond the "draperies of illusion" and the naivety of the moral as the absolute law that governs the relationships between individuals and states. Thus in the context of an ontology dominated by totalization, peace is at best a provisional phenomenon; that is, peace is merely a moment within war: "The peace of empires issued from war rests on war" (22).

In the horizon of war as the ontologically ultimate principle, there has never been a place for moral actions or intentions: "The state of war suspends morality" (21). Against the naivety of the moral, philosophical lucidity—or, philosophy understood as the exercise of lucidity par excellence—enjoins us to "catch sight of the permanent possibility of war" (21). If war delimits the real in its "very patency," its very structure and material, and if "the trial by force is the test of the real" (21), then it is an illusion to pretend to find even the smallest moral fact within the real.[2] To reason in axiological terms about the real is to abandon a substantive lucidity in order to see the ultimate principle of reality in war. Indeed, and again, moral vision obscures the profoundly agonistic structure of the real. We are "duped" by the moral insofar as it conceals the ultimate structure of the real, where morality is dismissed as a matter of principle. If war delimits the experience of being, then morality is nothing more than a hollow notion destined to distract the naïve, and all of those who will be made into dupes by it, from the ubiquitous state of confrontation that is the truth of the real.

The opening words of *Totality and Infinity* are thus disconcerting because they are devastating. They seem to utterly destroy the possibility of establishing, or reestablishing, the moral among human beings. They condemn a priori every attempt to build a moral philosophy worthy of the name, other than in the form of yet another illusion. The moral point of view is fraudulent in that it obscures the "very patency" of the real, the intelligibility of which emerges exclusively from war—wherein the moral has no place. Not to be duped by morality is to prefer lucidity to illusion; and, far from seeking to contradict Nietzsche, Levinas places the ethical intentions of his treatise wholly within the wake of the later. The opening lines of *Totality and Infinity* support the Nietzschean assessment according to which the moral is used to escape reality by way of a lie, and in this way, "What moral and religious judgments have in common is the belief in things that are not real."[3] The genealogical critique of the moral must be wholly taken up if we are to avoid rerouting the ethical project of *Totality and Infinity* toward an indeterminate "moraline."[4] The challenge issued here is thus not one of proceeding as if philosophy has not warned us or put us on the defensive against the naivety of the moral point of view, but rather to follow Nietzsche—in fact, to radicalize him—in the assimilation of morality to illusion, in a reality exclusively dominated by war. There is thus no need to follow Heidegger[5] in "proving by way of some obscure fragments of Heraclitus[6] that being reveals itself as war to philosophical thought." This is because philosophy at its best, with and after Nietzsche, recognizes "the very patency of the truth—of the real" in war (*Totality and Infinity*, 21).

Ethics, in the sense that Levinas elaborates in *Totality and Infinity*, will never serve the interests of a morality understood as the illusory consolation for a reality far too unbearable to accept for we who are human, all too human. In a way that is just as paradoxical as it appears, the ethical thinker is indeed obligated to begin by endorsing the Nietzschean analysis according to which "morality consists of words and is among the coarser or more subtle deceptions (especially self-deception) which men can practice."[7]

Ethics as the genuine overcoming of the horizon of war is possible, and indeed thinkable, if and only if we no longer begin by yielding to morality, understood as the mask of the permanent state of reality as war. Herein lies the paradox of a treatise aimed at the determination of ethics as first philosophy, but which from the outset dismisses morality as a practical possibility that is only viable and substantiated in a reality structured by war. "The state of war suspends morality; it divests the eternal institutions and obligations of their eternity and rescinds ad interim the unconditional imperatives" (*Totality and Infinity*, 21).

The challenge is thus a serious one: to successfully detach the destiny of morality from the occultation of war as the permanent state of reality— a state of which morality has, until now, been the servant. And yet how can this kind of detachment be possible if lucidity itself lies precisely in "catching sight of the permanent possibility of war?" (21). Is there not an insoluble contradiction between moral vision and this necessary clarity? Would not the former lead back to a fatal abandonment of the latter? Is it possible to rehabilitate morality without abandoning that necessary clarity, the very clarity which demands of us that we accept war as "the truth of the real"? Such is the gravity of the questions raised within the opening reflections of *Totality and Infinity*. If war does indeed have the last word on the real, it then seems logically impossible, short of renouncing lucidity in favor of illusion, to discern an authentically moral experience within the relations that human beings undertake together. And yet it is precisely the excavation of such an experience to which *Totality and Infinity* is devoted.

An ethical experience that does not amount to the continuation of war by other means does indeed exist. Therefore, to call this experience *moral* no longer amounts to being duped with regard to the permanent state of the real. And yet how exactly can we assign one area of experience to morality without deceiving ourselves about the real? It is from the perspective of this question that we must understand exactly how Levinas situates himself in the preface. His remarks certainly do not consist, contra Nietzsche, in contesting the deceptive character of the moral by rehabilitating the "moraline." Rather, the task is to position the rehabilitation of the moral within the horizon of a complete redefinition of ontology. It is only on this level that a challenge can be raised that would no longer undermine the Nietzschean analysis: to think the moral without naivety and without abandoning the exigency of lucidity.

That lucidity requires us to see the permanent influence of war as the absolute horizon of history, in a reality dominated by the concept of totality. And as long as the intelligibility of being is bound to the concept of totality, morality remains nothing more than naivety. In an ontology that assigns the real to "totalization" and the truth to history, morality is nothing more than an illusion of the naïve. The moral will recover its prerogative only once the insufficiency of the concept of totality to fully and exhaustively grasp the event of being (*l'événement de l'être*) has been demonstrated. Morality is impossible in a reality dominated by war, but totalization does not have the last word on being, because it does not saturate the horizon of experience. Morality does not recover its rights in a naïve refutation of the analysis of war but rather in the idea that, again, war does not have the last word on being and thus that totality and history do not pervade "the true measure of being" (22).

The elucidation of being will reach its full culmination—this being the central project of *Totality and Infinity*—when an eschatology of messianic peace is superposed upon historical totalization. This eschatology rests on an ultimate experience of being whose principle of intelligibility cannot be found within totalization. Such an experience is thus eschatological in the sense that it suspends the assignment of events of being to the continuity of war as the fundamental ontological framework of historical reason. In a reality dominated by totalization, the framework of being coincides with the deployment of objective reason, wherein the ordeal of war dominates and each event attests to the tragedy of confrontation.

Eschatology represents the advent of a regime of being that is not consumed by objective totalization. The former exceeds the latter in producing an experience of being liberated from history and the state of war to which it is bound. Eschatology thus denotes the emergence of a dimension of being that is no longer attached to the immanent course of reason in history but which consists in a relationship to transcendence or "a relation with the infinity of being" (23). As it "institutes a relation with being *beyond the totality* or beyond history" (22), eschatology suspends the historical destiny to which individuals are bound by the totality to which they belong. As long as the unfolding of being is governed by an ontology of totalization, no escape from war is even conceivable. In the context of the reduction of the real to the totality, the ontologically ultimate event is produced[8] by enlisting everyone in the effort of war. In this context, the mobilization of individuals by history constitutes the very event of all that participates in being, the event par excellence of all that is:

> The ontological event that takes form in this black light is a casting into movement of beings hitherto anchored in their identity, a mobilization of absolutes, by an objective order from which there is no escape. (21)

Taken by war, individuals are ordered to renounce the prerogatives of their own being in order to respond to a mobilization that requisitions their full participation, with no possible alternative, in an objectively determined order "from which no one can keep his distance" (21). That order at once annuls morality and dissolves the singular and unique identity of every human being. It transforms the individual into an object of history, an "ID number" with neither face nor voice. War, as Levinas attests, "destroys the identity of the Same" (21).

This is why being, for an individual, does not consist merely in being active or acting with only oneself in view, but rather in being forced along with everyone else to submit to the implacable event of the universal mobilization for war, a training for each in the dispossession of self. This mobilization thus compels the sacrifice of subjective aspirations in favor of the participation of all in the anonymous processes of history. Totalization entails a requisitioning of absolutes, a process through which it strips individuals of their own identities in order to transform them into instruments of the historical process. In the participation in history, *being* signifies nothing more than being a link, a tiny part of a totality which aims to relentlessly mobilize individuals in spite of themselves.

Eschatology on the other hand, contra history, designates an experience in which being is produced as transcendence, in other words, where individuals have *faces*, where speech suspends their teleological dispensation: "Peace is produced as this aptitude for speech" (23). Eschatology dramatizes "*existents [étants] that can speak* rather than lending their lips to an anonymous utterance of history . . . both involved in being and personal" (26, emphasis added).[9] To speak is to exist in the first person, to no longer draw the sense of one's being from historical reason and its "ruse."

The advent of language "breaks with the totality of wars and empires in which one does not speak" (23); speech is the mark of a being (*être*) that produces itself beyond the horizon of universal history and the permanent state of war to which it is tied. *To be* beyond history is to speak. To be enclosed in history, on the contrary, is to be situated before speech, which is to say, to not yet—or to not really—be: to be in the paradoxical mode of absence as phenomenon. To be in oneself is to express oneself. The thing in itself speaks; that which is transcendent speaks. The Other, insofar as he or she is exterior to the totality, speaks; as transcendent, he or she is never separated from expression. The face (*visage*) reveals the Other in his or her transcendence because the face as expression undoes every totalizing form which would aim to attribute a sense to it through its inscription in an objective system of signification.

It is in this sense that the face is a signification "without a context" (23); it cannot be exhausted by the sense that the totalizing act—or the historical totality—confers on it: "It *is* by itself and not in reference to a system" (75). It would thus be a complete contradiction to identify some "purely silent" aspect of the exterior transcendent being, in opposition to an "expressive part," which would reveal such a being extrinsically—as if it were not constitutive of this being to express and reveal itself. Therefore, if to be transcendent is to speak—that is,[10] to eschatologically suspend the grasp of totalization—then speech represents an absolutely constitutive dimension of the transcendence of being. This is why, following Kant, Levinas affirms that the thing in itself is transcendent, situated beyond phenomenality. However, this position does not signify a retreat into the obscurity behind phenomena; rather, it is a manifestation beyond phenomena in a relation to the noumenal that consists in expression. As soon as the face of the Other appears, it becomes a question of an expressive presence and not a phenomenon. The Other reveals his or her face—"ethics is an optics" (23)—because the face is *heard*. The face reveals the transcendence of the Other because, on its own, independent of any empirical act of speech, the face already speaks. That is, it undoes the intentional form that locks it into a signification that is extrinsic—originating in acts of constitution which themselves emerge from a transcendental ego—rather than intrinsic to it, whereby in its expression, and regardless of its objective content, transcendent being signifies itself in expressing itself.[11]

That messianic speech produces itself as the "aptitude for speech," means that there is a destiny for human beings other than the one imposed on us by history. But this alternative remains obstructed insofar as objective reason continues to govern the real, and insofar as being exposes itself as war—in other words, insofar as the eschatology of messianic peace does not superpose itself upon the "ontology of war" (22). Beyond history and war, beyond objective immanence, "the idea of being overflowing history" (23) has no place so long as totalization—or history—continues to suffocate the transcendence of being through its domination of the destiny of the world. The liberation of the world thus coincides with the production within being of an event that no longer depends on totalization, for which only an eschatological, and thus nonteleological, vision of being can take responsibility.

There is thus no transcendence of being without eschatology, even if, to this day, eschatology has been repudiated by philosophy: "Philosophers distrust . . . eschatology, [which] for them belongs naturally to Opinion" (22). Philosophers place the objectivity of evidence, from which results the perpetuity of war and politics, in opposition to the prophetic declaration of peace. As long as eschatology finds itself relegated to the rank of opinion—which philosophy, since its origins, has been called upon to discredit in the name of the truth of being—messianic peace will never be able to designate an event produced within being, independent of totalization, and war will remain the exclusive regime of ontology. Thus the True is opposed to the Good in the philosophical struggle against the naivety of the moral. It is for this reason that eschatology will only be able to reclaim its universal moral prerogatives once the situation of "the underlying rending of a world attached to the both the philosophers and the prophets" (24) is overcome by the superposition of eschatological ontology upon the ontology of war.

The superposition of eschatology onto history implies that eschatology, just as objective reason, brings about an event of being, which, however, no longer presents itself as objective evidence to consciousness. Philosophy rejects everything that does not fall under the regime of objective truth as being outside of ontology. The superposition of eschatology upon "the ontology of war" destroys the equivalence of objective truth and ontology, in liberating the experience of being from totalization.

Peace can only suspend the reduction of being to war—where the peace of empires is only the continuation of war by other means—once eschatology superposes itself onto the ontology of totalization. "Morality will oppose politics *in history* and will have gone beyond the functions of prudence or the canons of the beautiful to proclaim itself unconditional and universal *when* the eschatology of messianic peace will have come to *superpose itself* upon the ontology of war" (22, emphasis added). We are thus confronted with a decisive historical moment, an unprecedented situation within being, in which the event of being no longer coincides with the affirmation of war, and where totalization no longer saturates the exhaustive experience of being.

It will thus not suffice to say that the revelation of the face is eschatological, irreducible to history, nor even to prophetically announce the eschatological end of days. This is because insofar as this eschatology is not produced in being as relation to being, insofar as it does not superpose itself on the ontology that articulates objective reason in order to suspend the latter, eschatology will remain relegated to the level of subjective illusion, the naiveties that objective evidence will always be called to pulverize in the name of the ancient struggle of truth against the arbitrariness of opinion. Philosophy will remind eschatology and morality that being essentially reveals itself to lucidity as war.

War and politics will continue to triumphantly affirm themselves as the exclusive forms of ontology, and morality will remain confined to the naivety of a discourse powerless to describe the "truth of the real." It is thus in this sense perfectly essential, in order to raise the challenge unique to it, that *Totality and Infinity* should be a discourse on being and that Levinas does not abandon the language of philosophy for that of mysticism or prophecy. Such is the radical assessment of the opening pages of the preface: objective reason will always be correct in denouncing the naivety of these latter. The task is thus to counter the relegation of eschatology to the level of philosophically unfounded opinion by determining it as a relation to being, which, nevertheless, does not proceed from objective evidence, to the end of liberating ultimate events of being from the horizon of objectivity, and thus from history and totalization.

The advent of messianic peace thus requires the superposition, rather than the relegation, of "the extraordinary phenomenon of prophetic eschatology" (22), which is to say the opening of ontology to events that no longer draw their significance from the diurnal category of truth as representation or objective evidence, without at the same time falling back into the arbitrariness of opinion. The relation with the infinite is freed from opinion because the latter "vanishes like the wind when thought touches it" (25), even though "the Idea of the Infinite is in the mind before it lends itself to the distinction between what it discovers by itself and what it receives from opinion" (25). Exhumed from the subjective naiveties to which philosophy has relegated it, eschatology as idea of the infinite is thus clearly attributed the dignity of an experience of being properly speaking, an experience that is, moreover, originary, "if experience precisely means a relation with the absolutely other, that is, with what always overflows thought, the relation with infinity accomplishes experience *in the fullest sense of the word*" (25, emphasis added).

The superposition thus invoked signifies the double irreducibility of eschatology to either the rank of opinion or that of evidence, because "reduced to the evidences, eschatology would then already accept the ontology of totality issued from war" (22) and because "peace does not take place in the objective history disclosed by war, as the end of that war or as the end of history" (24). Peace as the end of war does not, however, mean the completion of history, but rather the suspension of its irresistible realization, by a relation to being situated outside the objective regime of totalization.

To superpose eschatology onto the ontology of war, and to enlist the aid of *Totality and Infinity* in so doing, is to interrogate the event of being that accomplishes the relation beyond history, without which messianic peace would remain relegated to the level of illusion that war rejects on principle. Eschatological peace thus realizes a dimension of being irreducible to the objectivity of impersonal reason and to the universality of war that results from it. Eschatology also reveals that access to being is no longer the exclusive prerogative of objective evidence: "Does objectivity, whose harshness and universal power is revealed in war, provide the unique and primordial form in which Being, when it is distinguished from image, dream, and subjective abstraction, *imposes itself* on consciousness? Is the apprehension of an object equivalent to the very movement in which the bonds with truth are woven? These questions the present work answers in the negative" (24).

It is for this reason that, no longer relaying objective evidence (which would only consolidate the hold of war), eschatology "does not introduce a teleological system into the totality," nor does it orient the totality, but rather, "Eschatology institutes a relation with being *beyond the totality* or beyond history" (22). The objective necessity to which totalization obligates events of being does not have the last word on being. Historical totalization does not coincide with the full measure of being, the exhaustive deployment of which demands something beyond the concept of totality—that of infinity. Totalization is made apparent in itself only in "the [side] of being that shows itself in war" (21).[12] The superposition of eschatology on the ontology of war liberates being from the exclusive format of objectivity, emancipates it from objective reason as the exhaustive measure of ontology, and thus permits the realization of the relation to the infinite as an originary event of being no longer inscribed within the horizon of totalization—that is, of war.

The superposition of eschatology on objective reason reveals the way in which being, in its full scope, is no longer measured in light of some singular objective totality, but henceforth equally and just as originally by the infinite as transcendence—as being beyond objective history. It is for this reason that the end of war, as the end of time, as heralded by eschatology, does not consist in the realization of the finality pursued by history. It consists, rather, in a relation to being that suspends historical objectivity in situating itself beyond the horizon of war, in the event of a relation to the infinite that is no longer the advent of a historical peace—which is merely a variant of war—but rather of a messianic peace. This latter coincides with the accomplishment of a relation to being under the guise of nontotalizable events; that is, essentially nocturnal events.

The existence of a *nocturnal deployment of being* means that all that is not revealed by the regime of objective evidence—the idea of infinity above all—can no longer be relegated to the level of opinion, consecrated to the universal domination of totalization and history over human beings. Consequently, there must be an ontology that establishes a place for ultimate events of being such that the advent of peace, as described here, will no longer represent the insidious relays of war continued by other means. Such events will no longer draw their significance from a Hegelian totalization or even from phenomenological constitution (Husserl) or the comprehension of the sense of being (Heidegger). The horizon of their deployment consists in a relation to being that overflows the light of objective evidence and of which all of these cases constitute various avatars. What Levinas calls a "primordial and original relation with being" (22) is nothing other than a relation to being that exempts itself from objectivity as the universal norm of ontology; it is a properly eschatological relation, liberated from history. The idea of the infinite deployed in this way, far from mere opinion or subjective illusion, is very much a relation to being, within which being reveals itself otherwise than in the mode of objectivity. It is thus beyond objective reason and the universality of war that results from it—which is to say, in the mode of nonadequation.

Being is thus not exhaustively produced in objective evidence or as objective event. Rather, another concept, that of infinity, is required in order to realize the transcendence of being in its originary exteriority to the objective order that totality articulates. Eschatology as the "[institution of] a relation with being *beyond the totality* or beyond history" (22), reveals being in its transcendence, which is, on principle, "non-encompassable within a totality and as primordial as totality" (23).

Nocturnal Dramas of Consciousness

The lexicon of being is clearly maintained in *Totality and Infinity* in 1961, unlike the text of 1974, which sought to break with it by way of that which is "otherwise than being." In *Totality and Infinity*, the regime of being is not an obstacle to the elucidation of the infinite; rather, Levinas presents its disclosure in terms of "the ultimate event of being itself" (28). The maintenance of the lexicon of being may seem just as surprising in the early Levinas as in the later works, as he is indeed concerned in both cases to move away from being in the strict sense and toward a regime that more and more clearly concerns itself with that which is "otherwise than being." Against every interpretive tendency to project the stakes and concerns of the text of 1974 back upon that of 1961, it must be kept in mind that the philosophy of nocturnal events deployed in *Totality and Infinity* has nothing in common with the constitutive project of *Otherwise Than Being*. The latter, it must be recalled, aims at a deduction of being that takes what is otherwise than being as its point of departure, within which "if transcendence has a meaning, it can only signify the fact that the *event of being*, the *esse*, the *essence*, passes over to what is other than being."[13] In 1961, however, the task yet remained of showing that being is not exhausted by totalization, and thus that ultimate events of being do not proceed from the ontology of war. The elaboration of the project of 1974 requires the inscription of the revelation of the face within the motifs of "illeity" and the "trace," and such an articulation has not yet been elaborated in *Totality and Infinity*.

From the point of view of *Totality and Infinity*, ethics and ontology are not mutually exclusive. There is very much a place within ontology for the revelation of the face—that is, for ethics—understood precisely as *ultimate event of being*.

Does the recourse to the lexicon of being nevertheless annul the distance, so carefully constructed within Levinas's earliest works, from Heidegger's fundamental ontology? The answer is an unequivocal no. For Levinas, neither totalization nor ontological comprehension saturates the horizon of being. It is for this reason that the maintenance of the lexicon of being in *Totality and Infinity* in absolutely no way compromises the critiques Levinas levels at the author of *Being and Time*. It could even be said that, contrary to *Otherwise Than Being*, the Levinas of *Totality and Infinity* is cautious precisely in order to avoid ceding the horizon of being to fundamental ontology, and to further avoid the assimilation of ontology to fundamental ontology.

There is a series of events of being—properly *nocturnal events*—that ontological comprehension is, structurally, in no position to take up. These nocturnal events occur within horizons beyond and other than those of comprehension and ontological unveiling. Thus Levinas does not claim in *Totality and Infinity* that we must pass from the register of being into that of ethics, but rather that fundamental ontology prevents the exhaustive elucidation of being from coming to full fruition. The latter requires that we take into consideration the revelation of the face as the ultimate event of being. For Levinas, contra Heidegger, awareness of the full deployment of being constitutively requires overcoming the prerogatives on which fundamental ontology rests—first and foremost of the restriction of events of being to the comprehension of being. The maintenance of the lexicon of being in *Totality and Infinity* is thus not evidence of a concession to fundamental ontology, but rather points up the fact that fundamental ontology is not in a position to exhaustively grasp ultimate events of being. It is in this sense that Levinas plumbs a properly nocturnal drama of consciousness, wherein being is deployed in events that the truth as *Aletheia*, as unveiling or disclosure, is constitutively in no position to grasp:

> Consciousness then does not consist in [equating] being with representation, in tending to the full light in which this adequation is to be sought, but rather in overflowing this play of lights—this phenomenology—and in accomplishing *events* whose ultimate signification (contrary to the Heideggerian conception) does not lie in *disclosing*. Philosophy does indeed dis-cover the signification of these events, but they are produced without discovery (or truth) being their destiny. No prior disclosure illuminates the production of these essentially nocturnal events. The welcoming of the face and the work of justice—which condition the birth of truth itself—are not interpretable in terms of disclosure. Phenomenology is a method for philosophy, but phenomenology—the comprehension effected through a bringing to light—does not constitute the ultimate event of being itself. (*Totality and Infinity*, 27–28)

Here we see that Levinas equally dissociates the question of being from both transcendental phenomenology and fundamental ontology. In each case, being finds itself surrounded—indeed, restrictively circumscribed—by a destiny that is not exhaustively its own. In the case of transcendental phenomenology, it is that of the truth as adequation; in the case of fundamental ontology, it is that of opening the truth of the sense of being articulated in its disclosure by human *Dasein*. In both phenomenological scenarios, the deployment of being finds itself assigned, in a limited way, to the truth as coming to light, as the adequation of being to the powers of intellection.

The measure of being would be limited to the light of representation, comprehension, or unveiling—whether this unveiling is *Lichtung*, a clearing, or not—capable of bringing it to light. And yet *Totality and Infinity* argues just as much against transcendental phenomenology as against fundamental ontology, that a constitutive dimension of being—the nocturnal face of being—does not surrender itself to human powers of discovery. Levinas recognizes, however:

> There is in Heidegger's "late philosophy" an impossibility for power to maintain itself as monarchy, to ensure its total mastery. The light of comprehension and truth streams into the darkness of incomprehension and non-truth; power, bound to mystery, avows its impotence. Thereby the unity of the existant seems broken, and fate, as errance, once more mocks the being that in comprehension means to govern it. (*Totality and Infinity*, 275)

Although Heidegger's later philosophy no longer raises the question of being in terms of the fundamental ontology developed in *Being and Time*, Levinas nonetheless continues to argue that for Heidegger, always, and despite the errancy of human beings, "the human being apprehended as power remains, in reality, truth and light. Heidegger hence disposes of no notion to describe the relation with mystery, already implied in the finitude of Dasein. If power is at the same time impotence, it is by reference to power that this impotence is described" (275–76).

Whether in terms of comprehension or unveiling, in Heidegger the unveiling of being is confined to the limited register of the unveiling of being as light and truth, an unveiling the intelligibility of which remains systematically dependent on a reference to human powers over being.

The discovery of nocturnal events by transcendental phenomenology or fundamental ontology, their inscription in the regime of truth (as adequation to the powers of the constitution of the phenomenon or of the comprehension of being), does not mean that philosophical discovery—or truth—is the originary destiny of such events in their ultimate character. The relation of humanity to being does not limit itself to the unveiling of the truth of being. Such a disclosure of being is always second; philosophy always arrives too late, when ultimate events of being, irreducible to the truth of unveiling, are already produced independently of the latter. Every disclosure of being is founded on an immemorial relation to being, fundamentally nocturnal and clandestine, where being overflows the objective norm by which it is measured and illuminated: "What counts is the idea of the overflowing of objectifying thought by a forgotten experience from which it lives" (28).

Ultimate events of being never allow themselves to be exhaustively redirected to the regime of philosophical discovery, which always takes hold of them retroactively. The relation to being affirms itself as such in a form of originary independence from the disclosure of being which is always second: "Philosophy does indeed dis-cover the signification of these events, but they are produced without discovery (or truth) being their destiny" (28). The nocturnal dramas by which being exhaustively produces itself thus designate events that find their point of departure within consciousness, but within a consciousness originally capable of departing from the horizon of its own selfhood and powers. That is, it is a consciousness capable of welcoming the excessiveness of the infinite, of receiving the latter in its originary nonadequation to the former's powers of constitution, comprehension, and disclosure. It is a consciousness that thinks the infinite in its idea beyond all illumination and unveiling. And yet it is because a separated consciousness originally thinks being beyond the register of truth—as adequation of being to the powers of comprehension—thinks, in other words, the nonadequation of being to its own idea, that the ultimate event of being accomplishes itself as infinition of the infinite, or the production of infinity: "The production of the infinite entity is inseparable from the idea of infinity, for it is precisely in the disproportion between the idea of infinity and the infinity of which it is the idea that this exceeding of limits is produced. The idea of infinity is the mode of being, the *infinition*, of infinity" (26).

It is in this sense that "consciousness then does not consist in [equating] being with representation" (27), and that phenomenology "does not constitute the ultimate event of being itself" (28). The production of ultimate events of being by consciousness does not amount in any way to the phenomenological paradigm of constitution, wherein the exigency of adequation takes precedence. Phenomenology amputates a fundamental dimension—an idea—from consciousness, constitutive of its essentially nocturnal originary drama. Traditional phenomenology forgets that "all knowing qua intentionality already presupposes the idea of infinity, which is preeminently *non-adequation*" (27). It is in this way that there is a more originary experience for consciousness than transcendental constitution.

This means that the epiphany of the face does not borrow its motives from the light of truth, which is to say, from consciousness's powers of constitution. By its originary overflowing of the phenomenological register of adequation, consciousness has always already opened itself to the idea of the infinite, that is, to the transcendence of the face. However, it would be erroneous to think that Levinas somehow turns from the regime of clarity and distinction to that of obscurity and confusion in order to describe the originary relation of consciousness to the face. It is certainly not a question, for Levinas, of saying that being in its nonadequation could amount to an event that is obscure for human beings, since that would once again reduce being to the negative measure of human powers. The transcendence of being, its infinition, entails surpassing our recourse to those powers in order to sound the event of transcendence.

To have the idea of the infinite entails neither welcoming an event that one cannot manage to understand nor losing oneself within the winding pathways of obscurity and the helplessness of intellection in the face of being. To welcome the Other in its excess is to no longer measure it, even negatively, or to reduce it to the incomprehensible. To have the idea of the infinite is to speak with the Other, to depart the inhuman—because silent—reign of illumination, in order to call to the Other and thus to be taught by him or her. In this sense, to comprehend being is, first and foremost, to be taught the truth of being by the Other, which means that there is no comprehension of being that does not have teaching—the originary event of revelation—as its foundation. In other words, the revelation of the Other-existent (*l'étant-autrui*) cannot, constitutively, arise from the question of the sense of being, since it is only from this revelation that such a question may be posed.

There can be no silent comprehension of the sense of being, as all comprehension of being rests on the metaphysical primacy of interlocution. The question of the sense of being is thus always a question that is addressed to someone. It is in this sense that the Other does not give itself over to thematization, not because the relation to the Other denounces the weakness of our powers of comprehension. The Other no longer measures itself by the standards of the criteria immanent to those powers, which is to say that it no longer measures itself negatively in relation to these criteria. The Other is not, therefore, first and foremost the one of which one speaks, but rather the one to whom one originally speaks; to speak to the Other constitutively supposes that one already speaks to someone. Put differently, there is no language of thematization without the originary dimension of the address that entailed by all recourse to language. To thematize the Other means that one already addresses oneself to him or her: The Other is first and foremost the interlocutor.

If Levinas does not renounce the lexicon of being in *Totality and Infinity*, it is certainly not in order to retreat to fundamental ontology, as could be inferred from a retrospective reading from the perspective of *Otherwise Than Being*. Rather, Levinas's goal here is to renounce the idea of fundamental ontology as the exclusive format of ontology. The complete deployment of being requires a departure from the still diurnal register of comprehension, in order to follow a nocturnal drama that at once escapes the transcendental powers of constitution and the sphere of selfhood of Dasein. The ultimate event of being, as an essentially nocturnal production, signifies the irreducible exteriority of being to the sphere of intellection, the comprehension of consciousness, or human existence. The exteriority of being to these powers of comprehension designates the idea of the infinite the concrete ordeal that coincides with ethics as the revelation of the face of the Other.[14] Such an experience of being overflows the register of our powers of comprehension by ethically calling them into question.

The attempt to dissociate being from the influence exercised over it by the powers of comprehension and the being of illumination had already been the subject of several lectures in the period immediately following the war, as part of the preparatory work of writing *Totality and Infinity*. "In Heidegger himself, where the contemplative side of spiritual life is subordinated to care, human beings are characterized by power, finite power, and events of being are conceived as comprehensions."[15] In the 1949 lecture "Pouvoirs et origine" Levinas recommends, on the contrary, that we

search within consciousness itself for an event that overflows it and which no longer formulates itself in terms of power. It is not an issue of finding some kind of exceptional content, but rather a new mode of consciousness; a new form rather than a new content. It is a question of separating the event of being and ontology, the event of being and truth—all while designating a place for truth within the general economy of being.[16]

It is not, therefore, a question of redirecting being to truth, but of inscribing the truth within what Levinas calls here "the general economy of being." If the truth is but one moment within the general economy of being, it is because the truth of being does not exhaustively saturate the horizon of being and because the truth of being does not allow for the taking up of being in its full deployment—that is, in its ultimate events.

The originary relation to being does not, therefore, amount to the truth of being. There thus exists a regime of being that does not allow itself to be either encircled by or reduced to the diurnal motifs of representation and comprehension, nor does being coincide with the ability of consciousness or of the existant (*existant*) to grasp it; together, these two facts constitute the profound sense of the nocturnal deployment of being that Levinas elucidates in and through the categories of the face, eros, and fecundity. The events of being to which these categories refer do not in any way allow themselves to be redirected toward comprehension or toward the projects of the existant. Such events exceed the constituent regime of power, or for that very reason, disclose and redirect us toward the nocturnal drama[17] of consciousness, by which the event of being successfully overflows thought and the projects that attempt to measure it. The infinitude of being thus cannot be dissociated from the accomplishment of such events, these nocturnal dramas of consciousness that break with the phenomenological exigency of truth as adequation.

This means that on this side of any transcendental deduction, consciousness carries out an originary movement that does not consist, first and foremost, in the adequation of being to representation, but rather in welcoming the way in which being exceeds human powers of comprehension; that is to say, it consists in the production—and not the constitution—of nocturnal events. This pretranscendental, originary movement of consciousness accomplishes what Levinas calls the "break-up of the formal structure of thought (the noema of a noesis) into events which this structure dissimulates" (*Totality and Infinity*, 28).

It is for this reason that consciousness no longer represents the exhaustive measure of being. The full development of being is no longer enclosed within the noetic-noematic correlation. In its originary exercise, consciousness overflows its own play of light in allowing[18] ultimate events of being to come to pass.

The constitutive powers of transcendental subjectivity no longer exhaustively encompass what Levinas calls "the general economy of being." Truth as the adequation of being to intellection thus no longer coincides with the originary destiny of being but falls within a moment shaped by its deployment. The originary dimension of that deployment henceforth returns to the nocturnal relation to being that consciousness maintains in the idea of the infinite, eros, and fecundity. Neither the noetic-noematic regime in Husserl, nor the existant (*existant*) in its selfhood in Heidegger, nor consciousness as a project of the "for-itself" in Sartre, can measure up to the expanse of being fully unfurled. The ultimate event of being is developed under the fundamental modality of the nonadequation and the exteriority of being to human powers of comprehension.

Thus we see that the originary event of being does not reside in its adequation to the constituent or revealing powers of consciousness or the existent, but rather in overflowing these in the nonadequation of being to the truth of being. Here, the way in which the infinite, in the idea of the infinite, overwhelms the finite is concretized in the relation to the face; the caress overflows all intentionality and fecundity saturates any notion of transcendence restrictively understood as a project of the existant. It is in this way that Levinas distinguishes the revelation of the other (*Autre*) to the same of all consciousness and establishes at the interior of this relation to the other a subdistinction between the revelation of the face, on the one hand, and eros and fecundity—those relations situated beyond the face— on the other. The relations to the other articulated by eros and fecundity are not reducible to any form of knowledge or to any disclosure but no longer coincide with the relation to the face of the Other. They proceed from "events that cannot be described as noeses aiming at noemata, nor as active interventions realizing projects" (*Totality and Infinity*, 28).

Nocturnal Phenomenology

Does the elucidation of nocturnal events entail the renunciation of all methodological rigor? It is a matter of leaving behind evidence in order to grant free rein to the arbitrariness of descriptions that no exacting method can control? How is it that the "revelation of infinity does not lead to the acceptance of any dogmatic content"? (25). For Levinas, it is less a question of completely renouncing the transcendental methodology of phenomenology than it is of renewing that method by way of its own guiding spirit, to the point of radicalization.

The transcendental method makes it possible to place naturalistic evidence at a distance, by its particular "way [of working] back and [remaining on] this side of objective certitude" (25), which rests on a fundamental methodological achievement. It is in aligning himself with an evident affinity with this method that the question becomes one of reviving a more originary experience than that of objective evidence. Nevertheless, the noetico-noematic structure of the experience of consciousness, made accessible through Husserlian phenomenological reduction—transcendental idealism—*do*es not consume this experience:

> For the way we are describing to work back and remain this side
> of objective certitude resembles what has come to be called the

transcendental method (in which the technical procedures of transcendental idealism need not necessarily be comprised). (25)

For Levinas, the critique of natural evidence does not end with a phenomenology determined by this noetico-noematic structure. The latter, as we have come to see, conceals originary events of being, rendering them clandestine. Transcendental idealism obliterates the originary movement of conscience, which does not originally consist in the constitution of phenomena—"in [equating] being with representation"—but instead consists "in overflowing this play of lights—this phenomenology—and in accomplishing *events* whose ultimate signification (contrary to the Heideggerian conception) does not lie in *disclosing*" (27–28).[19] Consequently, it is no longer a question of describing the experience of consciousness in its noetico-noematic structure but rather one of taking this structure as point of departure for the return of the movement of consciousness to its own energy. The latter would entail beginning with the constitutive noetico-noematic structure in order to exceed the play of lights and thus to emphasize those events that, obscured by noetico-noematic intentionality, do not appear to the gaze of intuition. The self-overflowing of consciousness, this overtaking of intention by its own energy, is accomplished in a re-descent to the level of those nocturnal events that support the noetico-noematic structure, unknown to intentionality's own work of illumination. In this sense, nocturnal events are never called to show themselves to phenomenological intuition.

The restitution of nocturnal events cannot coincide with a movement toward the "return to the things themselves" in which the latter would simply hand themselves over to phenomenological sight. On the contrary, nocturnal events can be obtained by overflowing that sight and the play of lights that organizes it. This excess is no arbitrary production, because it very precisely coincides with a deduction:

> The break-up of the formal structure of thought (the noema of a noesis) into events which this structure dissimulates, but which sustain it and restore its concrete significance, constitutes a *deduction*—necessary and yet non-analytical. In our exposition it is indicated by expressions such as "that is," or "precisely," or "this accomplishes that," or "this is produced as that." (28)

In this sense, Levinasian philosophy, in each stage of its deployment, is never a phenomenology of the visible. And yet the register of sight is surpassed precisely through the achievement of the very inspiration that guides the phenomenological process itself, in paradoxically demonstrating that the intuitionism of the latter no longer has a monopoly on the concrete.

This method of concretization thus distinguishes itself from the transcendental method of Husserl by assuring the passage—by way of rupture—from formal structures constituted by phenomenology to the dynamics of the events that underlie them and which return these structures to their concrete signification. Consciousness, when restored to its original productive energy, exceeds the game of lights of established phenomenology by shattering the formal structure of thought—noema and noesis. This movement coincides with a deduction that returns an established formal structure to its concrete signification. But how does this concretization oppose itself to simple exemplification, to the straightforward illustration of a formal possibility?

Concretization accomplishes a gain which is indispensable for phenomenology, in an elucidation of the concrete which entails an exit from the phenomenological play of lights, understood as the rupture, within nocturnal events, of the noetico-noematic structure. To successfully carry out the phenomenological investigation of the concrete means to surpass the phenomenological play of lights—that is to say, to accomplish these kinds of deductions—would be to shift into the regime of the nocturnal production, and no longer of the constitution, of phenomena. The restoration of the concrete signification of an established formal possibility thus introduces a discontinuity—a rupture—in which exemplification never comes down to the simple illustration of the possibility in question. It is in this way that it must be understood that the deduction that accomplishes this concretization is presented by Levinas as "necessary and yet non-analytical" (28), which means that concretization is not satisfied by the actualization of the possibilities contained within a formal notion. Rather, it more precisely returns this actualization to its own proper energy, which entails exceeding actualization by way of a priori possibilities that are contained by a notion—that is, through the emergence of possibilities inherent only in concretization and unintelligible outside of it.

For this reason, the concretization of a notion constitutes a nonanalytical deduction:

> "Concreti-zation" does not only reflect the possibility it concretizes, rendering explicit the articulations enveloped in it. Interiority concretely *accomplished* by the home, the passage to act—the *energy*—of recollection in the dwelling, opens up new possibilities which the

possibility of recollection did not contain analytically, but which, being essential to its *energy*, are manifested only when it unfolds. (154)

Every abstract analysis of a notion—limiting itself to the possibilities that it contains—detached from the concrete situations that put it into practice—from events that deploy its energy—is condemned to miss those possibilities that reveal themselves only in the concretization of the notion in question. Concretization assures the passage from a formal signification to nocturnal events that support it and thus restore its otherwise obscured concrete signification, and outside of which the intelligibility of a yet-abstracted notion remains imprecise and vague.

Levinas affirms that "the method practiced here does indeed consist in seeking the condition of empirical situations, but it leaves to the developments called empirical, in which the conditioning possibility is accomplished" (173). This method appears to inscribe itself within the continuity of the classic transcendental quest that seeks to elucidate the conditions of possibility of empirical situations. And yet Levinas goes much further and continues by affirming that the method practiced "leaves to *con-cretization* . . . an ontological role that specifies the meaning of the fundamental possibility, a meaning invisible in that condition" (173, translation amended). This means that the condition, removed from its situation, which is to say from its exemplification as concretization—as passage from a formal signification to the events that concretize it—remains imprecise and vague; that is, it remains underdetermined.

The intelligibility of a condition of possibility abstracted from its actualization overflows with imprecision. The description of the events that the condition renders possible allows for the specification of the very sense of the condition that conditions them, in such a way that the conditioned becomes in part the condition of intelligibility—on the model of the refinement and clarification—of that which conditions it. The concrete situation does far more than simply illustrate a possibility or a concept, it specifies its sense. A concept cannot be detached from the dimension of the concrete without losing something constitutive of its very intelligibility. So as Didier Franck has so magnificently shown in his own classic analysis,[20] the phenomenological method that Levinas deploys requires him to delimit a clear critical distance, from the perspective of *Totality and Infinity*, vis-à-vis *Being and Time*.

Levinasian phenomenology thus rests on the phenomenologically paradoxical liberation of the concrete from the intuitionism that guides transcendental phenomenology. The analysis of the concrete, understood as the completion of the phenomenological quest, thus begins with nocturnal events and a deductive method that is itself no longer tied to either intuitive grasping or forms of disclosure and instead overflows their play of lights by the restoration of consciousness to its originary movement. This is the essentially nocturnal, originary movement of consciousness that *Totality and Infinity*—beyond transcendental phenomenology—renews, little by little, at each step of its development.

CHAPTER 2

To Receive the Idea of the Infinite

For the sake of what will follow here, I want to emphasize that in the first section of *Totality and Infinity* Levinas begins by appealing to purely formal notions (of Platonic origin): the same, the other (*l'Autre*), the infinite, participation, and separation. He does this in order to, on a second pass, propose a deformalization of these very terms. The same finds its concretization in the happy self, separation in enjoyment, and the idea of the infinite in the revelation of the face of the Other (*autrui*).[1] In each case, as we have seen, the question is one of the inscription of a formal notion within a situation that concretizes it and thus specifies its signification.

The Fundamental Detour of Metaphysics

The exceptional character of the metaphysical relation is that in constituting relationships among the terms that it brings together, it maintains a separation among those terms that does not amount to the indifference of the same vis-à-vis the other.

The advent of the ethical relation, as a metaphysical relation, necessarily demands the constitutive precondition of an autonomous life separated from the other. Its advent brings about "the rupture of participation" in a substance that would be shared by the same and the other, and within which no separation—which is to say, no prospect of the overcoming of totalization—is conceivable. Such nonseparation would indeed entail the repression of the exteriority of the other—and thus of the ethical—in the communal participation of the same and the other in a common whole, which would grant the other an identity commensurable with that of the same. For this reason, totalization systematically hinders the deployment of the idea of the infinite, which is to say, the advent of the ethical as such.

Indeed, the idea of the infinite requires "the rupture of participation," in that this rupture conditions the necessary separation without abolishing ethics as a metaphysical relation. It is thus a question of the ability of the self (*le Moi*) to constitute itself within this "rupture of participation," with which the sensible life—or atheism—of the self separated from the "other being" (*l'Être Autre*) coincides.

The exteriority of the other being vis-à-vis the same as self (*le Même comme Moi*) thus requires a separated life. This is because, by immediately turning the same away from the other, this separation prepares the same for the revelation of the other as exterior, as something that cannot be attributed to the immanent schemes of the separated life of the self. It is in this sense that, unbeknownst to the egoist self, the economy within which the sensible life of the atheist self is deployed lays the groundwork for the advent of ethics.

The ethical relation thus first requires, paradoxically but constitutively, the achievement of a movement that opposes every spontaneous tendency to enter into an immediate relation with the other. In a totality that envelops the same and the other in a common speculative identity, "the rupture of participation" is crystallized in the sensation wherein the same emerges concretely as the separated self. This means that only a self that makes the experience of an integrally immanent life entirely his or her own—which is to say, atheistic, constituted by sensible enjoyment[2]—is likely to open himself or herself, by producing it (a point to which I return), to the infinite alterity of the other; in other words, only such a self can be ethically called. Put differently, this separation is the precondition of the emergence of language in the dimension of constitutively ethical interpellation. The revelation of the Other in the expression of the face addresses itself to a separated being. Without separation, without the interruption of the totality, the mobilization of language loses all power of invocation and thus prolongs silence. Within the totality, the speech of the Other, the face as expression of its transcendence, does not ring out. Here, rather, being tragically returns to a silent world—because a faceless world—of totalization. This is what Levinas means in the preface when he refers to "the totality of wars and empires in which one does not speak."[3]

The paradox in question here, in which separation is required for the metaphysical impact of the ethical relation, consequently entails nothing less than the absolutely constitutive risk that such a relation may not, in fact, appear. In other words, there is a risk that the ethical relation, against which the atheist depth of the separated life is measured, is not in fact— neither systematically nor analytically—entailed by the course of the life of the separated self, and is thus ever at risk of falling back into totalization. This assessment is only the inverse of the absolute sufficiency that the self must attain within sensible life in order to find itself ethically solicited by the Other. Put differently, it is the consequence of the self's immanent enjoyment, which is a true enjoyment if and only if this contented self can justly prefer it to the ethical, and thereby willingly sacrifice ethics on the altar of enjoyment.

This is also, however, just what prevents the relation of desire from cor- responding to a totalization. Desire, as Levinas concretizes it, is not a form derived from egoistic needs; it is not a logically necessary consequence of immanence. This means that the act of closing oneself off to the Other is the condition of our ability to meet the Other in his or her transcendence but also runs the risk of remaining closed off. In other words, the promise is ever at risk of a danger that desire, at a certain level, constitutively re- quires. In other words, the development of the theory of the atheist self, separated from the other, is thus a double-edged sword: It is a sign of the risk that the self may prefer to withdraw into itself. But this risk is at the same time constitutive of the possibility of an authentic opening up to alterity, understood here as exteriority. Only one who is able to remain radically indifferent—which is to say, only the one who is self-sufficient in his or her terrestrial happiness—can open himself or herself up to the ethical relation.

Levinas speaks of egoism as "the eventuality of all unpunished crimes," immediately adding that "such is the price of interiority, which is the price of separation" (61). Only a self that is fixed on enjoying the contents of the world is in a position, by this disposition or a spontaneous indisposition with regard to the Other, to escape entrapment within egoism, which is to say, by the very fact of its spontaneous closure, to receive the idea of the infinite.

Any subject cut off from this spontaneous aspiration to live first of all for-oneself (*pour-soi*)—Levinas reconstructs the Sartrean concept—finds himself or herself ipso facto incapable of desire. That is, such a subject is condemned to never be able to enter into the kind of relation with the Other in which the latter reveals himself or herself in his or her full inter-locutory scope, at once calling out to the subject and calling him or her into question. That altruism may never be spontaneous in human beings represents both a chance and a risk, but it is constitutive of the develop-ment of ethics as such.

We thus arrive a first conclusion: To begin by describing the separated condition of the atheist self certainly does not amount to turning away from the object of research invoked here. Rather, it is a commitment to the exhaustive description of the ethical relation, precisely because the latter deploys itself within the horizon of separation.

It is thus no surprise that Levinas devotes a large part of his analytical efforts to the description of the immanent life of the self separated from the other. But he certainly does not do so in order to show that there are empirical situations wherein the self lives without taking into account the existence of the Other—where the relation to the latter would not be always already the proper condition of the former.[4] Rather, he does so be-cause the complete descriptive deployment of the ethical relation requires a description for itself of the separated life of the self, that is to say, of the background of separation on which the metaphysical relation is constitu-tively grounded.

For this reason, the analyses of *Totality and Infinity* that are devoted to interiority in no way constitute a superfluous detour. Rather, they allow for the clear demonstration of the separation that is effectively at work in the relation between the same and the other that is articulated by the idea of the infinite. This means, therefore, that the ethical relation, as meta-physical articulation, essentially departs from a term—without abolishing it—defined in its profound ontological self-sufficiency, without which the trajectory toward another horizon, toward that "land not of our birth" (134) would remain perfectly indescribable. A treatise that takes ethics as its object of elucidation is inseparable from an analysis that first takes up the atheist separation of the same, following a detour the fundamental metaphysical necessity of which we must further elaborate.

Although subjectivity truly comes into itself through the ethical rela-tion, the wrenching away from egoism which that relation entails is in fact more ambiguous than it appears. The ethical overcoming of egoism cer-tainly does not consist in the annulment of the atheist conditions within which the separated and sensible life of the ego is forged, because the latter undergirds the revelation of the idea of the infinite.

The objects that language puts into circulation, as a result of their the-matization in words, are no longer the exclusive possession of a self that finds contentment in them. Rather, it remains absolutely constitutive of the possibility of their being put into circulation from the same to the other, that on the most basic level they are defined in reference to the atheist horizon of the self's enjoyment. If ethics is not egoism, and in-deed represents its exact inverse, the movement from the economic to the ethical still does not entail the abolition of the primary sense that the world assumes within the horizon of economic life—to the contrary, it is a fundamental requirement. This latter sense remains the precondition that undergirds the proper advent of ethics in its irreducibly metaphysical dimension, wherein the other reveals itself as other. Insofar as the ethi-cal relation coincides concretely with the generosity toward the Other for which the self is responsible, it presupposes the horizon of a possession which it comes to call into question. One who does not "possess"—the one who is not defined by hunger and the sensible satisfaction of that hunger—is not in a position to be unsettled by the ethical revelation as contestation. The latter is not, however, the contestation of—constitutively required—sensible happiness, but rather of its exclusive character.

And yet this contestation represents one of the concrete fundamental dimensions of the ethical calling out to the same by the other—that is, of the development of the idea of the infinite as such. In other words, this contestation can only take hold of a self marked by egoism. The horizon of subjectivity is defined by a constitutive, though not exhaustive, reference to the egoism of enjoyment.[5]

If this egoism does not define the self in its essence, but rather as a "phenomenon"—a point to which I return—this egoistic dimension, by its fundamental and radical deafness with regard to the very exteriority that it entails, constitutes the background of ethics. Without it, every attempt to elucidate the self in its truth, as a responsible subject, is inconsequential.

The Point of Entry of the Ethical Relation: The Same as Self

The imperative to exodus, as the departure toward elsewhere, which Levi-nas begins to describe from the first paragraph of *Totality and Infinity*, must be understood in terms of leaving a place wherein the same has fixed itself on itself. Such a place is constituted by that form of interiority in which the self is essentially defined by its own egoistic enjoyment and its contented self-sufficiency, where it is thereby separated from and indifferent to the other. When the same thus concretely constitutes itself as self, its egoistic affirmation coincides with a self-sufficiency that attests to the absence of a need for alterity, which is to say the satisfaction of all of its sensible needs. That the achievement of terrestrial happiness does not require the other, means that the encounter with the other by the same, which is now the separated self, is not inscribed within the register of need. Here the movement of the departure from the self does not aim at a return to the self but takes the form of an opening to alterity as such, to which *desire* as deployment of the idea of the infinite corresponds.

In this way, the aspiration that carries desire toward a "foreign country" that is truly other, that "desire for a land not of our birth" (33–34), is only conceivable from the moment in which the same establishes itself as the self whose self-sufficiency characterizes terrestrial happiness: "The Desire for the other, above happiness, requires this happiness" (62).[6] The advent of such happiness thus opens the possibility of a relation with an exteriority that no longer takes its own completion, which is to say the ultimate return of self to the same, as its goal. The sufficiency of the atheist self, egoistic and happy, is thus the necessary precondition of desire. At the moment of entry into relation with the other, the satisfied same is not out to fill some gap, and it is indeed only in this way that it can open itself to the idea of the infinite. The aspiration for the truth can only be born in one "who lacks nothing" (62). Desire accomplishes a leap beyond need, and it is in this that metaphysics consists. The advent of desire is nevertheless only rendered intelligible to the extent that its achieved by a being whose very existence is constituted by needs and their sensible satisfaction.

Happiness thus represents that form of satisfaction in which one lacks for nothing: a disposition that is ontologically essential to the deployment of the idea of the infinite and in turn to the possibility of ethics. It is thus to the extent that the self is sufficient, by itself, to itself, that it is able to elevate itself to the desire for the infinite, which is to say, to a relation that transcends the register of need and completion. It is to the extent that the Other does not contribute to the happiness of the self that the Other can be desired by a self that is already contented. That is, it is only in this way that the Other can reveal himself or herself in his or her radical exteriority, in relation to the life of sensible immanence in which the separated self is firmly grounded. Through the atheist disposition, the latter already assumes, in spite of itself and without yet knowing it, that the other does not have a place in the sensible existence of the self, that it does not belong to the framework of immanence in which the separated life of the ego unfolds.

It is in this sense that desire draws up a route, the course by which it will depart the terrestrial home wherein the self is already, without the other, quite contented. There can be no true departure, no transcendent movement, without a point of departure from which one releases and frees oneself. Without it, there is no perspective from which one could exit the register of assimilation to the identity of the same that would not remain perfectly illusory.

It is in this way that Levinas is able to reject the term "transcendence," in Sartre's sense,[7] entangled as it is in the immanence of a departure from a conception of self which rejects interiority, and is thereby cut off from any point of departure. Such a conception of the self thus precludes the possibility of a "trans-ascendant"[8] movement toward the alterity of any other—which is to say, the deployment of the idea of the infinite. Interiority is, indeed, constitutive of the possibility of an authentic departure from the self that would no longer mime Ulysses, but rather follow in the footsteps of Abraham,[9] in a movement without return, toward the absolutely other.

It is for this reason that the metaphysical alterity of the Other requires the precondition of the position of the self, a here-below positioned in relation to an over-there. The alterity of the Other only appears in its metaphysical dimension from the perspective of one who is "separated," which is to say, the perspective of the same as self. This separation is thereby constitutive of the transcendence of the other in its dimension of exteriority. Thus, far from demanding the annulment of the separated self, metaphysics presupposes it as its ineliminable condition. It is thus required for the paradox that the idea of the infinite—transcendence properly speaking—can be developed only within a separated ego, that is to say, an ego that is capable, on a very specific level, of maintaining its resistance to any form of transcendence. Egoism, as the mature form of self-sufficiency, as a kind of contented deafness to transcendence, constitutes the immovable point of anchorage—the position[10]—from which the idea of the infinite develops.

We must nevertheless clearly distinguish this articulation of the here as position and dwelling[11]—forms of egoism—from the relation between "the here" and the "over there" that Husserl elaborates in the fifth *Cartesian Meditation*.[12] The Husserlian theory of alterity is founded upon the doctrine of "analogical appresentation" that begins with the sphere of belonging (*appartenance*) proper to the ego. The here is defined as the absolute origin and zero-point of one's orientation in the world.[13] The Other is thus understood by Husserl to be an intentional modification of the ego: The other, over there, is constituted by the transcendental ego as another absolute origin and another zero-point in one's orientation within the world—that is, as an alter ego.

In order to avoid dissolving the distance between the same and the other through the transposition of the form of the same of the ego into an alter ego, the subject who finds himself or herself at the point of departure of that relation must not be defined as a universal ego. Levinas thus breaks with the Husserlian theorization that defines the subject as consciousness. For Levinas, the self is in no way an anonymous and impersonal "subject in general." It is not a question of some abstract conception of the self, but rather of a singular and contented self, irreducible to any generality or to any totality. It is a self defined by "the concreteness of egoism" (*Totality and Infinity*, 38). Only a self understood in this way can stand as the true point of access to the relation with the other, because such a self emerges from the act of separation from which—and only from which—the other can reveal itself in its relationship of absolute exteriority to the same. This seems to be the condition that allows the metaphysical relation to exempt itself from the schema of totalization.

The transcendental ego, to the contrary, would in fact eliminate the distance between same and Other by constituting the "over there" as another ego, as an alter ego—another here. It would thereby dilute the transcendence of the other, by abolishing its distance from the same. Such a consequence is not merely the result of the supremacy of sameness (*mêmeté*) but rather of a description of the ego grasped in all the sensible profundity of its sameness, which has not yet been brought to full fruition. The paradox thus requires that one be able to take up the elucidation of transcendence without starting from a complete description of the register of immanence.

Such a method must allow us to no longer discern subjectivity in terms of a subject of representation, but rather of a separated self, essentially defined by its contented inscription within sensible life. It is in this way that the metaphysical relationship fundamentally distinguishes itself from any transcendental deduction. Indeed, what Levinas calls "the production of the Infinite" (69) must be clearly distinguished from the "constitution" of the alter ego, and from any "transcendental constitution" in general.

To the extent that the transcendental ego remains a kind of generality, to the extent that it is not sufficiently the same—that is, enclosed within itself by and in the egoistic affirmation of its autarkic happiness—it leads the other back to a form of the same, to another my-self. The transcendental ego amounts to the absorption of the self within a generality and thus results in the abolition of the nontranscendental condition of possibility of the metaphysical relation as idea of the infinite.

The abolition of the self in its enjoyment would thus abolish the distance that separates the same from the other and would violently deny the alterity of the other insofar as this distance is the way of being of the transcendent, and because this distance can be neither maintained nor attested save for its origin in the self. The fixation of the self in its enjoyment preserves the fundamental separation required for the advent of the ethical relation. This fixation thus constitutes an ineliminable point of departure, the absence of which would compromise the development of the idea of the infinite. Indeed, in the idea of the infinite, the separated self thinks a being that is radically exterior to it, because it requires the separation of the self and maintains it in relation to the other: "The metaphysician and the other do not totalize one another" (35).[14]

It is for this reason that only the separated self can open itself to the other qua other. Atheism thus represents a paradoxical predisposition with regard to "religion," in Levinas's sense of the term, as "the bond that is established between the same and the other without constituting a totality."[15] The separation of the self and its maintenance as unabolished point of departure and the remnant of interiority on which the relation to the other is inexorably founded makes possible a departure from the self that would no longer return to the supremacy of the same over the other. The same surpasses itself in desire, but this surpassing in no way amounts to the effacement of the self, because it is only possible to the extent that the incommensurable within transcendence is experienced. And yet this ordeal can only be experienced by an ego that is in itself, by its own sensible life, profoundly separated. It is only from such a depth that the other can reveal itself in its infinite transcendence, which is to say as that which, radically, has no place in the universe of the subject, as the Most High, the ever distant.

The depth of a-theist life that the self reaches in its economic existence, at the same time as its preservation as ineffaceable point of entry into the relation with the other, thus has a positive significance. It is that which makes possible—though neither necessary nor ineluctable, that is, neither analytically nor dialectically deducible from the same, under pain of falling back into totalization—an opening to transcendence, which is the possibility of the solicitation of the Same by the other beyond itself.

It is for this reason that the eventuality of passing beyond the horizon of totality rests on the essential precondition of a positive philosophy of the self as sensible ego. That is, this overcoming rests on the elucidation—brought to term by Levinas—of the character fundamentally required for the emergence of the eschatological relation against which totalization is shattered, now capable of much more than the simple reduction of the alterity of the Other to a variation of the identity of the same.

There is thus nothing accidental about the order of exposition by which *Totality and Infinity* proceeds, and all that this progression entails. Levinas begins by unfolding a phenomenology of sensible immanence, before moving on to any elucidation of the infinite and its concretized translation in the epiphany of the face. And so, this priority of exposition has a metaphysical justification, but one that we must further clarify.

Separation and Metaphysics

Levinas advances two seemingly contradictory theses: on the one hand, an alterity "prior to every initiative, to all imperialism of the Same" (38–39), and on the other, an "alterity [that] is possible only starting from me" (40). This apparent contradiction is resolved by the theory of separation that Levinas articulates several pages following section B of the first part of *Totality and Infinity*, titled "Separation and Discourse" (53).

The revelation of transcendent being (*l'Être transcendant*) requires an inversion of the before and after, wherein "the after," as that which is conditioned, comes before that which precedes and conditions it. "Atheistic separation" refers to the act by which this inversion of the before and after is accomplished, an act fundamentally required for the deployment of the idea of the infinite. It is in situating itself before its own cause, indeed in ignoring that cause in atheistic indifference, that the self can then open itself to the revelation of transcendence by discovering after the fact the cause that precedes and conditions it from an ontological point of view. If this separation does not intervene in order to free the effect from its cause, the relationship between these terms will remain the prisoner of a relationship of totalizing commitment—thus proscribing, for all of the reasons that we have laid out here, the revelation of the infinite.

The initial period during which the subject deceives himself or herself with regard to his or her own ontological independence constitutes the fundamental event of separation. There is thus no possible revelation of the infinite without a being who begins by ignoring the very cause on which he or she depends. This primary and preliminary ignorance establishes a breach in the relationship of the subject to his or her own situation of real dependence; it delays the realization of that dependence, and that delay coincides precisely with the independence of the self.

This independence would thus be reducible to the whim of a subject ignorant of his or her own dependence, since the illusory anteriority of the ego with regard to the cause on which it depends has a genuine ontological impact. This illusory anteriority marks the advent of the independence of the self in relation to its own cause: "This illusion is not unfounded; it constitutes a positive event" (54), as Levinas affirms. The self lives in ignorance of its own cause, but that does not mean that it is *causa sui*. Rather, it means that it is constituted such that it can ignore its dependence and live as if it were independent. And yet its independence is located entirely within its illusory belief in its own independence. In other words, it is located in the possibility of the effect positioning itself before the cause, by ignoring the latter just as much as its own dependence on that cause.

This primary moment of ignorance represents a "dimension indispensable, in the economy of being, for the production of Infinity" (240). The idea of the infinite—presented by Levinas as a "marvel" (27), and of which the face is the concretized (or deformalized) (115)[16] manifestation—indeed requires, for all of the reasons that have been laid out thus far, the preliminary exposition of the separated self. Levinas is by no means ungenerous in his warnings on this point: "The atheist independence of the separated being . . . alone makes possible the relation denoted by this idea," and consequently, "the atheist separation is *required* by the idea of Infinity" (60). Without this inversion of signs, without this illusion or ignorance on the part of the self in relation to its own ontological situation, the idea of the infinite would not be able to reveal itself, and we would thus remain within the totalizing framework of the causal relation.[17]

In this sense, *Totality and Infinity* represents an exemplary rewriting of Descartes's approach in the *Meditations*: The discovery of the idea of the infinite, the possibility of an absolutely metaphysical relation to the other, is conditioned by a chronological inversion of the logical order that allows the effect—the moment of the discovery of the cogito—to position itself as being first in a chronological anteriority in relation to its own cause. That is to say, Levinas follows a path wherein the order of exposition does not coincide with the logical order; the two are out of phase. This "breaking with participation" (58) corresponds to the lack of logical-chronological synchrony that marks the advent of the interiority—or atheism—of the self.

In Descartes, the discovery of the cogito chronologically precedes that of infinity, where God is its foundation. Similarly, in *Totality and Infinity*, if the other is presented as "prior to every initiative, to all imperialism of the

Same" (38–39), then the infinite requires nothing more for its revelation than "beginning" with the atheism of the sensible ego.

For Descartes, the delay that separates the discovery of the primary foundation, the cogito, from the second, the infinite, constitutes the independence of the self. Here the infinite is logically prior to the cogito, and the delay is produced by the self's naïve ignorance. We are thus able to see the displaced or staggered relationship of the self to its own logically prior cause, the anteriority of which is only discovered after the fact. The self thus lives in ignorance of its own cause, which does not mean that it is *causa sui*, but rather that it can live *as though* it were independent of any prior cause. Further, the phenomenon "after the fact," engendered by memory, breaks with linearly determined historical time, where the present is understood in terms of that which precedes it. Through memory, the end of that which precedes something is dependent on what follows it in time; thus memory is defined by Levinas as the "inversion of historical time" (56). Through this inversion of historical time, I am no longer tied to my past as if condemned to some fate. That which precedes me ceases to weigh on the separated self as an inexorable necessity. Interiority thus marks the independence of the self in being, by the deferral of its dependence, and sensation coincides with this deferral.

The separation of the self is thus entirely contained within the absurd act of the chronological inversion of a logical truth, an inversion that is essential for the possibility of metaphysics. These passages within *Totality and Infinity* thus convey the fundamental lesson that any metaphysics of infinity which aims to begin directly with the infinite is doomed to failure. Levinas follows Descartes in the idea that the chronological inversion of logic, in which the cogito presents itself before its own foundation, represents a necessary detour for the discovery of the idea of the infinite. Short of the revelation of the infinite by its idea, the exteriority of the other in relation to the separated self is indeed without content.[18] It is through sensation that the relationship to a cause is deferred and the other is thus placed in a position of exteriority. It is only from this vantage that the other is then likely to produce itself as metaphysical, which is to say, to speak. It is to a sensible cogito, initially positioned within being independent of its own cause, that the infinite within the idea of the infinite reveals itself. Discourse becomes possible only through sensible self-identification. The content of the infinite cannot be dissociated from distance, which "enters into the way of existing of the exterior being" (35). And yet there is only distance in relation to a position distanced from the other, ignorant of the other—precisely that position where the separated self stands and lives. Only a separated being can have the idea of a being absolutely exterior to itself; that is to say, a being that appears—beyond one's own egoism—as the subject of revelation.

In this sense, the alterity of the other, in its content, is indissociable from the sensible—that is, separated—position of the self: "The transcendence with which the metaphysician designates it is distinctive in that the distance it expresses, unlike all distances, enters into the *way of existing* of the exterior being. Its formal characteristic, to be other, makes up its content" (35).

It is from this perspective that we may come to understand just how the infinite is produced in the idea of the infinite, in the two senses that Levinas elaborates in the preface of *Totality and Infinity*: as revelation and as effectuation (see 26). Prior to this separation, the other is not yet transcendent, since the same and the other are still participating in a speculative communal substance. But afterward—and before any revelation—the other is no longer either: The infinite transcendence of the other in its content is indissociable from the thought of the separated self. The idea of the infinite articulates this thought, and the other produces itself—that is, reveals and constitutes itself—as absolutely other in relation to it: "The transcendence of the Infinite with respect to the I which is separated from it and which thinks it measures (so to speak) its very infinitude. The distance that separates *ideatum* and idea here constitutes the content of the *ideatum* itself" (49).

In other words, the revelation of the other qua other coincides with the revelation of its distance from a self from which it is separated and who thinks it. It is from the moment that the self thinks the other from which it is separated—or that the other reveals itself to the self—that the infinite is produced in being. This is because its content consists in the "distance that separates *ideatum* and idea" (49), that is to say, in the idea of the infinite as infinition: "The production of the infinite entity is inseparable from the idea of infinity. . . . The idea of infinity is the mode of being, the *infinition*, of infinity. Infinity does not first exist, and *then* reveal itself" (26).

It is for this reason that Levinas insists that "it is in order that alterity be produced in *being* that a 'thought' is needed and that [a self] is needed. . . . 'Thought' and 'interiority' are the very break-up of being and the production (not the reflection) of transcendence" (39–40). It is indeed from the moment that the self, separated from the other, thinks the other, through the idea of the infinite, that the other produces itself in its infinitude. Moreover, the infinitude of the other coincides with its infinition—that is, with its infinite excess with regard to the thought of the separated self that it exceeds. It is thus a question of thinking "the paradox of infinity" with Levinas, the paradox "of an Infinity admitting a being outside of itself which it does not encompass, *and accomplishing its very infinitude by virtue of this proximity of a separated being*" (103, emphasis added). Thus "*the individual and the personal are necessary for Infinity to be able to be produced as infinite*" (218).

As I now examine in greater detail, it is in sensation that the irreducibility of being separated from the concept—that is to say, separated from the totality—is produced. As Levinas so succinctly formulates it, "Sensation breaks up every system."[19]

The system is demolished in the moment that I find myself in the first person—that is, in the moment in which I sense. Put differently, it is through sensation that I constitute myself as interiority, that is, as a sensible subject who is ignorant of the cause upon which I depend. In this sense, if it is truly through the immanence of the sensible and separated self that the infinite reveals itself, then such a revelation does not come from me—it does not emerge from my cognitive powers of constitution. Indeed, if that were the case, we would remain imprisoned within the immanent life of the same, and the relation of the same to the other would not produce itself in being.

As the concretized experience of the idea of the infinite, the social relation must be understood on the Cartesian model. It is indeed God "who has put the idea of infinity in the soul" (86). From the deformalized perspective in which Levinas situates himself, this means that the face reveals itself by itself, *kath'auto*,[20] and not in an objective/plastic form drawn from the self's powers of constitution, where it would be at risk of dissolving its infinite alterity in an intellectual form that issues from the same. Such a dissolution would attest to the falsely infinite character of this other, because it is constitutive of the being of the infinite that it produces itself by speaking. Indeed, to speak amounts, ipso facto, to the revelation of the Other itself by itself, unmasked and in all its nudity, which is to say that it undoes the plastic form that originates with the self's powers of constitution: "The Other alone eludes thematization" (86).

CHAPTER 3

The Sensible Depth of Being

At that moment we are thinking only of the other
person—thus says thoughtlessness.

—NIETZSCHE, *Daybreak*, §133

"Sensation Breaks Up Every System"

The psychism, as the subject's individualized first-person identity, coincides with the atheist sufficiency of the self, which is indissociable from the act of sensing, at the frontiers of which totalization comes to an end. Sensing (*le sentir*) suspends totalization, in that all sensation is fundamentally correlated to its bearer, the one who senses (*le sentant*). Through sensation, the individual no longer exists as an element, a link, or a means belonging to a totalizing and teleologically oriented process destined to envelop him or her, but rather affirms himself or herself as an irreducible singularity. Nevertheless, this dependence is not entirely surmounted, but rather postponed and deferred. The sensing being (*l'être sentant*) is certainly ontologically dependent, but in the mode of not-yet-being. Sensation offers a deferment to the dependent being by assuring its emergence in the first person as interiority. In the space of sensation, the self exists as will. This means that it is not yet at the mercy of a grand historical account, where the first person has already been effaced by the *Sinngebung* of the historiographer.

The historiographer is defined by his or her position within being: He or she is the one who outlives the will of individuals, the one who decides, in their absence, the significance of their work. When the will has disappeared, it can no longer answer for its actions or defend its deeds—that is, it cannot speak. It thus falls to the historiographer to attribute the ultimate signification to these singular destinies, by integrating them into the grand and totalizing account of universal history. And yet to sense is only to forestall this danger, to postpone its arrival; it is to be, paradoxically, at the mercy of universal temporality though not fully inscribed within it. Sensation thus coincides with the disjunction of universal temporality, with the emergence of the ontological anomaly that is the precarious independence of a being in the first person.

To sense is to depart from the anonymity of history; in other words, it is to suspend, for a time—the time of the will—the legitimacy of any third-person perspective applied to the individual. The sensible thus coincides with the temporary suspension of our ontological engagements, bracketing[1] our participation in the grand saga of universal history. The ego thus emerges within being as that which can no longer be brought within the narration of universal history. In other words, it is that which is not yet—already—too late, that for which everything remains possible. In sensible life, human beings stave off our inscription into the totality and affirm ourselves in the first person.

As the deferral of dependence, the suspension of historiographical time, and the temporary cessation of objective reason, independence is crystallized in sensation, itself understood as the radical principle of individuation from which humanity emerges in its plurality. To sense is to break with participation, which is to say, to exist in the first person: "Commencement and end taken as points of universal time reduce the [self] to the third person, such as it is spoken of by the survivor.[2] Interiority is essentially bound to the first person of the [self]. . . . The thesis of the primacy of history constitutes an option for the comprehension of being in which interiority is sacrificed."[3] By assigning it the purely epistemological role of the representation of reality, modern philosophy underestimated the reach of the soul as psychism, when "the original role of the psychism does not, in fact, consist in only *reflecting* being; it is already a *way of being* [*une manière d'être*], resistance to the totality" (*Totality and Infinity*, 54). To resist the totality is to live sheltered from totalization, which is to say, to be immersed in sensible life. As an activity of enjoyment, the psychism is thus a "principle of individuation" (59); indeed, "The particularity of the *tode ti* does not prevent the singular beings from being integrated into a whole, from existing in function of the totality, in which this singularity vanishes" (59).

Individuals thus no longer draw their status as extended beings from a concept. That fact in turn corresponds to the dissolution of the individual as such, which itself either amounts to resistance to totalization or not: "Individuals belonging to the extension of a concept are one through this concept; concepts, in their turn, are one in their hierarchy; their multiplicity forms a whole" (59). If each individual is defined as a psychic interiority by his or her own particular sensations, then the diversity of individuals cannot be integrated within the unity of a category or concept that holds them in common. Thus sensing does not engender the diversity of individuals, understood as a dispersion recoverable by some speculative identity, but rather brings about their plurality.

Through its radically individualizing capacity, sensation brings about the erosion of conceptual totalization at the moment in which sensing deploys itself. The social interlocution by which the infinite produces itself— to the extent that the social relation concretely articulates the idea of the infinite — constitutively requires plurality as a precondition. Without it, as we have seen, the same and the other would participate in the same whole that prevents the other from producing itself as infinitely other. In short, in order for the other to position itself outside of the totality, the same must first free itself from the prerogatives of the whole by emerging within being in the form of a psychism, that is, as a sensible interiority. There is thus no discourse without plurality, which is to say without interiority or psychism, understood by Levinas as "its egoist and sensible self-reference" (59). In the advent of a psychism by sensation, each is called to emerge in the form of an irreducible individual, that is, a separated interlocutor, as is required by the metaphysical face to face.

In his analyses of sensation, Levinas deliberately places himself in opposition to the Hegelian system: "Sensation breaks up every system" (59). But can we, for all that, simply forget that the *Phenomenology of Spirit* begins with an analysis that takes as its object the dialectic of "sensible certitude"? Is it not from just such a certitude that Levinas himself purports to begin? And yet in taking hold of the what is sensed (*le senti*) in its anonymity, Hegel would obliterate the constitutive implication of a sensing subject (*sentant*) by the sensed. This effacement explains the regimentation of "sensible certitude" within the system — as the first step in a systematic deployment of the "science of the experience of consciousness" that constitutes the *Phenomenology of Spirit*. In his analysis of the sensible, Hegel would have thus already lost sight of the fact that sensation always goes hand in hand with the affirmation of an irreducible sensing subject:

> Sensibility constitutes the very egoism of the [self], which is sentient [*sentant*] and not something sensed [*senti*]. Man as measure of all things, that is, measured by nothing, comparing all things but incomparable, is affirmed in the sensing of sensation. Sensation breaks up every system; Hegel places at the origin of his dialectic the sensed, and not the unity of sensing and sensed in sensation. (*Totality and Infinity*, 59)

In this way, it is by the "singularity of the sentient [being]" (59) that Eleatic being (*l'être éléatique*) and ontological monism annihilate themselves in becoming. Here becoming refers to the multiplicity of subjects who are radically individuated by sensation. To the integral manifestation of being within totalizing thought, Levinas opposes the act of withdrawal that represents sensible separation. The subject is no longer held in thrall to a universal reason, wherein it would only ever be one of many components in a system. Rather, he or she removes himself or herself from the universal stage of the world, in order, like Gyges, to withdraw into the secret of individuated life, and in turn to prepare yet another scene: that of the social, founded on interlocution. As Levinas says, "The real must not only be determined in its historical objectivity, but also from interior intentions, from the *secrecy* that interrupts the continuity of historical time. Only on the basis of this secrecy is the pluralism of society possible. It attests [to] this secrecy" (57–58).

"To Live From": Contesting the Utilitarian Schema

Enjoyment represents the concrete mark of separation: "Enjoyment accomplishes the atheist separation; it deformalizes the notion of separation, which is not a cleavage made in the abstract, but the existence at home with itself of an autochthonous [self]" (115). Enjoyment is crystallized in the activity of living from the contents of the world: "We live from 'good soup,' air, light, spectacles, work, ideas, sleep, etc." (110).

The description of enjoyment is a rejection of the relevance of the utilitarian schema to the clarification of the relationship of the sensible self to the contents of the world. Further, the total refutation of the instrumental schema entailed by the description of sensible enjoyment will go hand in hand with the contestation of the Heideggerian primacy of *Zuhandenheit* ("readiness-to-hand") as Dasein's primary mode of access to worldly beings (*étants intramondains*).[4]

The elucidation of the sensible depth of being leads Levinas to phenomenological descriptions that reveal, on this side of the Heideggerian horizon of the quotidian, a relationship between enjoyment and the contents
of the world that takes precedence over their utilitarian function: "What
seems to have escaped Heidegger—if it is true that in these matters something might have escaped Heidegger—is that prior to being a system of
tools, the world is an ensemble of nourishments. Human life in the world
does not go beyond the objects that fulfill it."[5] Through the modality of
enjoyment which constitutively binds me to the contents of the world, the
equipment (*ustensile*) that I use to serve myself, as something that brings a
practical finality into view, is itself already the source of sensible contentment; it is an object of enjoyment.[6]

In this sense, any means that serves the realization of a certain practical end in fact represents an end in itself within the horizon of enjoyment
and is, as such, perfectly independent of its inscription within a system of
references. To live the contents of the world means that all content has
value, first and essentially, for itself. Enjoyment is attained on the level of
the mobilization of a piece of equipment in the service of the realization
of a practical end, to the extent that every piece of equipment is in the first
place for itself, independent of its reference (*renvoi*) to an extrinsic purpose.
It is a source of contentment, of enjoyment, or displeasure: "Tools themselves, which are-in-view-of . . . become objects of enjoyment" (*Totality and
Infinity*, 133).

The activity of eating is thus not reducible to the function of the realization of the organic end that consists in keeping us alive. Sensible life
doubles this activity of satisfaction, which we procure in the very activity
of accomplishing it: "Even if the content of life ensures my life, the means
is immediately sought as an end, and the pursuit of this end becomes an
end in its turn" (111).

It is in this sense that Levinas can affirm that "the uttermost finality of
eating is contained in food."[7] Nutrition serves no larger function beyond
nutrition itself—or, more precisely, every worldly (*intramondain*) being
serves some end, and is also in itself an end for the sensible beings that
we are. This means that, short of its utilitarian function, the status of the
worldly being is first and essentially that of a form of nutrition. The hammer already by itself produces a sensible satisfaction in the one who uses
it, which is in no way dependent on a network of practical returns. The
same will be the case for the use of the hammer as such, independent of
its purpose; it too is a source of celebration or of suffering. Every object
or activity that tends toward some end is already an end in itself, which is

to say, a source of sensible contentment. Enjoyment decouples a tool, or an activity toward a certain goal, from the finality or the point of reference that is its support. This kind of detachment is concretely produced through either the joy or suffering brought about by the activity itself, the exaltation or contrition of sense, which awakens the object in virtue of its being an object (and not as a piece of equipment inscribed within a "network of practical relations"). In this sense, the activity of feeding oneself in order to live is already valuable as nourishment: "Enjoyment is precisely this way the act nourishes itself with its own activity. . . . Life's relation with the very conditions of its life becomes the nourishment and content of that life" (*Totality and Infinity*, 111–12).

Enjoyment further consists in redoubling the third person point of view by the first person point of view. The anonymous accomplishment of life in the third person aims at obtaining contents that serve the utilitarian functions of life. These contents are thus understood as "the fuel [*carburant*] necessary for the 'functioning' of existence" (111). The emergence of the separated subject—of enjoyment—redoubles this exclusively neutral and objective point of view, by superposing on the third person activity of eating in order to live the act of nourishing oneself by this activity itself (to eat is to live). Thus from "the point of view" of sensibility, the aim of life—enjoyment—is already attained in the very activity of maintaining life. Even if "we live from our labor which ensures our subsistence," we live from this activity more fundamentally because that labor itself "fills (delights or saddens) life" (112).[8]

Nourishment, understood as a means tied to an end, is itself already an end for sensibility—sensibility that is elevated by all nourishment in enjoyment. One enjoys food for itself, independent of the practical end that it serves:

> Here lies the permanent truth of hedonist moralities: to not seek,
> behind the satisfaction of need, an order relative to which alone satis-
> faction would acquire a value; to take satisfaction, which is the very
> meaning of enjoyment, as a term. The need for food does not have
> existence as its goal, but food. (134)

The worldly being, understood as nourishment, is thus for nothing other than itself. Enjoyment is thus attained through the suspension of its referential function: "To enjoy without utility, in pure loss, gratuitously, without referring to anything else, in pure expenditure—this is the human" (133).

The idea that the objective of nourishment could in reality be already contained within nourishment itself is the great secret of sensible life, which remains unknown to fundamental ontology and which only an analysis of sensibility as enjoyment can reveal: "Things are always more than the strictly necessary; they make up the grace of life" (111–12). This grace of life, inherent in its detached contents, in the enjoyment that these latter procure for us in their horizon of return, constitutes the very substantiality of things, their sensible depths. To sense is to be in contact with such substantiality, which, for this reason, may not be reestablished in the Heideggerian perspective of the *Zeughaftigkeit* ("equipmentality"): "The structure of the *Zeug* [equipment, tools] as *Zeug* and the system of references in which it has its place . . . do not encompass the substantiality of objects, which is always there in addition" (133).

Overcoming the Ontological Horizon

For Levinas, the Heideggerian apparatus of everydayness does not permit us to take into account the independence within being that is achieved through sensible enjoyment. Indeed, "the recourse to the instrument implies finality and indicates a *dependence* with regard to the other, living from . . . delineates *independence itself*, the independence of enjoyment and of its happiness, which is the original pattern of all independence" (110, emphasis added).

And yet, as we have seen, the independence of sensible life as happiness is never ethereal or otherworldly. The transitivity of the "living from" very much entails a dependence with regard to worldly contents: "It is the joy or the pain of breathing, looking, eating, working, handling the hammer and the machine, etc." (110). What is, then, the nature of such a dependence, capable as it is of avoiding any contravention of the sovereign independence of the being that draws its happiness from the contents of the world? It is that, as we have seen, the model advanced here frees itself from any third-person schema, conceiving of the self, short of its sensible affirmation, as an objectively determined substance. Such a conception confuses enjoyment with a purely organic activity of subsistence. It remains on the anonymous level of substances and things in which enjoyment loses its intelligibility. It is for this reason that we must consider sensible enjoyment in the dimension of its excess (*surcroît*) in relation to the objective order of substances. However, Levinas insists that "the dependence of happiness on the content is not that of the effect on a cause" (110–11).

It is thus fundamental to understand that if enjoyment consists in "entering into relation with something other," then "this relation does not take form on the plane of pure being" (112–13). The plane of pure being, as it is understood here, refers to objectively determined nature. The affirmation of the self in enjoyment, however, entails the overcoming of such an anonymous framework: "Happiness, in which we move already by the simple fact of living, is always beyond being, in which the things are hewn" (113). Further, for a given being, the accomplishment of enjoyment carries with it nothing in terms of the actualization of its proper nature, but rather falls under what Levinas calls "a triumph inconceivable in the order of substances" (113). In this respect, it is impossible to assimilate the independence of enjoyment to the purely ontological independence of a substance. The depth of our sensible inscription within being gives us access to things as nourishment, which is to say, to the contents of life that engender happiness. The intelligibility of happiness, which is inseparable from the affirmation of the self within being, could not even find the criteria to which it corresponds within the objective order of substances.

For Levinas, it is a question of describing the dimension of excess (*surcroît*) in relation to the ontology from which sensible enjoyment proceeds. To be happy does not coincide, in any instance, with the pure, anonymous, exercise of being: "Enjoyment is an exaltation, a peak that exceeds the pure exercise of being" (144).

The "triumph . . . in the order of substances" (113) and the overcoming of the ontology that it entails, is not reduced to the description of one being among others on the neutral level of ontology. It is rather a question of distinguishing the density of sensible happiness from what Levinas calls the "bare fact of life" (112), or put differently, the pure fact of being detached from the transitivity of sensible life as related to the contents of the world. In the moment that its sensible dependence is extirpated, the self ceases to be. There is thus no self that could understand the exaltation of sensible happiness, which is to say, no self for which being could be reduced to the pure, anonymous exercise of being. The naked existence of the self is thus a contradiction in terms, as "naked existence" corresponds to the negation of the self. The transitive significance of the verb "to live" attests to the indissoluble connection that ties the life of the self to sensation, which is to say, the contents of the world that constitute the value of life above and beyond the anonymous plane of being. Thus, such a life could not be identified with the pure and naked fact of being, as such a life always exists in the first person—that is, exalted. It is in this way that Levinas can affirm, contra Sartre, that "life is an existence that does not precede its essence" (112).

Within the life of the self, there is nothing of the existential desiccation of an existent for whom essence coincides with existence. It is a contradiction to abstract human beings from their happiness, and thus our existence from our essence. That essence consists entirely in an excess, represented by sensible happiness, with regard to the anonymous framework (*plan*) of being. Sensible happiness in turn entails the effectual overcoming of the framework of being, which results from its being coupled with the framework of having (*l'avoir*).

The being (*l'être*) that I am is an existent (*étant*) that cannot be dissociated from the contents that I enjoy (*jouir*), which is to say, that I have (*avoir*).[9] To be in sensible relation with the world is to have the things that I enjoy, in such a way that my being—insofar as it is separated—ceases to be, once dissociated from their possession.

It is to the extent that the sensible self enjoys—that it is an ontically charged existent—that its being does not amount, as it does for Heidegger, to "the naked will to be, an ontological *Sorge* [care] for this life" (112). Contra Heidegger and Sartre, the being of the existents that we are does not amount to the naked fact of existence, it is not intelligible independent of the ontic charge that constitutively weighs on this existence, that is, which defines it in its proper density:

> Life is *love of life*, a relation with contents that are not my being but
> more dear than my being: thinking, eating, sleeping, reading, working,
> warming oneself in the sun. Distinct from my substance but consti-
> tuting it, these contents make up the worth [prix] of my life. When
> reduced to pure and naked existence, like the existence of the shades
> Ulysses visits in Hades, life dissolves into a shadow. Life is an existence
> that does not precede its essence. Its essence makes up its worth [prix];
> and here value [valeur] constitutes being. (112)

It is crucial to understand that the ontic content of sensible life is absolutely required by and for the advent of the ethical as such. In order to fully and clearly grasp this point, it must be understood that it is the notion of possession that serves as the paradigm for the analysis of enjoyment. Thus to enjoy contents is to possess them; it is to have these contents. My separated being is not abstractly isolable from this possession, this having, which confers an essence on it. There is absolutely no question of departing from this ontic density, in order to, for example, assume a purely ontological, purely verbal, condition, precisely at risk of losing sight of the subject called to responsibility. It is constitutive of ethics, and for its advent, that such a subject be understood in his or her full ontic density, which is to say that such a subject possesses contents that the revelation of the Other calls into question. Indeed, the implication of possession constitutes the concrete basis of the experience of the infinite—of the idea of the infinite—that is, of ethics. The advent of ethics remains unthinkable without the precondition of possession, that is, of enjoyment and its deepening within the dwelling (*la demeure*) (as we will show further below).

Put differently, neither the Dasein of Heidegger nor the Sartrean for-itself possess a "format" suitable for the revelation of the other qua other, that is, for the advent of ethics. The idea of the infinite cannot reveal itself to an existent who would be without ontic consistence, who would not be essentially defined by possession, which is to say an existent for whom the dimension of being would not be doubled by that of having. Life is inseparable from the value for which it is constitutively responsible through the enjoyment of the contents of life. Enjoyment thus reveals the fundamental priority of the ontic for ontology, of the happy condition of the self for every ontological, verbal, condition. This means that the *Seinsfrage* (the question of being) does not take priority in defining the kind of existents that we are:

> The upsurge of the self beginning in enjoyment, where the substantiality of the I is apperceived not as the subject of the verb to be, but as implicated in happiness (not belonging to ontology, but to axiology) is the exaltation of the *existent* [étant] as such. The existent [étant] would then not be justiciable to the "comprehension of being," or ontology. One becomes a subject of being not by assuming being but in enjoying happiness, by the interiorization of enjoyment which is also an exaltation, an "above being." The existent [étant] is "autonomous" with respect to being; it designates not a participation in being, but happiness. The existent [étant] par excellence is man. (119)

The priority of the axiological and the ontic for the ontological—of existents with regard to being and the question of being—is made explicit by the fact that enjoyment consists in the exaltation of an existent whose destiny is not exhausted in egoistic happiness, an existent whose authenticity is no longer bound up with existential solitude. But the paradox means that the revelation of the irreducibility of the existent to any ontological solipsism is only conceivable as such beginning with an analysis of the sensible condition of human beings as the objects of a full phenomenological elucidation. Before existents are in any way called to being, the existent is above all that existent exalted in sensible happiness. Such an existent is for this reason the subject on which the ethical may exercise its influence, the one to whom the ethical appeal is addressed. Put differently, he or she is the one to whom the idea of the infinite reveals itself, the one who is defined, first but not essentially by the satisfaction of needs, by the situation of hunger and the act of nourishment. We see once again the point at which the "rupture of participation" by happiness—as exaltation of the human being—constitutes the foundation of the event of sociality. Here still, however, we must not lose sight of metaphysics in its properly experiential dimension. It is very much the deformalization of the idea of the infinite that remains, always, the central concern of Levinas's analyses, which means that the act of nourishing oneself concretely prepares for the metaphysical experience.

Happiness and Independence

Happiness (*bonheur*) breaks with the framework of the ontology of nature, and as paradoxical as it may appear, it is through the satisfaction of needs that this rupture is accomplished. For formal logic, this would seem to invoke nothing less than a contradiction, and it must be explicated: "In formal logic the structures of happiness—independence through dependence, or I, or human creature—cannot show through without contradiction" (115).

Here, however, we must show some caution. Our inscription within being, as profound as it is, does not so much represent our integration and participation in the natural order, but rather the opposite. It is by way of sensible, terrestrial enjoyments and the immanent happiness that they engender that the radical independence of the self is affirmed. As a regime of separation, the sensible precisely signifies that the one who senses exempts himself or herself from the ontology of nature, and that his or her happiness is the affirmation of the sovereign independence within being. It is from here that the challenge to the causal model of the containment of the phenomenon of happiness emerges: "To this problem the notion of causality can bring no solution, since it is precisely a question of a self, a being absolutely isolated, whose isolation causality would compromise by reinstating it in a series" (119). And yet it would seem as though need would clearly inscribe our being within nature and that, moreover, need would constitutively entail a dependence on the location of that of which we are in need. How is it possible then that such a dependence is not only incapable of annulling the sovereignty of the self but in fact consolidates that sovereignty?

The dependence of need would only contravene sensible happiness if a given need is exclusively defined in terms of suffering from some lack. The "counterpart" (114) of the lack produced by need can be explained by the fact that this lack participates fully in the reality of happiness; indeed, "enjoyment is made of the memory of its thirst; it is a quenching. It is the act that remembers its 'potency'" (113). The extirpation of any need within the causal order, the capacity inherent in need to engender the happiness of the self, originates with that which the human being enjoys missing and depending on, precisely because this lack, the memory of thirst, plays a constitutive role in the realization of happiness as the satisfaction of needs. No satisfaction is possible without the memory of the lack provoked by need. To have a need and to satisfy that need are the two moments of happiness. The satisfaction of happiness is thus not the contrary of lack but rather implies it. There is no satisfaction that has not made the test of lack its own. The lack thus does not mark a condition of misfortune but rather constitutes the condition of happiness, in that enjoyment is only a sensible satisfaction to the extent that it comes not from the extirpation of a lack, but rather its fulfillment. Thirst recalls happiness in the satisfaction of past thirst, and that recollection is constitutive of enjoyment as such. The latter thus coincides with the satisfaction of needs.

To the extent that lack participates in sensible satisfaction, the human being loves to lack and thus "thrives on his needs; he is happy for his needs" (100). From the moment at which they become the effective conditions of happiness, lack and dependence, vis-à-vis the sensible contents of the world, are thus no longer suffered: "That man could be happy for his needs indicates that in human need the physiological plane is transcended, that as soon as there is need we are outside the categories of being" (115). In other words, that which frees need from the objective framework of nature is nothing less than the "complacency" (114) of human beings with regard to our own dependence. The redoubling of dependence, by the complacency that human beings witness instead, thus annuls the tragic condition referred to by the existentialist perspective that insists on the misfortune of human thrownness (*Geworfenheit*).

It is for this reason that Levinas equally rejects the assimilation of happiness to the ataraxy of the soul: A soul incapable of being exposed to the test of lack and dependence would never be in a position to know the apogee of satisfaction as accomplishment, that is, as sensible happiness. The soul in the state of ataraxy cannot know happiness, as ataraxy maintains participation. Thus "it is not correct to say that happiness is an absence of suffering. Happiness is made up not of an absence of needs. . . . Happiness is accomplishment: it exists in a soul satisfied and not in a soul that has extirpated its needs, a castrated soul" (115). Happiness is not to be found in the absence of needs but in their satisfaction. It is in this sense that happiness is not split between mastery and dependence, but rather accomplishes "mastery in this dependence" (114).

I develop in greater detail below the idea that there is no happiness without work, which is to say that there is no happiness without the deferral in time of our material conditions of dependence with regard to the unfathomable positivity of the sensible element.

The Depth of the Sensible Element

Enjoyment coincides with sensation, which means that to sense is to mark a rupture within the continuity of being—which is to say, to exist in the first person as an independent self. To sense is to break with all participation. And yet such a rupture is only the inverse of the extremely radical character of our sensible depth within being. Sensibility is the ongoing exposure of the sensible. It is taken directly from the sensible element that continuously nourishes it. The alimentary dimension of the sensible exterior is essentially understood through infra-objective contact with the exteriority of the world, which develops on the level of sensibility. Consequently, sensibility is less concerned with objects than with those properly elemental sensible qualities contained within the objective substrata of the built world: "The element has no forms containing it; it is content without form" (131). The infra-objective universe of sensible qualities is situated on this side of the objective world. Our sensibility is plunged into it. The alimentary dimension of an object thus does not come from its objective form, nor from its function as a tool, as we have seen, but from the qualities that such a form contains, in other words, from its sensible materiality. The sensible world is a world made of qualities that are independent of the objective substrates that contain them: "The pure quality of the element does not cling to a substance that would support it" (132).

This pre-objective universe, preceding any ambient world, and into which our sensibility reimmerses us at each instant through the enjoyment of sensible qualities, is what Levinas calls the "element." To be sensible is thus not to be concerned with objects, but to find ourselves radically thrust into a universe of formless qualities. Sensibility is nourished by the continuous flux of its contact with such qualities. The "element" is not the correlate or the vis-à-vis of the self, but the "milieu" within which sensibility is immersed. Prior to our representation and manipulation of existents, sensibility sinks its teeth into the element. Sensibility does not exercise a grip on things but rather on the primordial background of the element from which things issue. Things[10] emerge—by work—from the primordial depth of the element, which constitutes the originary matrix of sensibility, the sensible depth of the contemporary elemental world of our enjoyment, which coincides with a pure, and formless, sensible content. This pure, formless content is characterized by the fact that the element is essentially neither delimited nor deliminable. Sensibility returns to the element in its originary depth within which—to the point of disquiet[11]—our sensibility is embedded.

That which embraces the universe of existents is thus not primordially revealed, as it is for Heidegger, by a functional complex of equipment wherein each existent is related to other existents because they collectively form what Heidegger calls *Bewandtnisganzheit*, a "functional totality" or "totality of references." That which embraces existents is not revealed on the level of a functional totality, but rather composes the elemental milieu within which sensibility is immersed. The milieu of the element cannot be appropriated and is the background that embraces all things. It is the foundation from which things are carved out via the grasp that the laboring hand[12] exercises on the element. The sensible element makes itself available, in its depth, as an existent to no one, which is to say as earth, sea, light, city. If the element thus contains the very possibility of things within it, then conversely, nothing contains the element.

It is in this sense that, by its sensible depth, the element stands as a ground that is itself without ground, a content without form. If the element embraces all things, nothing embraces the element; it is a content that nothing can contain, a depth that nothing will ever be able to exhaustively plumb. The element is thus what Levinas calls the *there is* (*l'il y a*) in *Existence and Existents*.[13] In that book Levinas describes the *there is* as the degree zero of existence: the pure state of existence, existence without existent, existence in its pure affirmation, verbal and anonymous, which is to say, existence uncircumscribed by a substantive. The *there is* defines itself by the fact that no substantive, no existent, may come to delimit the anonymous verbality of existence. The category of the element proceeds from such indefiniteness—the mark of its sensible depth—which does not share the format of any existent or of any substantive-existent (*étant-substantif*).

Both the object and the element present themselves to perception from a single side (*face*),[14] but unlike the element, the object becomes present to perception in a side that is not necessarily the same in all cases. In contrast to the element, that we only perceive an object by one of its sides does not mean that only a single and unique side exists from which it would be possible to perceive it: The object may offer itself to perception from the front or from the back. For the element, however, there is no possibility of substituting one side for another. Not only do we perceive the element from a single side, but in opposition to the object, this side is unique. The element is the endless and indefinite prolonging of a single side that loses itself in the nowhere. "The depth of the element prolongs it till it is lost in the earth and in the heavens" (*Totality and Infinity*, 131).

The series of aspects through which we perceive the same object supposes that the object is maintained across all adumbrations. The objective coinciding of a back- and front-side is made possible by the identity or the substrate of the thing in question. The element, to the contrary, as element without substrate, content without form, does not articulate a back and a front, to the extent that such an articulation presupposes the invariance of a foundation. Such an invariance entails that it would be the same object that is perceived from the front or from behind, so that to perceive the object from one side means that it is perceived from one of several sides, without which the passage from one side to another would introduce discontinuity into the objective substrate targeted by the act of perception. The element is the content from which forms are carved out, but it is not, as such, itself delimited by anything: "The pure quality of the element does not cling to a substance that would support it" (132).

To the extent that the very notion of the "side" of an object is inseparable from the system of impressions that articulates it, the description of the element cannot be reduced to the application of a concept as limited— that is, determined by the horizon of the object—as that of a "side": "To tell the truth, the element has no side at all" (131). The idea of presenting the element through a singular impression or adumbration is not only in contradiction to the very notion of an impression, but leads to a misunderstanding of the element as some*thing* that one could approach, that is, something still in the mode of a determined existent. On the contrary, to the extent that the element is a sensible content without form, "The relation adequate to its essence discovers it precisely as a medium: one is steeped in it. . . . The adequate relation with the element is precisely bathing" (131–32).

In this way, our relation to the liquidity of liquid does not consist in the act of approaching it, but rather commingles with our sensible immersion in it: "The liquid manifests its liquidity, its qualities without support, its adjectives without substantive, to the immersion of the bather" (132). One cannot approach the element as one would a thing, because to approach it would presuppose that one could exercise an overarching grasp on it, or that one could take advantage of a distance in relation to our sensible immersion in it. And yet our sensibility is always already situated within the element. Through our sensible condition, we are always within the element. This means that there is no point from which one could either approach it or exercise a distanced, theoretical grasp on it. The element thus does not stand in opposition to thought, but it is first and foremost the milieu that embraces the sensible condition, and, from there, it supports and conditions any initiative of subjectivity. In this way sensibility does not enjoy the constituted object, but rather sensible qualities that the object contains: "Sensibility coincides with enjoyment enjoying an 'adjective' without substantive" (161). Enjoyment is rendered sensible in the element, the immersion of sensibility in a universe of pre-objective qualities. Sensibility bathes in sensible materiality. The world that precedes any ambient world is the non-unified world of the elements, within which, prior to any intentional initiative, our sensibility is embedded.

Whereas representation intentionally targets objects, our sensibility, by its originary adherence to the sensible element, causes us to regress into the enjoyment of qualities without form. The anteriority of the sensible materiality of elements to any ambient world—radically preceding any *Zuhandenheit*[15]—is that of an affective content, which is not essentially destined to inscribe itself within an objective form and which is not a sensible material that awaits or lacks an objective form. Sensible material precedes objective form; it is always detachable from the objective form within which it is embedded, and enjoyment, or sensible contact with the element, accomplishes this detachment by plunging us back into the world of qualities without form: "Sensibility establishes a relation with a pure quality without support, with the element" (*Totality and Infinity*, 136).

Enjoyment frees elemental content from the sensible, which delimits the objectivity of the form. For this reason, and through sensibility, the world is never exhaustively solidified in the world of objects. Sensible qualities are constitutively autonomous in relation to objective forms. In this sense, enjoyment reveals the sensible superabundance of the elemental content within any stabilized form. This signifies that the world of the element does not exhaust itself in any objective world, that the sensible exceeds any constituted objectivity. Sensible material is never assignable to an objectively determinate form: "Things come to representation from a background from which they emerge and to which they return in the enjoyment we can have of them" (130). "In enjoyment the things revert to their elemental qualities" (134). Unlike the intentionality of representation, sensibility does not target an object, since enjoyment causes the shattering of the element in the object; sensibility enjoys the elemental content with which objects are suffused.

It is in this way that Levinas can insist that "sensibility does not aim at an object, however rudimentary. . . . Its proper work consists in enjoyment, through which every object is dissolved into the element in which enjoyment is steeped" (137). In this sense, the sensible exercise of enjoyment shatters the elemental essence of the world just as it veils the objective world, the world constituted by identifiable objects, and the surrounding world of equipment. The element, including the grasp of our sensibility on it, radically precedes all of these. The immersion of sensibility within the sensible element outlines the contact with what Levinas calls the "reverse of reality" or the "the bowels of being" (132).

This explains why the affective content of the sensible material to which sensibility adheres precedes any representational content. Levinas speaks of it as "the world which precedes me as an absolute of an unrepresentable antiquity" (137). Our sensibility is thus immersed within a sensible rather than an objective world, replete with affective qualities without substrates. Enjoyment returns us to this infra-objective world of qualities without form.

From a phenomenological point of view, the primacy of the element on the objectively stabilized world entails the blurring of the neatly defined distinction between the constituent subject and constituted object of intentional representation. By virtue of the depth of our sensible embeddedness in being, the stability of this world is destined to remain precarious, to break apart in enjoyment. Indeed, the subject-object distinction noted here, as a result of the sensible condition of the existents that we are, is never unilateral. It is in this way that prior to *Totality and Infinity* Levinas could advance the thesis of a "ruin of representation,"[16] in an article inspired by the accomplishments of Husserl's phenomenology of the sensible.

The "ruin of representation" means that the poles of subject and object no longer occupy the neatly defined spaces conferred on them by classical representationalism. Indeed, the constituted object has a constituent affective content available to it, which compromises the exhaustiveness claimed by the transcendental activity of constitution. By virtue of the radical anteriority of the elemental world to representation—the nourishing world in which the sensible self is immersed—and to any objective knowledge, it is revealed that representation can never exhaustively constitute the sense of phenomena. One dimension of the world, the irreducible exteriority of the constituted object, escapes the acts of constitution of transcendental consciousness: the world in its very sensible depth.

It is thus a question of thinking the radical pressure that sensation places on representation, and the irreducibility of the former to the latter—that is, the originally noncognitive nature of sensation and its proper autonomy in relation to the global register of objective knowledge: "Sensation recovers a 'reality' when we see in it not the subjective counterpart of objective qualities, but an enjoyment 'anterior' to the crystallization of consciousness, I and non-I, into subject and object" (*Totality and Infinity*, 188). We must investigate the anteriority of sensation, as originary adherence to the sensible element, for every epistemological division that neatly delimits the distinction between the constitutive and constituted register. Levinas's analysis blurs any such transcendental distinction.

Enjoyment reveals the impossibility of reducing the constituted to the position of the intentional correlate of the constitutive acts of transcendental consciousness. Every constituted object reveals itself through enjoyment just as much as it occupies the position of the constituent, which is to say the sensible nourishment of the self: "The world I live in is not simply the counterpart or the contemporary of thought and its constitutive freedom, but a conditioning and an antecedence. The world I constitute nourishes me and bathes me. It is aliment and 'medium' ['milieu']" (129). Indeed, "Representation is conditioned. Its transcendental pretension is constantly belied by the life that is already implanted in the being representation claims to constitute" (169).

Where representation brings us to a position of contemplative disengagement with the world, Levinas not only invites us to think the disjunction of the sensible in relation to the register of representation but the latter with regard to the former as well. Sensation refers us to the primary breakdown of our sensibility within the element, which the register of representation is constitutively unable to recover. This delay between representation and sensation refers to the elemental depth of the world, to its originally nourishing—and thus nonexhaustively constitutable—character. It is in this way that the sensible resoundingly denies transcendental representationalism. Against any representational distancing of the world, Levinas rather insists on the radicalness of our sensible condition: "I am always within the element" (131); "to sense is to be within" (135).

The Inverse of Intentionality

In *Totality and Infinity*, Levinas contests the primacy of intentionality by way of the excessiveness of the infinite that presents itself to the self in the face-to-face encounter. But very little has been made of the line of analysis that traverses his earliest phenomenological elaborations, in which he challenges the privileging of theoretical intentionality from the ground up. In other words, he does not begin with transcendence in these early works, but instead departs first and essentially from the condition of the sensible life of the separated self. If the term "counter-intentionality" has been so frequently used to describe the relation to the face, it is often in order to reinforce the extent to which Levinas is first and foremost—and doubtlessly short of any counterintentionalism—a philosopher of the limits of intentionalism.[17]

Here I would like to concentrate more specifically on this lower limit of intentionality, which represents the register of sensation for Levinas, and of which enjoyment is the originary manifestation, as we have seen. It is a question of attempting to bring to light all of the originality of the phenomenology of sensibility—as the "intentionality of enjoyment"—that Levinas deploys, in the radical rupture that it establishes with the register of phenomenological constitution. However, the phenomenology of sensibility does not content itself with merely subverting the latter, but rather annuls it entirely in a renewed understanding of intentionality, the exercise and deployment of which itself entails the abandonment—if not the outright extinction—of the transcendental paradigm. For Levinas, intentionality, properly understood, leads to the overcoming of the representational framework. As we have seen, his thought reveals the overflowing of intentionality by its own intention, which is to say, the fact that the intention of intentionality, as a matter of principle, can never be exhaustively reduced to the status conferred on it by transcendental idealism. It is this kind of intentionality, understood as enjoyment, freed from any transcendental assignation—in short, "de-transcendentalized"—which concerns us here.

In 1959, in a volume commemorating the one-hundredth anniversary of the birth of Husserl, Levinas published the foundational article "The Ruin of Representation," which reappeared in 1967 in *Discovering Existence with Husserl*.[18] There, Levinas reminds us that "phenomenology is intentionality" but still warns against the kind of reductionist reading that he attributes to Sartre:

> But there was protest against the idea of a subject separated from its object before Husserl. If intentionality meant no more than that consciousness "bursts forth"[19] toward an object, and that we are immediately in the presence of things, there would never have been phenomenology. ("Ruin of Representation" [hereafter RR], 115)

This critique of the Sartrean interpretation of Husserl's intentionality provides Levinas the occasion to put forward an alternative understanding of the key concept of phenomenology, the echo of which will persist until the distinction developed in *Totality and Infinity* between representation and enjoyment. In the text of 1959, beginning with the Husserlian notions of the "horizon" and the "implicit," Levinas shows that intentionality can no longer be understood to consist in a single representation targeted by an ego constituting the sense of the transcendental object. Rather, intentionality is inscribed within an implicit horizon that cannot itself be constituted: "Intentionality thus designates a relation with the object, but a relation essentially bearing within itself an implicit meaning" (RR, 115).

This kind of assertion may surprise the reader of the early Levinas, who, in this initial phase of his phenomenological elaboration, inscribed the Husserlian conception of intentionality within an extension of the most traditional form of representationalist objectivism.[20] In "The Ruin of Representation," composed during the period in which *Totality and Infinity* was being edited, Levinas presents intentionality as a concept in complete rupture with the representationalist economy. Representationalism left no space for the dimension of the implicit; to the contrary, "The object is at every instant exactly what the subject currently thinks it to be" (RR, 115).

The dimension of the implicit that intentionality entails would, however, bring about the ruin of representationalism, to the extent that "by contrast, intentionality bears within itself the innumerable horizons of its implications and thinks of infinitely more 'things' than of the object upon which it is fixed" (RR, 116). Through its opening to the object, and to the horizons supposed by such an opening, intentionality entails the irreducible anchorage of explicit vision within the horizons of implicit sense, resistant a priori to objective thematization. Levinas emphasizes that such horizons demonstrate an absolutely irreducible potential, which for this reason does not fall within a "diminished or slack form of the 'actual'" (RR, 117).

Intentionality thus anchors thought within horizons that envelop the object but which, in opposition to the object, can never become the object of representation, other than to engage those implicit horizons within which all representation is irreducibly inscribed. This notion of a horizon signifies a "conditioning of conscious activity in potentiality" (RR, 116), which subsequently compromises "the sovereignty of representation" (RR, 119).

Intentionality thought through to the end leads to the shipwreck of representationalist intellectualism, because, as intentionality, "thought is no longer either a pure present or a pure representation" (RR, 116):

> This discovery of the implicit, which is not a simple "deficiency" of or "fall" from the explicit, appears as a monstrosity or a marvel in a history of ideas in which the concept of actuality coincided with the absolute waking state, with the lucidity of the intellect. (RR, 116)

Although, in its prototypical form, the Levinasian concept of intentionality continues to refer to Heideggerian ontology (at least in "The Ruin
of Representation," 115), this would not prevent Levinas from continuing to work beyond fundamental ontology, the form of reversibility that
emerges from Husserlian intentionality, and as a result of which, "being
is posited not only as correlative to a thought, but as already founding the
very thought that nonetheless constitutes it" (RR, 116). Later, Levinas will
affirm that "intentionality means that all consciousness is consciousness of
something, but above all that *every object calls forth and gives rise to the consciousness through which its being shines, and in doing so, appears*" (RR, 119).

And yet it is sensibility that comes to obstruct the possibility of an exhaustive constitution of the object. The introduction of sensibility into the
representational equation thus entails the reversible future of the relationship of constituent and constituted: "Sensuous experience is privileged,
because within it that ambiguity of constitution, whereby the noema conditions and shelters the noesis that constitutes it, is played out" (RR, 119).

The sensible inscription of the transcendental ego thus disturbs the univocality of the distinction that marks off the constituent ego from the constituted object. This inscription reveals that "the world is not only constituted but constituting. The subject is no longer pure subject, and the
object no longer pure object" (RR, 118). This means that in every intentional act there is a paradoxical reversibility of the constituent and constituted. Levinas would retranslate this idea in 1961, arguing that being is not
only a position of objective correlation—that is, of a content constituted
by the act of giving sense (*Sinngebung*) of the constituent transcendental
consciousness—but equally in the position of nourishing the constituent
subject itself. This paradoxical dependence of the constituent with regard
to the constituted that nourishes it would mark for Levinas the definitive
extinction of the modern paradigm of representation.

Indeed, in "The Ruin of Representation," Levinas constantly under-
scores the way in which "the ideal of a total actuality can only come from
an abstract view" (RR, 120), forgetful of the concrete, "and in a sense, car-
nal" (RR, 120), conditions of sense itself. Everything within sense is not,
therefore, illuminated; things grasped within the light of representation
are preceded by the nourishing character of those very things themselves,
delimiting the depth of our sensible installation within being. Contents are
not essentially the correlates of abstract representation but are rather always
already the unobjectifiable sustenance that the self enjoys in nourishment.

In *Totality and Infinity*, Levinas draws out the implications of the reversibility of constituent and constituted that he inherits from Husserl and Heidegger, in attempting to think "the intentionality of representation" through "the intentionality of enjoyment." The latter form being very much understood in terms of phenomenological intentionality in its impact on the register of representation. Within that register—which, in *Totality and Infinity*, Levinas integrates with Husserl's approach in his *Ideas*—there is no place for the full deployment of intentionality understood as that reversible relation by which the constituent future of the constituted would be accomplished.

In the "intentionality of representation," the constituent and constituted each have their fixed position. That is to say that each has a place determined by the irreversibility of the relation that comes from the same—the constituent transcendental ego—to target the determination of the other, the object thus constituted. The position of the unconditioned instance emerges from the first of these terms, and that of the conditioned instance from the second.

"The intentionality of representation" is defined by the adequation of the object to the thought that invests it, and it thus requires from the latter its assignment to the identity of the same. The object targeted by representation, the other fixed on by intentional representation, thus remains commensurate with the identity of the same. In a conception determined by the unconditioned primacy of representation, objectivity results from the sponsoring movement of sense that begins with the transcendental ego, from which the "total adequation of the thinker with what is thought" results (*Totality and Infinity*, 123). In this way, the object of intentional representation "falls under the power of thought" (123).

Such a demand for adequation would be inseparable from the Husserlian notion of the "noema," which Levinas identifies with representation as constituted by a transcendental consciousness sustained by sense: "The value of the transcendental method and its share of eternal truth lies in the universal possibility of reducing the represented to its meaning, the existent to the noema, the most astonishing possibility of reducing to a noema the very being of the existent" (127).

In representationalist logic, the same determines the other in its sense of being, such that the relation of the same to the other remains unilaterally determined by the same. The other, as noematic correlate of intentional consciousness, does not introduce any genuine alterity to the extent that the latter issues from the free exercise of the constituent powers of the transcendental ego. Levinas emphasizes that within intentionality restrictively understood as representation, "uprooted" (123) from its primary context, the non-self does not exceed the boundaries of the self. Phenomenological constitution describes an absolutely unilateral movement of the constitution of the same in relation to the other: "The same is in relation with the other but in such a way that the other does not determine the same; it is always the same that determines the other" (124). Representation thus entails a nonreversible relation in which the constituted is founded on the constituent.

As representation, intentionality at once conditions and constitutes the other, all while remaining absolutely unconditioned itself. If the non-self is conditioned by the constituent ego, there is no instance in which the reverse is also true. It is for this reason that Levinas can so decisively affirm that only where representation has the last word on intentionality would we find ourselves obliged to think the relationship between the same and the other in the form of an irreversible relationship founded on one unconditioned pole: "We are far from thinking that one starts with representation as a non-conditioned condition! Representation is *bound* to a very different 'intentionality,' which we are endeavoring to approach throughout this analysis" (126).

The alternative intentionality that Levinas describes is, in fact, *enjoyment*. Enjoyment offers intentionality a new amplitude, one that calls into question the restrictive premises on which representationalism rests, as the latter detaches intentionality from its concrete conditions. We see the method that Levinas introduced in the preface at work here, and it is a question of nothing less than the deduction of "the intentionality of enjoyment" from transcendental idealism. In other words, the task is to begin with transcendental idealism in order to arrive at a conception of intentionality as enjoyment, by way of the deduction and rupture of the formal noetico-noematic structure.

The elucidation of a movement that is originally at odds with intentionality, is thus no longer understood in terms of the light of transcendental constitution, but rather emerges from the rupture of the noetico-noematic structure, which was itself the result of the inscription of intentionality within the concrete horizons of sensibility. The deduction—or concretization—proposed here thus culminates in the expansion of the constituent sphere to the constituted itself of transcendental idealism or, in other words, in calling into question the unilateral division of the phenomenological poles of constituent and constituted. Transcendental idealism reduces—by putting in parentheses—the exteriority of the non-self to its sense of being constituted by the sponsoring acts of consciousness, wherein "the object's resistance as an exterior being vanishes" (124). Clarity, the work of representation, thus announces "the disappearance of what could shock" (124).

However, "the intentionality of enjoyment" presents a structure that is fundamentally different from that of "the intentionality of representation." This structure consists in assuming the exteriority that suspends the transcendental reduction, which is to say in immediately living this exteriority for itself: "The intentionality of enjoyment can be described by contrast with the intentionality of representation; it consists in holding on to the exteriority which the transcendental method involved in representation suspends" (127). The needs of the body, which arise in the exteriority of the world, situated below all objectification, "affirm 'exteriority' as non-constituted, prior to all affirmation" (127). In other words, the constituted is never entirely reduced to its status as constituted. The irreducibility of the constituted to that status—the way in which the constituted contests this very status—takes into account the profound nature of its role as nourishment of the same. The movement against which "the intentionality of enjoyment" responds brings into being objects constituted by consciousness just as much as those contents that already constitute, by nourishing[21] it, bring into being the sovereign activity of constitution deployed by intentional consciousness. The "intentionality of enjoyment" thus describes a kind of backward intentional movement, in which the world, to the extent that this activity of constitution deploys itself, undoes that activity, because the aliment already nourishes the activity of the constitution of consciousness. The anteriority that thus comes to light is that which "conditions the very thought that would think it as a condition" (*Totality and Infinity*, 128).

In the intentionality of enjoyment, that which consciousness constitutes thus paradoxically becomes that which conditions the activity of constitution itself. The intentionality of enjoyment entails the future conditioning and anteriority of the world with respect to the consciousness that constitutes it, a future engendered by this very activity of constitution, the unilateral status of which is in turn placed in check. This means that the more consciousness constitutes reality, the more the test of the primordially nourishing—that is, inconstitutable—character of the world intensifies. And it does so following a movement to which intentionality opposes itself, under the effect of its own constituent activity, coming about in the mode of that which is already constituted—nourished—by the very thing that it constitutes.

It is important to note that Levinas insists that "it is not that this conditioning is only noticed after the event," but rather that "the originality of
the situation lies in that the conditioning is produced in the midst of the relation between representing and represented, constituting and constituted"
(128). This means that the more the constituent activity deploys itself, the
more the situation of the constituent ego is then changed, through the paradoxical effect of this kind of intentional activity, modified by enjoyment.
Within the universal and unconditioned center of the constituent activity,
the ego comes to find a "condition in its own product" (129), which is to
say that it becomes interior to the very exteriority that it constitutes. In
other words, the formal modification of the terms of representation by
enjoyment entails the reversibility of the movement that begins with the
same in order to determine the other. At the same time that it constitutes
the exterior, the ego finds itself already embedded within the world that it
purports to constitute.

In this way, such a world reveals the underlying elemental nature from
which its anteriority to the self becomes—as the activity of constitution occurs—absolute, which is to say that it cannot be reabsorbed into a
noetic-noematic correlation. The reversibility of the terms of representation produced by enjoyment thus entails, contra representation, that the
more I constitute the world, the more the world constitutes me. Moreover, it means that the constituted future of the world entails ipso facto its
constituent future. It is for this reason that in enjoyment, the constituted
incessantly contests its position as constituted by exposing the elemental depth of the world, by way of the very movement through which the
same constitutes the other: its status as that aliment the anteriority and
conditioning of which are absolute in relation to an ego immersed within
the world that it constitutes, that is, in relation to an ego that is no longer
transcendental but already sensible.

It may be said that as enjoyment, intentionality advances in reverse. In
it, all transcendental progress (in terms of constitution) draws the regression of the self toward its primary condition as sensible subject, essentially
enveloped by the world of the element that contains it. All intentional acts
lead to the reversal of these terms following a process through which the
constitution of the object simultaneously results in the constituent future
of the constituted: the revelation of the always already nourishing character of the world that envelops the self.

The "represented" is no longer exhaustively reducible to its noematic
status, as it is at the same time the content by which the self that constitutes it always already lives: "The represented turns into a past that had

not traversed the *present* of representation" (130). Enjoyment reveals the irreducible depth of the sensible inscription of the self within the world, a depth that the register of representation could never, constitutively, come to fill. This reversal of intentional activity that is produced by enjoyment also brings about the future condition of the conditioned, a modification that comes to solidify the excess of the aliment with regard to any represented reality: "This sinking one's teeth into the things which the act of eating involves above all measures the surplus of the reality of the aliment over every represented reality" (129).

In representation, exterior reality exhausts itself in the noematic system. Enjoyment, in contrast, reverses the unilateral relationship of same to other, in a relation of dependence constitutive of the self vis-à-vis the non-self. In enjoyment, the other cannot be constitutively reduced to the identity of a constituted product. This is because enjoyment modifies the very sense of the intentional relation, by giving rise to the becoming-condition of the constituted and overthrowing the unconditionality of the transcendental ego—betraying, in intentional activity, its primary condition as an essentially sensible subject who already enjoys the contents that it constitutes.

In the "intentionality of enjoyment," the conditioned becomes the condition of a self conditioning itself, thus revealing the nourishing source on which noematic activity always already rests. The represented object is therefore not renewable exclusively in its status as represented; it becomes that which, by way of an absolute anteriority, already supports and nourishes the very activity of representation: "The represented turns into a past that had not traversed the *present* of representation, as an absolute past not receiving its meaning from memory" (130). In enjoyment, intentionality thus finds itself in the situation of having come to the point of surrender, beginning "from the point to which it goes, recognizing [its past self] in its future" (129, translation augmented); it finds, in other words, its own constituent origin within its correlate.

In a way that does not correspond to a position of excess, or a universal and unconditioned center in relation to which the world becomes the object of a disinterested contemplation, but rather by its sensible and corporal[22] existence, the ego shows itself to belong to the world that it constitutes. It is like the artist that Levinas describes, who finds himself descending from the canvas he is in the midst of painting (128). The intentionality of enjoyment is thus at once a rejection of the myth of absolute withdrawal, the mythology of representation as the disinterested act of placing the world at a distance. Rather, the world that theoretical vision places at a such distance exists in fact, and above all, at a primordial level of great depth: It is the world from which I live and the world in which my sensibility is immersed. This primary and absolutely radical inscription means that it is indeed impossible for consciousness to reduce the world to the format of a noematic sense. There is no act of exhaustively distancing the world that "precedes me as an absolute of an unrepresentable antiquity" (137), which means that the world that I constitute obscures the primordially nourishing richness of the world as that which "bathes me," in Levinas's terms: "The world I live in is not simply the counterpart or the contemporary of thought and its constitutive freedom, but a conditioning and an antecedence. The world I constitute nourishes me and bathes me" (129).

Further, the world is not opposite the subject, it does not face the subject—only the Other stands facing me. The world is first and fundamentally the "milieu" that "bathes" the sensible ego, and which comes to be revealed by the intentional reversibility of enjoyment.

This thus describes the paradoxical, constituent movement from the self toward the world in already living from its contents, which is to say in assuming the elemental depth of the latter—of which constituted objectivity is merely the facade. The future conditioning and anteriority of the world in the intentionality of enjoyment renders our sensible inclusion in the world indelible. It also, therefore, affects the register of representation, the transcendental purity of which is constantly contradicted by the irreducibility of our sensible implantation within being: "Representation is conditioned. Its transcendental pretension is constantly belied by the life that is already implanted in the being representation claims to constitute" (169).

Consequently, to target something outside of myself entails, by my corporeal existence, that I am always already within the interior of the exteriority that I target and constitute. It means that, by the reversal of representation in enjoyment, I become myself already within reality. The equivocal status of reality—at once constituted and constituent—denies the possibility of its exhaustive reduction to a noematic sense: "The 'failure' of the constitution of the objects from which one lives is not due to the irrationality or the obscurity of those objects, but to their function as nutriments" (147). Enjoyment thus causes the constituent nucleus of the world to appear behind the facade of the constituted, that is, the richness of its inconstitutable alimentary depth, the unconditioned source of the sensible self, the exaltation of which is enjoyment.

Despite all this, Levinas's goal in these analyses is not to plunge us headlong into a critique, let alone a deconstruction, of objectivity. It is rather a question of showing that the sensible self is not, by its own resources, in a position to grasp the world in its objectivity. For the sensible subject, the world is first and foremost a fundamentally equivocal world of enjoyment, or what Levinas calls "the anarchy of the spectacle" (90).

As such, Levinas is concerned with the rejection of phenomenological transcendentalism, wherein the ego purports to monadically achieve the thing itself, or to do so by following the monadic coordination of an inter-subjective community. It is thus a question of thinking the foundation of objectivity from teaching, by demonstrating that objectivity requires much more than the register of the single vision to which representation has reduced its destiny. Namely, it requires a surplus of language or, in other words, a relation to the exteriority of the Other: "Representation is not a work of the look by itself, but of language" (189). As we will see further below, metaphysics as revelation and discourse—that is, as teaching—is the condition of intentionality.

The noetic-noematic structure of transcendental phenomenology thus obscures the nocturnal events that support it and by which it lives, the events of enjoyment and teaching in particular. The deduction by rupture of the noetic-noematic structure restores intentionality to the concrete horizons that determine it. Every structure of illumination, every intuition, rests on the double priority of a life enjoying the contents of the world and language as principle of the phenomenon in its presence to sensible perception.

The Primacy of the Sensible

By the depth of our sensible immersion in a world of pure qualities, which lacks both form and substrate, it must be recognized that "the senses have a meaning that is not predetermined as objectification" (188). This kind of assessment has been rejected by the philosophical tradition, which assigns the intelligibility of the sensible to the norm of objectivity. There, sensation is reduced to either a representational content or to the subjective face of an objective content. Such a conception assumes an understanding of the epistemological distinction between subject and object, but the sensible life of the ego—which is in contact with the element—radically precedes and thus denies this distinction: "In other words, sensation recovers a 'reality' when we see in it not the subjective counterpart of objective qualities, but an enjoyment 'anterior' to the crystallization of consciousness, I and non-I, into subject and object" (188). To obscure the affective depth of our sensible installation within being is to reduce sensation to a representational content, and to thus set up the "objectivity of the object" (cf. 67, 76, 94, 96, 188, 209) as the measure of the non-self.

The archaic plenitude of our sensible implantation within being has its own autonomy; it does not organize itself according to a teleology of cognition. Sensation is not an amputated or diminished knowledge, and sensibility is neither "a fumbling objectification" (187) nor "an inferior theoretical knowledge" (136); indeed, "sensibility is of the order of enjoyment and not of the order of experience" (137).

By reducing sensations to the "structures of objectivity" (188), philosophy has ipso facto granted a kind of elevated dignity to certain senses. Indeed, "we reserve a transcendental function for visual and tactile qualities, and leave to qualities coming from other senses only the role of adjectives clinging to the visible and touched objects" (188). For an entire tradition that has taken up sensation as a function of objectification, "the object disclosed, discovered, appearing, a phenomenon, is the visible or touched object. Its objectivity is interpreted without the other sensations taking part in it" (188). Here Levinas recalls the thesis of Heidegger, according to which the primacy accorded to vision entails not only that we accord an epistemic value to vision—a value not granted to the other senses—but that the general form of vision serves as the paradigm for all sensible experience. Whether a given sensible experience engages sight or another sense, "It is incontestable that objectification operates in the gaze in a privileged way" (188). "As Heidegger, after St. Augustine, pointed out, we use the term vision indifferently for every experience, even when it involves other senses than sight" (188).[23] The regimentation of sensibility within the work of knowledge ineluctably entails the becoming-paradigm of vision.

And yet enjoyment is not reducible to what Levinas calls "the qualitative speculation of an object" (188) and is thus not reducible to the paradigm of vision. Further still, however, the theoretical view does not depend only on the gaze that the philosophical tradition has raised up to this privileged status of the paradigm of all senses. For Levinas, objective evidence essentially depends on language, and finds its metaphysical condition in teaching, which coincides with the presence of the Other. If "objectification operates in the gaze in a privileged way" (188) within the philosophical tradition, for Levinas the gaze alone does not suffice for the objectification of the world. Objective representation requires the welcoming of the face, which is to say that it requires language, the departure from economic solitude. There is thus, as such, no isolated theoretical view, as all theoretical perspectives engage the metaphysical primordialness of the face, that is, the entry into language—which is only language in the fullest sense by and through the teaching that it dispenses. Thus, enjoyment is irreducible to objectification and therefore to the primacy of sight over the other senses to the extent that enjoyment is not representational, but rather primordially affective. But, further still, in order for sight to adopt a representative content, it requires more than the gaze, more than sight to bear on the thing: It requires the welcoming of the Other, the revelation of the face, and the teaching that accompanies its epiphany. Sensibility "is not to be interpreted in function of objectification" (187); objectification supposes more than sensibility and more than the gaze. The surplus that objectivity supposes is nothing other than the exteriority of the Other to the self, the surplus of society and the obligation that crystallizes in the experience of teaching.

The philosophical tradition thinks objective representation independent of its metaphysical condition and for that reason privileges the senses of sight and touch. The privileging of vision refers to the notion of the idea, and the privilege accorded to touch refers to the notion of the concept understood as a grasp of being, as *Begriff*: "The hand takes and comprehends [*La main prend et comprend*]" (161). As discussed in chapter 5, the seizure of the element by the hand is constitutive of the comprehension of being as passage from being to having (*de l'être à l'avoir*): "The intelligibility of the concept would then designate its reference to the seizure by labor by which possession is produced. The substantiality of a thing lies in its solidity, offering itself to the hand which takes and takes away" (*Totality and Infinity*, 161).

Regarding vision, Levinas highlights a continuity from Plato and Aristotle to Heidegger. Vision indeed supposes light, and yet light causes a defined existent to appear to the gaze, within a space that it also illuminates, but which is itself nothing (*rien d'étant*). Vision sees within a field that is not itself any "thing": "Vision is therefore a relation with a 'something' established within a relation with what is not a 'something'" (189).

This function of vision, which inscribes something within a space which is not something, can be found in Heidegger, where the primacy of nothing of being (*rien d'étant*) in relation to "something of being" (*quelque chose d'étant*), something which is, denotes the distinction between being and the existent (*l'être et l'étant*). Being in Heidegger is, indeed, no "thing"—it is not an existent: "For Heidegger, an openness upon Being, which is not a being, which is not a 'something,' is necessary in order that, in general, a 'something' manifest itself" (189).

Thus in every case from Plato to Heidegger, "the relation of the subject with the object is subordinated to the relation of the object with the void of openness, which is not an object. The comprehension of an existent consists in precisely going beyond the existent, into the open. To comprehend the particular being is to apprehend it out of an illuminated site it does not fill" (190). The open space is the very site of being, which does not commingle with any existent. The openness to existents is not an existent itself, although this void is the very precondition of the manifestation of existents. Levinas sees a continuity from Plato to Heidegger here, because as he explains, the light can cause an object to manifest only to the extent that it has already cleared the space. The light is thus the precondition of the emergence of things within the ground of the void of openness, which is itself not something: "The light makes the thing appear by driving out the shadows; it empties space. It makes space arise specifically as a void" (189). The light allows the hand to traverse the void of this space in order to touch and grasp the object. Vision maintains the object within the void, which thus serves as the origin from which an existent comes to manifest. Levinas speaks of the "void of illuminated space" (cf. 190–91) out of which objects appear, but an object as such cannot completely suffuse the entirety of this open space. At the same time, this space, which places the object at a distance from the subject, is in no way an absolute or insurmountable interval that would separate the self from the Other. To the contrary, what we have instead is a passable space, one that is traversed by the hand and the grasp that it exercises.

It is for this reason that vision is never entirely independent of the operations of the hand. To the contrary, Levinas describes the depth of the grasp of vision in great detail, in a way that reinvokes the Heideggerian dimension of *Zuhandenheit* (readiness-to-hand), as vision opens a surmountable distance, which in turn invites the hand to exercise a grasp on a given existent. It is by the hand that the object is seized and understood, which is to say that the object only begins to take on a particular signification in relation to other objects graspable by the hand. For Heidegger, this signification emerges in relation to other existents in the capacity of manual tools inscribed within a network of return and within relations of *Bewandtnis* ("involvement," or "*tournure*" in French). At the same time, Levinas questions whether such a movement—rendered possible by the light of illumination, where "vision moves into its grasp" (191) and where an existent assumes a signification from the hand that seizes it—actually marks any form of transcendence: "Space, instead of transporting beyond, simply ensures the condition for the *lateral* signification of things within the same" (191).

If Levinas's doubts here are correct, it means that we must place the slanted or lateral relationship of vision to objects inscribed within a traversable space—because "to traverse it is not equivalent to transcending" (190)—in opposition to a face-to-face relation with the Other, the existent par excellence. A transcendental movement can be described only by a face-to-face relationship because such a relationship approaches the other across an absolute distance that the relation to the Other does not abolish. In the relation to the Other, insofar as it consists in that linguistic work wherein an existent signifies itself by itself—which is to say, remains exterior to the same—the distance separating the self and the Other is maintained. For this reason vision is not a transcendental movement, and thus falls short of language, because it does not breach the horizon of the same, within which existents are always approached in an indirect way, never head on.

In other words, for vision, the space between the self and objects is always surmountable. It is traversable (and traversed) by the hand, which vision incites to grasp the object, in order to attribute a relational significance to it. However, it is unclear whether or not the signification that originates with the grasp of the hand on an existent in turn allows for a challenge, as in Heidegger, to the philosophical primacy of theoretical vision, in favor of a pre-theoretical horizon of sense, where existents would be defined by their manipulability. Vision intensifies with touch, which is to say, with the grasp that the hand exercises over the object. The significance that ensues from the grasp depends in reality on the space opened by vision: "By the hand the object is in the end comprehended, touched, taken, borne and *referred* to other objects, clothed with a signification, *by reference to* other objects. Empty space is the condition for this relationship. . . . Light conditions the relations between data; it makes possible the signification of objects that border one another" (191).

The void produced by the work of light is neither nothing nor nothingness. Indeed, there is a mode of plenitude to it, although, as Levinas specifies, "its 'plenitude' nowise returns it to the status of an object. This 'plenitude' is of another order" (190). Indeed, "If the void that light produces in the space from which it drives out darkness is not equivalent to nothingness, even in the absence of any particular object, *there is* this void itself" (190). It is disposed toward a particular form of presence, which once again raises the insistent affirmation of the "there is" (*l'il y a*).

Beneath every positive object, the presence of the absence of all positive existents subsists within the positivity of the "there is." The "there is" coincides with the positive insistence of the absence of a positive existent:

"The negation of every qualifiable thing allows the impersonal *there is* to arise again, returning intact behind every negation, whatever be the degree of negation" (190). In the context of the analyses undertaken here, the "there is" corresponds to the void of the space produced by the light, insofar as "the light makes the thing appear by driving out the shadows; it empties space" (189).

By the action of the light that clears this space, there remains not exactly nothing, nor yet something, because the "there is" is that which remains when there are no longer any existents. However, it is not a question of something that is no longer, because the "there is" returns us to the degree zero of existence, to existence insofar as it is no longer the existence of any *existant*.

And so even if the light "drives out the shadows" in order to clear the void from which all beings emerge and appear to vision, it does not dissipate the murmur of the "there is." If the void is not something, but rather the precondition of the very appearance of things, then *there is* this absence of being and *there is* this void. The dissipation of the shadows, which coincides with the opening of the void, at once demonstrates that the void is completely undetermined and that *there is* this absence of something. If, in "driving out darkness the light does not arrest the incessant play of the *there is*" (190), how is it that vision does not then expose itself to the horror of the "there is" that Levinas describes in *Existence and Existents*? If the persistence of the "there is" cannot be suspended, how can "vision in the light" represent "the possibility of forgetting the horror of this interminable return" and thus "[approach] objects as though at their origin, out of nothingness"? (190–91).

The answer is to be found in the mode that characterizes the separated life of the self as sensible life. Economic life defines itself precisely by its naïve indifference to the infinite. Prior to any self-consciousness, "living from" consists in leading a life defined by self-sufficiency. Such a life is not preoccupied with the infinite, which is to say that it affirms itself in an atheist independence, ignorant and satisfied in a way that crystallizes in the absolute contentment of the elemental world in which it is actualized by sensible enjoyment. Thus the register of the sensible inscribes itself within a constitutive ignorance of the infinite, and enjoyment does not preoccupy itself with the infiniteness of the element that it enjoys. Rather, it comes to be sated despite the infinity of the element.

Enjoyment, as the principle of the individuation of the concrete self, allows for an anonymous relation to the element, which suspends the infinite regress of the "there is." Enjoyment is not a latent pleasure, nor an amputated thought, and thought is not the measure of sensibility. It is for this reason that the satisfaction of enjoyment effaces the infiniteness of the element, on which sensibility exercises its grasp: "Objects *content* me in their finitude, without appearing to me on a ground of infinity. The finite without the infinite is possible only as contentment. The finite as contentment is sensibility. . . . The objects of the world, which for thought lie in the void, for sensibility—or for life—spread forth on a horizon which entirely hides that void" (135). "Sensible 'knowledge' does not have to surmount infinite regression, that vertigo of the understanding; it does not even experience it. It finds itself immediately at the term; it concludes, it finishes without referring to the infinite" (136).

By its finite satisfaction, naïvely indifferent to the infinite, enjoyment is what allows vision to suspend the horror of the "there is." This is why "vision in the light is precisely the possibility of forgetting the horror of this interminable return, this *apeiron*, maintaining oneself before this semblance of nothingness which is the void, and approaching objects as though at their origin, out of nothingness" (190–91). As the work of sensibility, and thus as agreeableness, vision allows for the effacement of the murmur of the "there is": "Vision is a forgetting of the *there is* because of the essential satisfaction, the agreeableness of sensibility, enjoyment, contentment with the finite without concern for the infinite" (191). Thus, sensibility does not suspend the "there is," but rather our exposure to the "there is."

And so it is by way of the enjoyment inherent in sensible life that the incessant game of the "there is" does not stop itself, but rather forgets itself. This forgetting allows vision to serve as a relation to the void, experienced as the originary space from which all beings emerge. To the extent that the self does not relate to the infinite in sensibility, the void of the open space cannot represent the absolute interval from which the Other reveals itself. The horizon of vision remains the horizon of the same, even "a modality of enjoyment and separation" (191). The philosophical privilege attributed to vision, where objects appear from a presumed origin, thanks to the occultation of the indefinite, cannot for that reason be confused with the regime of objective truth. The latter supposes an overcoming of the economic horizon—that is, language—as the precondition of the revelation of the infinite in the face of the Other. It further supposes, therefore, not the void of the open space, nothingness as the ground of objects, but rather the presence of a positive existent that, because it signifies itself, gives a principle to the world that overcomes the equivocation of its immediate sensible appearance. That principle is precisely what is missing in purely sensible life, which Levinas calls both "relative and egoist" (193).

CHAPTER 4

The Terrestrial Condition

From the Transcendental Ego to Geworfenheit

In the early period of his phenomenological development, the Heideggerian concept of *Geworfenheit*, or "thrownness," presented itself to Levinas as a potential alternative to Husserlian representationalism, though he would later move away from thrownness and toward an elaboration of jouissance, "enjoyment." The question, then, is how the capacity of enjoyment to contest the primacy of representation—which entails the inclusion of the subject within the sensible element—is so radically distinguishable from the tragic condition of a being thrown into existence. The latter would indeed contradict the mere happiness of the atheistic separation that delimits the preliminary horizon of the sensible self, which is to say the existent constitutively disposed to the reception of the idea of the infinite. Moreover, and as I have attempted to show, the phenomenological elucidation of the position of the self within the sensible element is distinguished from thrownness in that the former annuls any reference to power, which undergirds the very intelligibility of the concept of thrownness. But to understand just what motivates Levinas to take up this increasingly explicit critical distance with regard to the existential condition of the thrown-being, I must proceed carefully, step by step.

In his 1930 *Theory of Intuition in the Phenomenology of Husserl*, Levinas deliberately inscribes Husserl's transcendental phenomenology within the Heideggerian horizon of the "question of being." Here in his first book, where the young Levinas proposes to "study and present Husserl's philosophy as one studies and presents a living philosophy,"[1] his goal is to show just how phenomenology can come to establish "a new conception of being."[2] This new conception would stand in opposition to naturalist ontology, which masks the origin of being insofar as it is "directly tied"[3] to the "life" of consciousness.

Husserl's phenomenology thus allows for the discovery that, owing to its intentionality, the life of consciousness is characterized by the fact of being "in the presence of transcendental beings,"[4] which is to say that "being is nothing other than the correlate of our intuitive life, because the latter does not aim at representation but always at being."[5] But in spite of Levinas's general enthusiasm for Husserlian phenomenology, its ontological reform remained unsatisfying. Indeed, even though Husserl had been able to reveal the relationship of intentional life to existence, he could not, as Heidegger had, elucidate the fundamentally temporal and historical character of intentionality.

Husserl would thus remain a prisoner of the classical schema founded on the "primacy of theoretical consciousness," in which the transcendence of existence (*l'exister*) is restrictively conceived in terms of the relationship of an object to consciousness. It is for this reason that, in Husserl's thought, where the concrete world is reduced to "a world of perceived objects, above all else," that his phenomenology, unlike fundamental ontology, could not bring to light what Levinas calls "the historical situation of man."[6] Levinas thus laments the fact that for the founder of the phenomenological tradition himself, history remains

> constituted by a thought; it in no way commands the fact of intentionality and intellection themselves. The genetic phenomenology through which Husserl will later seek to discover the "sedimentary" history of thought, deposited in constituted things, will not surmount his antihistoricism.. . . Thus, the mind, in Husserl, ultimately appears foreign to history.[7]

For Husserl, thought stands at a distance from history, and intentionality is consequently divested of any form of historicity. Levinas insists that in Husserl, time "does not exist prior to the mind, [and] does not engage it in a history in which it could be overwhelmed."[8] On this model, consciousness is not dependent on its historical situation; rather, it is history that

depends on consciousness for its sense of being: "History itself is constituted by a thought; it in no way commands the fact of intentionality and
intellection themselves."[9]

Whereas Husserl contents himself with "the suprahistorical attitude of
theory,"[10] Heidegger, for his part, in posing the question of sense, begins
with the temporality and historicity of human beings, which much more
profoundly raises the question of our existentiality. The Levinasian notion
of "the historical situation of man," regrettably absent in Husserl, is thus
illuminated by the Heideggerian concept of thrownness.

Thrownness refers to the fact of the existence of Dasein, what Heidegger calls its "facticity." Dasein exists in the mode of a project (*Entwurf*), but
always as a project thrown (*geworfen*) into the world. As such, Dasein finds
itself always already thrown into a situation that is not of its choosing. In
other words, thrownness refers to the fact that Dasein always opens possibilities against the backdrop of other possibilities, themselves already realized or missed. This relationship of displacement with regard to its own
origins is constitutive of the thrown condition of Dasein: "The subject is
neither free nor absolute; it is no longer entirely answerable for itself. It is
dominated and overwhelmed by history, by its origin, about which it can
do nothing, since it is thrown into the world and this abandonment marks
all its projects and powers."[11]

It is from this perspective that Levinas lauds the fact that the question
of sense in Heidegger is decided within the thrown existence of Dasein.
Here, even first-level intellection is in fact always already overwhelmed
by the actual situation in which the finite existant finds himself or herself
thrown. Thus in the capacity of being-thrown, Dasein experiences itself as
an origin that by definition cannot be recaptured. For Dasein, the temporal mode of being-thrown does not itself arise within existence; indeed, a
gap that it constitutively cannot fill separates it from its own origin: "Dasein is not itself the basis of its Being [*der Grund seines Seins*], inasmuch as
this basis first arises from its own projection; rather, as Being-its-Self, it is
the Being of its basis."[12]

Contra Husserl, Levinas thus valorizes the Heideggerian idea that intellection can never really grasp the de facto situation in which the finite
existant finds himself or herself caught up. In this way, to exist is to assume the precondition of a situation from which it is constitutively impossible to distance oneself: "Heidegger's *In-der-Welt-sein* affirms in the
first instance that man, because of his existence, is always already overwhelmed."[13] From this perspective, "Self-evidence is no longer the fundamental mode of intellection. The drama of existence, prior to light, is

the essential part of spirituality. . . . Existence is irreducible to the light of self-evidence."[14]

To the contrary, to affirm as Husserl does, that "at the basis of every intention—even affective or relative intentions—representation is found" is to inevitably "conceive the whole of mental life on the model of light."[15] It is for this reason that the sense articulated by temporal existence entails an irreducible opacity. There is, before all else, intellection of the always already accomplished, and sense no longer takes the form of the representation of an object; it "no longer has the structure of a noema."[16]

In this respect, Heidegger's thought certainly constitutes a decisive moment in the crisis of the sovereignty of representation. In Levinas's early phenomenological meditations, we find the idea that all intellection necessarily rests on a condition that can never itself be objectified, an origin that the light of intellection can never recover.[17] Thrownness refutes all of our intellective powers, thus undermining the supposedly sovereign register of representation:

> For Heidegger, human beings possess absolutely no means of departure
> from our condition. . . . Human beings do not find within ourselves
> the absolute point from which we could dominate the totality of our
> condition, from which we could consider ourselves from the outside,
> from which we could at least, as Husserl would have it, coincide with
> our own origins.[18]

From Geworfenheit *to Position*

Despite Heidegger's influence on Levinas's early phenomenological meditations, it would be a mistake to simply assimilate the challenge presented by the sensible installation of our being within the element to the primacy of representation, that is, to a Heideggerian notion of thrownness. In both cases, existants are radically immersed within a situation that overwhelms us, and which thereby controverts our pretensions to mastery. As we have seen, the sensible condition of being brings about the inversion of constituted and constituent, and thus reveals the inconstitutable depth of the element as that which nourishes the self. There is thus no form of enjoyment that would not be ineluctably affected by the unsettling depth of the sensible element. Indeed, Levinas emphasizes that "the freedom of enjoyment thus is experienced as limited. . . . The happiness of enjoyment . . . can be tarnished by the concern for the morrow involved in the fathomless depth of the element in which enjoyment is steeped."[19]

Although this disquiet emerges from the very depth of our sensible in-stallation within being, it would be inaccurate to describe the radical nature of that installation in terms of thrownness:

> The sensible world, overflowing the freedom of representation, does
> not betoken the failure of freedom, but the enjoyment of a world,
> a world "for me," which already contents me. The elements do not
> receive man as a land of exile, humiliating and limiting his freedom.
> The human being does not find himself in an absurd world in which
> he would be *geworfen*. (*Totality and Infinity*, 140)

The sovereignty and independence of happiness are not suspended by the element's inundation of sensibility; the element disturbs but does not annul enjoyment. For this reason, to interpret Levinas's reevaluation of the sen-sible within his description of our being-in-the-world in terms of thrown-ness is to fundamentally misconstrue his conclusions there. Indeed, to do so would amount to projecting the problematic of power onto the position of sensibility, when in fact the former does not constitutively belong to the latter. It would further amount to a description of sensible existence as deficient or lacking with regard to some absolute identity, one that could genuinely challenge our condition as thrown-beings, and thus to equate our sensible position with some kind of ontological dereliction.

And yet such a conception in fact rests on a perfectly abstract repre-sentation of the self, as if subjectivity could be conceived independently of its concurrence with sensible happiness. The attempt to understand the position of our sensibility in terms of some kind of ontological degradation relies on an ideal self, severed from the sensible context from which its very emergence as self cannot be dissociated. As I have tried to show, subjectiv-ity is radically inseparable from sensation. It is for this reason that "one cannot first posit [a self] and then ask if enjoyment and need run counter to it, limit it, injure it, or negate it: only in enjoyment does the [self] crys-tallize" (144). To enjoy is to touch the element; the archaic contact with the element coincides with the fact—always already so—of touching the earth and thus with the originary effort to be held by and remain with it. To be me is to be supported by the element, which is to say, to grasp the earth, and to have a position.

The radical anteriority of the element, within which my sensibility is immersed, entails that my contact with it, the fact that I grasp it, precedes and envelops any relational activity that would originate with me and reach toward the world (understood as the object of theoretical or practical ac-tion). Position is prior to any initiative of subjectivity. Indeed, the fact that my position is the foundation on which any practical or theoretical activity rests attests to the radical nature of the anteriority in question: "The bit of earth that supports me is not only my object; it supports my experience of objects. . . . The relation with my site in this 'stance' [*tenue*] precedes thought and labor" (138). If it is possible for me to be here below, in contact with the objects of my focus, it is because I am always already here. To think the radical nature of our installation here is to break with any analysis that consists in reintegrating our sensible condition within a problematic of human powers.

Although thrownness certainly reveals the limits of the powers that we, as existants, have over our own being, it only does so to the extent that the existential apparatus continues to accord an importance to the notion of power: "The fact that we have not chosen our birth seems to constitute the great scandal of the human condition. And it is a scandal, due precisely to the exceptional prestige enjoyed by the notion of power, and the idea of freedom which undergirds it. . . . The obsession with power continues to dominate the philosophy of existence."[20] Further,

> The novelty of the modern critique of reason in relation to all other irrationalisms consisted in challenging the possibility of positioning oneself outside of the situation, which is the most radical opposition to idealism. But the conception from which this critique proceeds does not renounce the idea of power. Thus the inability to grasp the entirety of existence—the limits of our power, which results in the loss of the infinite—still appears tragic to us; it still appears as thrownness.[21]

It is equally legitimate to accept, following Heidegger and Sartre,[22] that any exercise of power inscribes itself within the foundations of a terrestrial condition that is itself the basis of power, but which, as such and by definition, is itself immune to the exercise of power. All power rests on a condition that cannot be phenomenologically reduced to the structures of representation, and over which no totalizing transcendental grasp could ever take hold: "Power holds no sway over the position from which it is established."[23]

In this way, it makes little sense to equate the lack of any influence over the origin with the tragic in thrownness. Indeed, it would be perfectly erroneous to understand this condition as a deficiency that afflicts our powers, as some kind of absurd and tragic limitation inherent in them:

> This disparity between the power of the subject and the very supports upon which that power rests—the foundation necessarily presupposed

by such power—is singularly impoverished by that famous "I did not
desire my own existence" from which so much recent philosophical work commences. . . . With regard to these powers, it is that over
which power holds no sway; but everything that is outside of power
does not simply amount to subjection or servitude. And yet this is precisely the deficient interpretation given by Heidegger and Sartre.[24]

Our originary situation is a position which locates consciousness, and
that localization of consciousness is prior to any positive or negative reference to powers: "The situation is beyond activity and passivity."[25] In order to describe this localization of consciousness, which is again prior to
any consciousness of localization, Levinas uses the language of Sartre, and
speaks of an "extreme in-itself," or a "movement in place,"[26] preceding
any ecstatic movement away from the self and toward the world. It thus
becomes a question of an affirmation of self that, unlike the Sartrean for-
itself, does not in any way amount to a negation of the in-itself. As an affirmation that precedes any active or passive affirmation, position coincides
with what Levinas calls "all of the weight of being."[27]

Thus transcendence is not the originary phenomenon. The ecstatic departure from the self, which correlates with the comprehension of being
supposes—prior to any transcendence—the preeminence of an existent
here, rooted in being, which is to say an ego inscribed within the sensible.
Before being-there, I am here, which is to say that I am sensible:

> My sensibility is here. . . . Position, absolutely without transcendence,
> in no way resembles the comprehension of the world by the Heideg-
> gerian *Da*. Its is not the care for Being [*souci d'être*], nor a relation with
> existents, nor even the negation of the world, but its accessibility in
> enjoyment. (*Totality and Infinity*, 138)

In this respect, the separated self does not primarily consist in Dasein's
assumption of a verbal condition, but rather an ontic condition: a sensible
position that weighs on being. The ego "is not, for its part, some arbitrary and floating being, but rather *weighs upon being*; it is, as Descartes
put it in such a marvelously precise way, *a thing which thinks*."[28] Levinas
thus speaks as much in terms of position as he does of this "weight which
the subject possesses."[29] The radically and ontologically prior weight of
consciousness—the localization of our consciousness as irreducible, prior
to and constitutive of the possibility of the consciousness of our localization—precedes the existant's call to ontological unveiling and discovery.

This term "position" designates the condition on which the exercise of constituent, comprehensive, or revealing power is inexorably founded: "Power does not float in the air;"[30] "thought has a point of departure."[31] Position as a foundation in being is thus beyond the reach of power. Position precedes the regime of transcendental constitution just as it precedes the existential regime of the project, understood as the way of being of human beings in Sartre: "The *here* of the position precedes all comprehension, any horizon, and all time."[32]

Position proceeds from an ego that begins by being here before being there, which only affirms itself as transcendence on the precondition of the affirmation of a self that is withdrawn, which is to say radically deaf to the call of transcendence.[33] Such deafness betrays the material foundations of power, and reveals that the exercise of thought does not come from nowhere but rather from an existent essentially bound to a position—which is to say, an existent essentially created, a point to which I return.

That any consciousness has a condition is perceived and understood by the philosophies of existence as the experience of a limitation of our powers, as what Sartre calls the facticity of consciousness. It is in this way that Levinas summarizes Sartre's position concerning the unavoidable conditioning of consciousness: "Consciousness is the mode of existence of a being who can [*peut*], and from there in turn, the relationship with the beginning is a relationship to that which one cannot [*peut pas*]. This relation appears as a limit and as a misfortune."[34]

Levinas refuses to assimilate the conditioning of consciousness to some kind of tragic facticity. He refuses to conceive of the conditioning of consciousness in terms of either a limit inflicted on our powers or the misfortune of a thrown and absurd factical condition. Contra Sartre, Levinas considers the conditioning of any activity of consciousness to be the refuge and the security of the existant: "For us, this foundation of power in being is not an obstacle to power, but rather its very condition, its privilege, its refuge and, in some sense, its glory."[35] The localization of consciousness prior to the consciousness of localization is thus not to be understood as a limit inflicted on power, or the misfortune of a thrown and absurd condition, but, again, as the refuge and the security of the sensible existent.

This security is the security of a base, which allows the existent committed to the world to withdraw into himself or herself, to cut with his or her worldly commitments in the act of sleeping. To be here, prior to being-there means for Levinas to have a localization, to be localized before thinking my localization, which is to say to possess the permanent capacity to withdraw into myself, into my own material condition, conceived as my shelter, and for that reason as the glory of human reality:

> The thought which instantly spreads itself within the world retains the possibility of gathering itself again here. It never detaches itself from this *here*. Its origin is its springboard, its refuge and its security. Consciousness is precisely the fact that the impersonal and uninterrupted affirmation of "eternal truths" can simply become a thought; that is to say it can, in spite of its sleepless eternity, begin or end in a head, illuminate or extinguish itself, escape itself: the head again falls upon the shoulders, and one sleeps. This refuge is open, in its very exercise, to thought.[36]

Every truth engages the material existence of a thinker, defined not by his or her openness to the truth, but by his or her capacity to withdraw. True thought begins and ends within a head, a head that sits on the shoulders of a concrete human being, immersed in sensible being, which is to say, in a position to suspend the anonymous wakefulness of eternal truths, in order to withdraw again into slumber. The philosopher, because he or she is first and foremost grounded in being, is precisely the one who can resurface on the other side of his or her effacement before the eternity of the truth, the one who can always return to the terrestrial condition that supports the exercise of his or her powers, "within the sanctuary of eternity and universality."[37]

An essential dimension is therefore missing from those descriptions of being-in-the-world that mask the material weight of the position which serves as ballast for every exercise of power. Power has a provenance that is itself irreducible to the horizon of power, whether that power is limited or not in the first place.

This provenance is rooted in the depths of our sensible installation within being, from which the emergence of the self can never be decoupled, lest we fall back into the tribulations of idealism—still latent in thrownness and which Levinas therefore denounces. However, if the subject's foundation within being is not a condition of misfortune but rather constitutes the refuge of the self, then we, as sensible existents, have no ontological unity. If the self identifies itself with an ontological unity, its integrity would be necessarily contradicted by its conditioning, which one could justifiably interpret in terms of ontological degradation: "because the being conceived as a unity could never admit any limitation, even that of its own origin."[38]

If position, and thus the pressure of the sensible element on the self which it entails, is not a position of misfortune for the subject, but rather a condition of security, and if the element that envelops it does not menace us but rather bathes and protects us, it is because our sensible condition as existents cannot be dissociated from our creaturely condition. The intelligibility of the sensible self therefore presumes the precondition of an ontological event the consideration of which allows for the definitive demarcation of the sensible being from the subjectivity of any condition of thrownness. The "transfiguration of the curse of *Geworfenheit* [thrownness] into glory"[39] can, nevertheless, become intelligible only once the reform of ontology, occasioned by the event of fecundity, comes to term.

The Ontological Background of Position:
The Plural Existence of Fecundity

For Levinas, the fact of being impotent toward our origin can be experienced as a tragic condition only from the perspective of an extremely conservative version of ontology, namely, the version adopted by idealism and existentialism after it. This conception has conceived of being in terms of unity since Parmenides, a unity whose ontological integrity is necessarily challenged by its immediate conditioning, understood as tragic facticity:

> Helplessness with regard to the origin is tragic when it is a question of a subject who is absolutely singular, and who finds himself opposed by virtue of the fact of never having chosen his own origin. This helplessness is also, to the contrary, the very security of a being whose existence is related to the event of fecundity: the security of the creature.[40]

Within the existentialist fantasy of replacing a birth that we have not chosen with a self-elected origin, there is thus a profound solidarity with the Eleatic idealism that has dominated ontology since Parmenides: to contain being within the unity. The tragedy of existence does not consist in a lack of power over our origin, but rather in the reduction of being to identity. Levinas contests the idea that "identity" is the proper format for the exhaustive deployment of the plan of being. Reduced to identity—the idea that being is identical to itself, and is thus one—ontology remains underdetermined.

As a result, the existentialist vision of the thrown condition of being-in-the-world commits the fundamental evaluative error of adopting the idealist understanding that a chosen birth would be somehow less tragic than thrownness. But the tragic within existence does not originate in our inability to dominate our own condition, but rather in the reduction of being to the permanence of identity, because "substance is precisely that which does not recommence."[41] "Substance" here is synonymous with a return to self that fixes the subject to an identity to which its being is assigned and reduced. Substance coincides with the aging of being (*vieillissement de l'être*). The renewal of being, its rejuvenation, does not entail a departure from the framework of being (*plan de l'être*), but rather its pluralization in fecundity, by the father-son relationship. Here, the substance of the father is renewed in that of the son, without being identical to the son—which is to say, without being identical to itself, and without, for all that, ceasing to be. In fecundity the father becomes the son, which attests to a discontinuity between the same and the other, a scission of identity, constitutive of ontology as multiple: "On the level of the logic of Parmenides, to free oneself from one's identity without effacing being would be meaningless."[42]

We must therefore think, contra Parmenides, a noncorrespondence of ontology and identity. Being is not limited to the "exercise of being" of an existent identical to itself. The father does not cease to be in the son; he is his son, but the identity of the son cannot be reduced to that of the father. Such a reduction would risk the dissolution of the very transcendence of the act of begetting, by which the father emerges as other in his son. In such a scenario, the son could only ever be an avatar of his father, which is to say a modification of the same:

> The evasion of the self is no simple recommencement of the subject. It is constituted in the relation to the Son. Paternity is not only a renewal of the Father in the Son, and his confusion with the latter. It is also an exteriorization of the Father in relation to the Son: a pluralist existence. There is a multiplicity contained within the verb "to exist," which the most self-assured existentialist analysts necessarily fail to recognize.[43]

The ontological impact of fecundity brings about an ontology capable of taking up the discontinuity of the same and the other. It translates the inseparability of being from its own multiplication, by which being renders itself infinite.[44] However, here the infinity of being is no longer marked by a continuous or consistently identical presence, nor is it the infinite continuation of the soul, but rather coincides with the infinite renewal of being across generations. The act of fecundity is an act of getting outside oneself, an act of transcendence, by which the same emerges as other, irreducible to the identity of the same. By this intrinsically ontological act, being transcends itself and becomes infinite. Without an elucidation of the ontological reform that is entailed by the event of fecundity, the transfiguration of thrownness into glory—the passage from the primacy of the existential *Da* to the here of position—would remain perfectly unintelligible. Without the nocturnal event of fecundity, brought about through the rupture of phenomenological intuition, it would be impossible to describe the terrestrial condition of human beings in any terms other than those of the tragic form of thrownness. The primacy of sensible happiness over any condition of misfortune becomes intelligible only once the nocturnal event of fecundity is elucidated, which in turn opens up the sensible depth of our being-in-the-world. It is thus fecundity that exhausts the reference to power and allows us to grasp the depth of our foundation in being.

We can only think an existent primordially defined by the here, which is to say by a sensible condition, on the precondition of an ontology marked by the event of fecundity. The ontological implications of that event allow us to understand just why our terrestrial condition is not inscribed within the register of power. In other words, the lack of power over our own origin does not come from an ontological unity that must be reconquered, but from the profound plurality of existence itself, which does not require any recovery or synthesis of identity. In this way, the event of fecundity allows us to think a relation to the origin that does not consist in a relation of power: "In a pluralist existence, our powerlessness with regard to the origin loses its tragic sense; it is a necessary aspect of this pluralist existence."[45]

It is not, therefore, that my origin escapes me, as it can be understood to tragically escape me only if being is conceived in terms of a unity. But by the fecundity and the intrinsically plural character by which it is instead characterized here, the terrestrial condition can no longer be seen as something tragic. That condition instead becomes the mark of an ontology that cannot be dissociated from the succession of generations, wherein the father transcends himself in the son but is not confounded with his son. By the ontological plurality of which he is the very signature, the son does not live out his creaturely condition in suffering and misfortune. Understood as an engendered being, the son proceeds from the pluralization of the father. And if being is constitutively plural, then there is no suffering for one to live through exterior to one's origin. Material conditions thus become the security of a base, of a position, in which the subject, as an essentially sensible being, which is to say an engendered being, finds himself or herself grounded.

Disquiet and Recourse

The dependence on the space of the other—that is, of the sensible—does not therefore contradict happiness. To the contrary, it represents the condition required for happiness to emerge in being in the form of the separated self. However, although Levinas does contest the characterization of thrownness as originary, he does not dismiss the concept altogether. The sensible self is never sheltered from dereliction. Indeed, we must recognize here a character that is essentially derived in relation to the primary condition of happiness, quite the inverse of certain existential and existentialist analyses. Even if thrownness does not originally define the terrestrial condition, it may still define its possible degradation.

Enjoyment is not originally thrown; it is a dependence that is overcome, a sovereign dependence. The dependence of need in no way contradicts the sovereignty of the self, but is, to the contrary, its very condition. Sovereign sensibility is thus a sovereignty that does not suffer from its state of dependence, a sovereignty that remains unthinkable without the dependence of need, because it renounces the predicates of idealism. However, this dependence can become a form of suffering and absurdity, because the very dependency that happiness articulates—which is not primarily thrown, but is rather sovereign happiness—remains a disquieted sovereignty. It is disquieted because it is held in the grasp of the fathomless depth of the sensible, which, as "content without form"—even if it does not directly menace the instant of enjoyment—will never fail to remind the subject of the depth of his or her own inscription within the alterity of the element. The transitivity of "living from," constitutive of the sovereign mastery of the self, entails its precariousness, the fact that it is constantly at risk of degrading into a total dependence on the non-self, which is to say, into indigence.

Enjoyment evinces the grasp of the same on the other. And although that grasp never amounts to the other's influence over the same, it always threatens to become so: "In sensibility itself and independently of all thought there is announced an insecurity. . . . Enjoyment seems to be in touch with an 'other' inasmuch as a future is announced within the element and menaces it with insecurity" (*Totality and Infinity*, 137). In this way, because it is exercised on a depth without ground, enjoyment never exhaustively masters the element that it enjoys. Although its mastery is incontestable, it is also incontestably limited. "The indetermination of the future" (141) affects enjoyment. The disquiet of indigence brings the horizon of every act of immediate enjoyment—that is, unmediated by labor—into view. This means, therefore, that the dependence of enjoyment does not hinder its mastery; it is a "mastery in this dependence" (114). It does not condemn the self to the absurdity and misfortune of a thrown condition but rather exposes its sovereignty over being to the menace of a future of privation and misery.

This menace entails the absence of neither mastery nor happiness, the misfortune of dereliction, but rather attests to the limited character of the mastery that enjoyment exercises over elemental being: "The perfidious elemental gives itself while escaping" (141). This limitation does not hinder the happiness of enjoyment but rather tarnishes it:

> The happiness of enjoyment flourishes on the "pain" of need and thus depends on an "other"; it is a stroke of good fortune, a chance. But this conjuncture justifies neither the denunciation of pleasure as illusory nor the characterizing of man in the world as dereliction. (144)

It is in this sense that the life of need comes into its full expression only once it is coupled to the labor from which its definition can never be dissociated. If need is the mark of a sovereign self within being, this need consolidates itself by laboring on the element. In other words, this sovereignty would contradict itself if it were content to simply enjoy the element from which it draws pleasure without laboring on it. True sovereignty evokes the indigence that conjures the horizon of immediate enjoyment without hindering it. Immediate enjoyment crystallizes a short-term happiness that does not evoke the uncertainties of the future, although its independence coincides with its future dependence. In this sense, its immediate sovereignty signifies the imminence of its subjection.

And yet any sovereignty thus menaced still lacks sovereignty. Even if the self seeks to concentrate itself within the instant of plenitude that procures the immediate enjoyment of the non-self for it, such a state can never annul the indetermination of the future, experienced in the discomfort brought about as the depth of the element tarnishes anxious enjoyment. This disquiet does not amount to dereliction, but rather announces it as an ineluctable consequence which need does not inscribe within the time of labor. Disquiet announces the imminence of indigence and privation, which do not define need as an originary state, but rather as the ineluctable prolongation of the separated condition of the self. The mythic fascination with the unfathomable depth of the element equally represents one of the possible destinies of the disquiet that manifests itself in enjoyment. This leads to the pagan exaltation wherein the mystery of the element is deified in an anonymous—faceless—polytheism, in other words, a situation wherein the wrong sort of infinity, the sensible indefinite, prevails over the development of the idea of the infinite.

For this reason, the pagan world is a world without speech, made up of "faceless gods, impersonal gods to whom one does not speak" (142). The epiphany of the face, "where precisely an existent [*étant*] presents itself personally" (142), stands in opposition to the anonymity of the element. The element leads to a night in which no nocturnal event can be produced: the unfathomable night of the *there is* (*l'il y a*) in which—as content without form—the element loses itself. The *there is* is a night without event, because it is an existence without existant (*existant*), its ordeal is that of a verbal affirmation devoid of any substantive.

To the contrary, however, the revelation of the infinite reveals a perfectly positive event: the production of an existent in the process of infinitation, which is the idea of the infinite. However, at the same time, the risk of paganism attests to a separation already accomplished and thus preparation for religion in the true sense is indeed inevitable. This is why, originally, all separation is an anxious separation. Happiness is always accompanied by the experience of the strangeness of the elements within which sensibility is originally immersed. Enjoyment is therefore also affected by the ever-imminent danger of falling back into anonymity, where dependence has the upper hand over the fragile independence of sensible happiness. And yet to be originally exposed to such a menacing future is not necessarily to be condemned to a condition of indigence because "insecurity menaces an enjoyment already happy in the element" (142). It is for this reason that the limitation of immediate sensible happiness does not coincide with thrownness:

> Limitation is not due to the fact that the [self] has not chosen its
> birth and thus is already and henceforth in situation, but to the fact
> that the plenitude of its instant of enjoyment is not ensured against
> the unknown that lurks in the very element it enjoys, the fact that joy
> remains a chance and a stroke of luck. (144)

If the self does not originally embrace the condition of an existent thrown into the world (*un étant-jeté*), then the threat of indigence marks a deficit in the sovereignty which labor and possession come to fill. Sovereign life, constituted by the satisfaction of needs, does not stop at immediate enjoyment; the sovereignty of need intensifies in labor: "Need is *also* the time of labor: a relation with an other yielding its alterity" (116, emphasis added). Sovereignty is contemporaneous with enjoyment, but because it is always menaced by indigence and a disquiet that immediate satisfaction can never abolish, it increases in labor and possession. Indeed, to the extent that enjoyment marks a kind of independence through the deferral of dependence, labor and possession, themselves understood as "a relation with an other yielding its alterity," represent the constitutive dimensions of the life of need. Sovereignty is the contemporary of enjoyment, but because it is always menaced by indigence, a disquiet that immediate satisfaction can never abolish, this sovereignty deepens in labor and possession. To the extent that enjoyment marks independence and defers dependence, labor and possession, as relation to the other who yet "retains his [or her] alterity" (see 255), represent constitutive dimensions of the life of need.

A life that does not leave the self the possibility of consolidating its sovereignty through labor and possession, inevitably leads to a degradation of the self in thrownness. Far from being either originary or existential, thrownness is the symptom of a socially disorganized world, in which the satisfaction of needs is transformed into indigence because we lack the necessary time for the labor required to domesticate the unfathomable depth of the element: "To conceive of need as a simple privation is to apprehend it in the midst of a disorganized society which leaves it neither time nor consciousness" (116).

Contra existentialism, Levinas invites us to consider the social conditions that give rise to the material misfortune of human beings rather than relegating the latter to an ontologically fixed position. Thrownness does not existentially impose itself but rather always does so either in a socially determined world that lacks time or — following a Marxist analysis — in a universe in which workers suffer under the exploitation of their labor power:

> The limit case in which need prevails over enjoyment, the proletarian condition condemning to accursed labor in which the indigence of corporeal existence finds neither refuge nor leisure at home with itself, is the absurd world of *Geworfen-heit*. (146–47)

The world of thrownness essentially marks a deficit of sociality. A world in which we lack time or where need is reduced to indigence and privation rests on the repression of the idea of the infinite, which, as the form of sociality par excellence, liberates the time needed for the full and genuine satisfaction of needs. In other words, the idea of the infinite frees the time needed for a life in which labor, in a form unlike that of the proletarian condition, is not exiled from enjoyment. In a world so socially disorganized, the contents of the world lose their nourishing status and become nothing more than the "fuel" needed for the reproduction of exploitable labor power.

That the essence of need consists in the deferral of dependence, means that immediate enjoyment does not exhaust the concept of need. Labor and possession are thus included as constitutive dimensions in the description of economic happiness. Human beings are therefore not condemned to thrownness. Thanks to labor, the degradation of happiness into indigence is in no way ineluctable. Labor, as recourse and remedy, responds to the undetermined future of the element, in the reversal of dependence and independence in privation:

> Labor can surmount the indigence with which not need, but the uncertainty of the future affects being. . . . The pessimism of dereliction is hence not irremediable—man holds in his hands the remedy for his ills, and the remedies preexist the ills. (146)

Thus, as we have seen, it is in a world where sociality is perverted that indigence can encroach on happiness, and, therefore, that labor as recourse requires the idea of the infinite.

And yet have we not begun from the inverse relation? Is it not sensible happiness that would condition our opening up to the infinite? But it now seems as though desire takes precedence over enjoyment, because desire grants need the time necessary to domesticate the mythical depth of the element through labor: "Labor, however, already requires discourse and consequently the height of the other irreducible to the same, the presence of the Other" (117). Such a reciprocity, wherein the conditioned becomes the condition of its own condition, means that the movement from need to desire does not entail the exclusion of the former. The person who satisfies his or her needs is also the person who desires, and vice versa: The one who desires does not refuse the enjoyment of needs, at the risk of no longer being in a position to desire. The existent who possesses the idea of the infinite is precisely the one who, at the level of his or her sensible installation in being, leads a separated life, which is to say a life constituted by needs and their satisfaction.

Need and desire refer to states that are irreducible to each other, although the advent of desire, in its discontinuity with regard to need, does not entail the neutralization of the life of need. Desire depends on need—or egoism, in other words—which itself requires desire: "Indeed the time presupposed by need is provided to me by Desire; human need already rests on Desire" (117). However, this means that desire, following a virtuous circle, reinforces its own condition of possibility, and that the sensible life of the ego is consolidated beginning with the relation to the infinite, without which the apologetic dimension of the self could not produce itself within being: "The light of the face is necessary for separation" (151).

There is another decisive situation in which the infinite is summoned for the advent of interiority, but which cannot, however, correspond to that of discourse. Rather, it designates a relation to the Other beneath discourse, where the Other reserves its transcendence in order to permit the self to gather itself, and in that way allows the self to labor and to possess. The situation in question corresponds to the reception of the infinite under the modality of the feminine.

CHAPTER 5

The Utopia of the Dwelling

The Gentleness of the Feminine

Labor allows for a deferral of the dependence on the sensible and makes possible the mastery of the uncertain future of the element through the establishment of possession. For all that, however, labor in turn supposes the dimension of recollection (*recueillement*), which does not emerge from the singular fact of the ego. Recollection requires the presence of the Other in all of his or her discreteness, the infinite according to a specific ontological modality, in which the other qua other reserves its transcendence. The Other does not reveal himself or herself to the self in an expression and from the height of discourse, but in the modality of the feminine, which is to say, essentially, as gentleness.[1] Although the Other necessarily interferes with and interjects himself or herself into the life of the solitary ego, he or she does so not in order to destroy the solitude of the latter, nor to question the exclusivity of its enjoyment—which brings about the ethical situation—but, quite the contrary, to consolidate the latter within the category of recollection.

In this sense, the feminine certainly does not bring about an ontological modality more specific to women than to men, but rather the capacity of the Other qua other (*Autrui en tant qu'Autre*) to escape discourse by emerging in being in the mode of gentleness. And yet there is no gentleness without the intention of gentleness, which is why recollection—the concrete situation of which coincides with habitation within the dwelling[2]—requires the Other: "By virtue of its *intentional* structure gentleness comes to the separated being from the Other."[3]

The feminine is thus a constitutive aspect of the Other (*Autrui*), whether male or female, insofar as they are other (*Autre*). The Other is always in a position to reserve his or her transcendence, in order to reveal it, not through discourse, but rather "as the primordial phenomenon of gentleness" (*Totality and Infinity*, 150). There is thus no labor without recollection and no recollection without this "delightful 'lapse' of the ontological order" (150), which represents the feminine gentleness of the Other. The phenomenon of habitation as the concrete accomplishment of recollection, is thus in solidarity with the completely withdrawn presence of the Other.

Labor and Utopia

For Heidegger, the being-in (*être-dans*) of authentic Dasein does not carry with it the sense of inhabiting (*habiter*) proper to everydayness. In authenticity, Dasein occurs to itself in the mode of "not-being-at-home" (*das unzuhause sein*) and of "uncanniness" (*Unheimlichkeit*).[4] Levinas emphasizes, to the contrary of these ontological analyses, the primary sincerity of the concrete fact of dwelling, constitutive of the genuine opening to the alterity of every other understood concretely as the welcoming of the Other into a dwelling-place. Yet again it is by the separation of which it is the concrete energy that the dwelling consecrates an opening to the Other as absolutely other. Indeed, the dwelling can remain sealed, closed to the other, in order to maintain the separated being (*être séparé*) in its self-containment, in an ontologically radical self-sufficiency—attesting to the breadth and depth of the separation. But it is for this reason that the welcoming of the Other, accomplished by the open door of the dwelling-place, is realized in the guise of a discourse, as the ethical production of the infinite. The closure of the self is not a subjective illusion, but rather an ontological event, the eventuality of which is necessary for a separated ego to be able to receive the idea of the infinite:

The possibility for the home to open to the Other is as essential to the essence of the home as closed doors and windows. Separation would not be radical if the possibility of shutting oneself up at home with oneself could not be produced without internal contradiction as an event in itself, as atheism itself is produced—if it should only be an empirical, psychological fact, an illusion. (*Totality and Infinity*, 173)

From here, we can see just why the rupture of authentic Dasein with the familiarity of the habitation (155)[5] ipso facto precludes the development of the idea of the infinite—where the latter corresponds, in Levinas's ontology, to the ultimate event of being itself. As he says, "The social relation itself is not just another relation, one among so many others that can be produced in being, but is its ultimate event" (221).

Habitation coincides with the concrete actualization of the recollection proper to a separated being. In this way, the objective representation of the world is not merely the fact of an abstract subjectivity subtracted from the concrete phenomenon of habitation; it is rather the fact of a separated subjectivity that inhabits a dwelling. Such habitation allows the subjects to distance themselves from the world, in contrast to the immersion of sensibility within the element. This aptitude for recollection and for the representation that concretely offers up separated life within a dwelling— or, more precisely, the constant possibility of renouncing the world of elements in favor of a retreat into one's dwelling—opens the distance necessary for the possibility of labor and possession to exercise a grasp and a mastery over the uncertain future of the element.

In this way, the home is not some "tool" among others within a totality of "appearances," because a genuine system of "implementation" or "equipmentality" requires that the dwelling be the commencement, the starting-place, of any finalized human activity: "The privileged role of the home does not consist in being the end of human activity but in being its condition, and in this sense its commencement" (152). Human beings are thus neither thrown into existence nor subtracted from it in a position of absolute retreat. Between openness and closure, situated within the elements and yet at once de-territorialized, the dwelling makes the articulation of interior and exterior possible, constitutive of the experience of human separation. For the one who inhabits a dwelling, to be outside does not only signify the status of "being outside," uneasily exposed to the elements, but rather, at the same time, entails the possibility of being at home, within the dwelling, which is to say never entirely or completely outside.

For the one who stands outside, the dwelling itself accounts for this internal movement. This distance from the elements offers the separated self the possibility of exercising a grasp on being through labor and possession. This is why, far from being reduced to one thing within the world among others, or even a single piece of equipment within a system of equipment, the dwelling is the thing from which the situation of all other things is determined: "The home, as a building, belongs to a world of things. But this belongingness does not nullify the bearing of the fact that every consideration of things, and of buildings too, is produced out of a dwelling. Concretely speaking the dwelling is not situated in the objective world, but the objective world is situated *in relation* to my dwelling" (152–53, emphasis added, translation amended).

The exceptional status of the home (*étant-demeure*) in relation to other existents (*étants*) arises from the dimension of welcoming, which is itself at once constitutive of and inseparable from the withdrawal of the face that inhabits it. This is what Levinas calls "the feminine as category," as a mode of being of the face, which is independent of any empirical division of the roles apportioned to men and women. The dwelling concretizes the dimension of recollection constitutive of the separated life of the self, expressed and represented by the feminine. For that reason, the dwelling is the existent that allows the things of the crafted, built world to be gathered up, arranged, and possessed. And so its exceptional status comes not from being an existent that one welcomes, but rather that existent by which the act of welcoming is itself made possible. The dwelling is thus characterized by the fact that it renders possession itself possible, through the dimension of welcoming that is constitutive of it: "The home that founds possession is not a possession in the same sense as the movable goods it can collect and keep. It is possessed because it already and henceforth is hospitable for its proprietor" (157).[6]

Levinas refuses to assimilate—at least not without targeting Heidegger anew—the localization of the separated subject to some kind of "pagan rootedness," which is to say the self's dependence on and participation in a place in which it is inscribed: "Enrootedness, a primordial preconnection, would maintain participation as one of the sovereign categories of being, whereas the notion of truth marks the end of this reign. . . . The inner life, the [self and] separation are uprootedness itself" (60–61).

Enrootedness impedes the subject's independence in being, because the independence of the separated being (*être séparé*) is only fully thought through by Levinas in the fundamental coincidence of the subject's position in a place with the subject's independence from that place: "By virtue of the psychism, the being that is in a site remains free with regard to that site; posited in a site in which it maintains itself, it is that which comes thereto from elsewhere" (54).[7] The dwelling thus concretely accomplishes the double challenge, constitutive of the status of separation, in which the being situated in a place realizes its independence from that place, through the possibility, provided by the dwelling, of withdrawing itself to another place.

It is in this sense that the dwelling is utopian; it does not in any way inscribe itself within the milieu of the elements. In suspending the immediate contract with the element, the dwelling opens up the possibility of a retreat to a radical elsewhere, which is only other than the intimateness of "my home," the place wherein the self can gather itself, and to which it always arrives from elsewhere.

The home makes it possible to close off the space of exteriority, but it is a closure proscribed by the immediate contact of enjoyment. The possibility of closing the window entails a distancing of exteriority. This closure represents the possibility of suspending any and all relation with the elemental and thus sustains the independence of the gaze that opens itself to the world. To relate to the elements in this way, via the home, is thus no longer a form of contact, but is rather a form of relation. It is a relation to nature as what stands before the gaze that no longer enjoys the element but is now able to contemplate it as a world: "The ambiguity of distance, both removal and connection, is lifted by the window that makes possible a look that dominates, a look of him who escapes looks,[8] the look that contemplates" (*Totality and Infinity*, 156).

Labor consists in the transformation of elemental nature into a world of identifiable things; labor "*arouses* things and transforms nature into a world" (157). This prolonged and ongoing work brings things forth from the depth of the element. It is an operation of determination: The determined thing depends on the activity of detachment produced by labor on the elemental depth of being. Such detachment is the work (*oeuvre*) of a hand that extracts and fashions things from the anonymous element. The discovery of the world is thus correlative with labor, and labor thereby precedes any theoretical perspective.

The things that come to be possessed through labor are inscribed within a duration that was missing in a direct relation to the element, which had exposed immediate enjoyment to insecurity. The future of the element within the dwelling is no longer marked by the insecurity of a "nowhere," as entailed by the unfathomable sensible depth of being. The things that issue from labor, which become the goods held within the dwelling, presuppose the suspension of the menacing independence of the element, which is accomplished by the grasp of possession. The latter allows for things to be obtained and the possibility of their repatriation in the home as movable things (*choses-meubles*), or furnishings.[9]

Through labor, "The element is fixed between the four walls of the home, is calmed in possession. It appears there as a thing, which can, perhaps, be defined by tranquillity—as in a 'still life.' This grasp operated on the elemental is labor" (*Totality and Infinity*, 158). Possession, within the dwelling, presupposes labor as the activity of seizing and bringing things forth from the anonymity of the elements. Labor thus consists in the substantialization of the element. Through the transformation of the element into things, labor assures the passage from enjoyment—understood as the contact between sensibility with the formless qualities of the element—to the possession of things that are durable because they are substantial.

Through labor and the possession that results from it, the self overcomes the regime of immediate consumption and liberates itself from its vicissitudes: "To possess by enjoying is also to be possessed and to be delivered to the fathomless depth, the disquieting future of the element" (158). In essence, possession neutralizes the menacing weight of the element. And yet it must be noted that Levinas still thinks of enjoyment on the most immediate level as a possession. Indeed, as we have seen, the self is immediately constituted as that which is what it is because it has, because, through enjoyment, it possesses—which is to say, through the possession of contents.

However, because enjoyment does not endure, it is in a precarious position. As "possession without acquisition," enjoyment "'possesses' without taking" (158). As enjoyment, possession exhausts itself at the very moment of its consummation. Labor, to the contrary, suspends the immediate exaltation of the element by making possible an enduring possession, a form of possession in which sensible qualities are consigned to a determinate substratum. Because it places the sensible qualities of the element into such substrata, labor releases the sensible condition of the separated self from the disquiet of the future. It ensures the passage from a universe composed of anonymous and independent elements to a universe of determinate and possessed things. Indeed, labor entails such an ontological modification, which in turn allows being to close the originary gap that characterizes the register of having (*l'avoir*): "Labor recoups the lag between the element and the sensation" (141). The element thus no longer coincides with the anonymous element that exceeds the self, exposing the latter to an unfathomable alterity, but rather becomes, through the transformation of labor, that which the self possesses from this point forward in the form of enduring things.

Labor thus suspends the ontological independence of the element. The grasp of possession neutralizes the ontological nucleus of the element, the source of its autonomy and menacing indifference. Indeed, "The other in which it jubilates—the elements—is initially neither for nor against it" (164). The thing is thus nothing more than the element, but the element severed from its menacing depth. In other words, the thing is that element whose being is mastered in possession, which is to say that it is the element whose ontological independence has been suspended and replaced by fully possessed movable-existents (*étants-meubles*).[10] In the possession of things, the future of the element no longer overwhelms the self.

The thing is also, therefore, nothing more than the element, because it coincides with an element whose ontological independence has been neutralized and, in other words, whose being has been anesthetized. Put differently, through labor and the possession that results from it, the being (*l'être*) of the element becomes the having (*l'avoir*) of the self: "Possession neutralizes this being: as property the thing is an existent that has lost its being" (*Totality and Infinity*, 158).

There are no things but for the suspension, by labor, of the ontological nucleus of the element, the origin of its menacing independence; in other words, there is no possession without the neutralization of being. Subsequently, that which *is*, from this point forward only *is*, in the full sense, to the extent that it is possessed. The element becomes some thing only through the suspension of its being. Here, the ontological frontiers of the element no longer exceed those of the self, which is to say that we are now dealing with being insofar as it is possessed by someone (the self).

In this way, the sensible prolongation of the element no longer menaces the self, and consists in a reserve of enjoyment and happiness, mastered in the form of things possessed within a dwelling. The thing, the emergence of a substrate through labor, is nothing other than the element circumscribed by possession. In possession, the future of the element is no longer beyond the grasp of the self. It is through labor that the element is given such substantial form. And so things, extracted from material and possessed, are nothing other than the element, mastered by the self. Here elemental being no longer is, independent of the self, but becomes that which I have; in other words, that which being is, no longer exceeds the measure of the self. The future of the element in the possession of things is thus no longer marked by the indeterminate excess of the *there is*, but is rather, from this point on, extended into the future that is mastered and circum-

scribed by the self. In this way, Levinas displaces the categories of fundamental ontology and argues that the comprehension of being is deployed at
the level of the grasp of the possession of being, which labor and possession
accomplish: "Ontology is a relation with things which manifests things;
the ontology that grasps the being of the existent is a spontaneous and pre-
theoretical work of every inhabitant of the earth" (158).

The comprehension of being therefore designates the original seizure
of being, realized in the possession of the element. It is the thing as thing
which results when the being of the existent (*l'être de l'étant*) is seized, which
reduces the indefiniteness of the element. The element is thus understood
and no longer exceeds the limits of the self, which is to say that the element
is suspended in order to become the possession of the subject. Things are
the result of grasping and possessing being. Things delimit being insofar
as they are possessed; they refer to the element the being of which is seized
in the sense of an effective grasp of the self on the non-self. In possession,
being is no longer something that escapes me, but rather something that
I comprehend—that is, something whose alterity has been neutralized.
Possession is nothing other than being circumscribed by the very limits of
comprehension, which is to say, ipso facto, a being (*être*) transformed into
a having (*avoir*).

Prior to ontology, and the comprehension of being that it realizes, being is indifferent to the self; it is not yet known, which is to say that; it
is not yet encircled by the self in possession; it is what Levinas calls the
"incomprehensible format of the surrounding medium [*milieu*]" (166). It
is this foundational indifference that makes being something menacing,
because being is unconcerned with the future of the ego, which it exposes
to indetermination, that is, to the threat that its happy condition will de-
grade into misfortune. The thing is the existent by which being is known,
or put differently, by which it becomes my possession. It is no longer being
as anonymous element, but instead a thing that I have. The thing-known
(*l'être-compris*), the thing as substance or constant presence, results from the
comprehension of being, understood as an effective grasp on the element.

The thing *is* being insofar as it is no longer unrestricted or in itself, but
rather for me or non-me-for-me, the non-me severed from its alterity, established as that which I possess. To comprehend the being of the existent
is to possess it in the form of something substantial and durable. We must
therefore return to the separated condition of the self in order to elucidate
the ontological vocation of human beings to comprehending being, concretely understood as coming to possess the element through labor. From
here, the comprehension of the being of the existent—through which

the worldly register of the existent is opened, in the sense that, following Heidegger, there are no existents but for the background of the preliminary comprehension of the being of existents (*l'être de l'étant*)—would find its full phenomenological production within the analysis of effective labor. Here, the comprehension of being consists in this relation of an effective hold over being, from which worldly existents manifest, precisely as those things possessed by the subject.

Indeed, the things that we have emerge from the elemental ground, but only in the suspension of its independence—which is to say the element circumscribed within an ontology—from which the formlessness of elemental being gives way to those forms of the same that invest the world and divide it into so many possessed substantives. We must therefore come to understand the grasp of the being of existents (*l'être de l'étant*) in its literal and pre-theoretical sense. From there, the relation to the existent, understood as a tool, depends on such a modification, which emerges from the materiality of our sensible and laborious condition: "Every manipulation of a system of tools and implements, every labor, presupposes a primordial *hold* on the things, possession, whose latent birth is marked by the home, at the frontier of interiority" (163).

We see in these passages on labor another recovery of Heideggerian conceptuality. The analyses of the hand, present in the substantive *Hand* of *Zuhandenheit* and *Vorhandenheit*, are here placed under the aegis of labor, as Levinas presents the hand as the organ of work. The hand articulates a relation to the elements that does not consist in their enjoyment. The hand is instead related to being in its ongoing labor, which is to say, by "separating its take from immediate enjoyment, depositing it in the dwelling, conferring on it the status of a possession" (159). However, this operation of the hand is possible only to the extent that "the hand qua hand cannot arise in the body immersed in the element" (163), which means that the hand proceeds from interiority and that its movement is not ecstatic. This is why, for Levinas, the function of the hand precedes existence, understood as project and transcendence. Prior to any project, the movement of the hand does not target exteriority but rather the return to the self, and is for this reason a form of economic interiority: "The hand accomplishes its proper function prior to every execution of a plan, every projection of a project, every finality that would lead out of being at home with oneself" (159).

The movement of the hand is not transcendent and centrifugal, but circular and centripetal. Its labor articulates a movement that aims at a return to the self, by acquiring things from the elements, with the goal of gathering them up within the interiority of the dwelling as things possessed. The home thus remains the horizon of labor; the dwelling constitutes the very possibility of work. The activity of labor is indissociable from the return home of objects garnered from the elements—objects that the self arranges and possesses insofar as they may be gathered up within the dwelling. The dwelling, the home, "my place," is thus the constitutive horizon of those analyses that take the labor of the hand for their object, and it is for this reason that the reference to interiority prevails over any exterior, outward-looking focus. Labor is thus "not a transcendence" (159), and the movement of the hand is an "Odyssey where the adventure pursued in the world is but the accident of a return" (176–77). Labor must therefore be essentially understood as a movement of interiorization.

Through possession, the world is thus populated with substantives and substrata, with objects fixed under the aegis of permanence: "Possession posits the product of labor as what remains permanent in time, [as] a substance" (160). The subsisting presence of the thing is essentially understood as a reserve, which is to say as the enduring fixation of elemental qualities. However, because substance coincides with the suspension of anonymous being, the substantial world produced by labor is in fact falsely substantial, because it lacks ontological autonomy—it is in short, for-myself (*pour-moi*) rather than in-itself (*en-soi*). Hence the oxymoronic characterization of being that results from labor. Indeed, it is a question of "a being of pure appearance, a phenomenal being; the thing that is mine or another's is not in itself" (162). It is because it is not in-itself, but rather draws its substance from subjective possession, that the substantiality of possessed things remains inconsistent and relative: "The substantiality of a thing, correlative of possession, does not consist in the thing presenting itself *absolutely*" (162, emphasis added).

Because things can never be "in themselves" under the regime of possession, their identities can always be modified. This relativity manifests within the anonymous circuit of monetized exchange. Things drawn from the anonymity of the element fall back into the "anonymity of money" (162). Indeed, "because it is not in itself a thing can be exchanged and accordingly be compared, be quantified, and consequently already lose its very identity, be reflected in money. . . . [Its] permanence disappears forthwith in the phenomenality reflected in money" (162). The thing possessed may be sold, exchanged, converted into money; its identity is never absolute. Its permanence and consistence thus only endure relative to the dwelling. The thing possessed is therefore not the absolute thing in itself—which results from language and the presence, in person, of the Other—

but rather something the identity of which remains precarious, which is to say just as exchangeable as it is transformable into something else.

The Laboring Body

It would be inconceivable to completely remove the self from determinism. Enjoyment brings to light the impassable insecurity entailed by the activity of living from the element. As we have seen, the dependence of need is in fact a happy dependence. In this way, the separated self is never disembodied or immaterial, its independence does not emerge from some *causa sui*, but rather from the manner of being of corporeality, which takes shape in enjoyment. Nevertheless, the independence of the self as an ontological affirmation in the first person remains an uneasy independence, because the immersion of our sensibility within the element exposes sensible happiness to the immanent threat of its degradation in thrownness. "Living *from*" and enjoyment simultaneously describe independence and yet highlight the risk of dependence tied to any form of lived enjoyment. More precisely, the movement of separated life brings to light the sovereign independence of a being in the form of the temporarily avoided, though never abolished, risk of total submission.

Sensible life is a life of respite. To the extent that its exposure to the risk of collapsing into the anonymity of material is constitutive of its affirmation, the joyous body, glorious and delivered from any material dependence, thus loses any trace of an immaterial body. The sovereignty of the joyous body is never absolute, which is to say, never absolutely or unequivocally acquired. Rather, such a body is defined by its equivocation: Irreducible to materiality, enjoyment does not eliminate the participation that constantly threatens to take the upper hand over this independence so precariously obtained. For Levinas, "Life is a body, not only lived body [*corps propre*], where its self-sufficiency emerges, but a cross-roads of physical forces, body-effect" (164). Sovereignty can never suspend the obsessive fear of its alienation from the other by whom it lives: "In its deep-seated fear life attests to this ever possible inversion of the body-master into body-slave, of health into sickness" (164). The body is not reducible to its physical materiality, because it is a "rupture with participation," a happy and sensible affirmation of the self. But this irreducibility cannot be understood in terms of removing the living body from the physical world, insofar as the subjective affirmation that it conveys results from an adjournment of its participation in the reign of objective materiality: "The world life acquires and utilizes by labor, is also the physical world where labor is interpreted as a play of anonymous forces" (165).

The body is thus never entirely a lived body (*corps propre*),[11] a subject-body, but always a potentially subjected body, a body virtually redirected to the non-self of materiality in the extreme dependence revealed by malady and privation. The impossible, exhaustive assignment of corporeality to the subject-body, divested of any naturalistic determination, evinces the fragility and ambiguity inherent in terrestrial happiness. As we have seen, the ego defers the risk of the inversion of the materiality of its needs into the sur-materiality of privation, through the distance vis-à-vis the elements that the dwelling makes possible, and the labor that results from that distance. This is why the separated body is a laboring body, essentially defined not by its spatiality, but rather by its temporality. It is thus a question of a body that works and suspends its materiality, which is to say a body that defers its participation in the objective world of bodies.

The subjective body, that is, the temporal body, completely engrossed in laboring effort, is defined as that very particular body which is not yet entirely objective and spatial, and thus attests to a materiality deferred in time. The materiality of the laboring body is thus something that virtually—though not actually—troubles the self. Furthermore, the laboring body is never my own body[12] (*corps propre*) in that it takes root in a material being that is deferred by the activity of the body. It is thus always a question of an ambiguous body, at once subjective and objective, and thus neither exhaustively one nor the other; it is a subjective body, because it is not yet an objective body, subjective because virtually objective, which is to say consciousness: "The ambiguity of the body is consciousness" (*Totality and Infinity*, 165). Far from proceeding, as Sartre does, from the nihilation of the in-itself, Levinas argues that consciousness is actually defined as an in-itself that has been deferred, virtualized, and differentiated, that is, as a dis-identification through deferral, or a deferred identification. In this way, it is not the body that incarnates consciousness, but rather consciousness that dis-incarnates corporeality: "Consciousness does not fall into a body—is not incarnated; it is a dis-incarnation—or, more exactly, a postponing of the corporeity of the body" (165–66).

It is in this sense that, unlike Sartre, such an ambiguity does not demonstrate the finitude of my thrown-freedom, but rather shows that my freedom is an essentially precarious, suspended phenomenon: "Freedom as a relation of life with an other that lodges it, and by which life is at home with itself, is not a finite freedom; it is virtually a null freedom" (165).

Consciousness coincides with a body held between sovereignty and dependence, neither absolutely sovereign nor absolutely material. Put differently, such a body is sovereign because it remains material, possessing the time necessary to defer, through its labor, its own submission to the material exteriority on which it depends.

Consciousness is thus identified with a material life constituted by the deferral of its own materiality or, in other words, with a fully material body participating in a physical world of bodies, but in the future tense. Consciousness thus does not intervene on the level of enjoyment, which only knows the immediacy of consummation, but rather corresponds to a life in which enjoyment is consolidated by the efforts of labor, and where being is conscious because it benefits from the time necessary to postpone its own decline: "To be conscious is precisely to have time . . . to be related to the element in which one is settled as to what is not yet there" (166). This laboring body, differing in its dependence, is thus the ambiguous body that coincides with the conscious beings (*l'être conscient*) that we are. The existential project, oriented toward the future, does not exhaust the phenomenon of consciousness. Consciousness does not aim to exceed the present in favor of a future toward which it projects itself, but rather to fundamentally defer the maturation of the present: "not to exceed the present time in the project that anticipates the future, but to have a distance with regard to the present itself, to be related to the element in which one is settled as to what is not yet there" (166).

In this way, for the one who labors—that is, for a consciousness—the persistence of a thing is never absolutely definitive. It is rather as an interval on which he or she is neither absolutely dependent, nor over which he or she exercises absolutely mastery, but within which the lineaments of the separated subject take shape. The latter is identified with a body that temporizes its own materiality in labor. As such, the ineluctable does not yet strike the conscious being which defers, through its labor, the maturation of its full participation in the materiality of being.

Being in Itself: From Silence to Speech

If, as discussed, the work of the hand outlines a centripetal movement of the interiorization of the sensible exterior, such a movement does not occur without leaving traces of its passage. Interiorization is an effective movement that happens in exteriority. We thus find here the vestiges of a passage, the indices that attest to the existence of a laboring being. These indices of the activity of interiorization are the detritus that laboring activity leaves in its passing. Labor does not abolish the exteriority of elements that it transforms into a habitable world, because it is inhabited by a laboring body—which is to say, gathered up within a dwelling. The one who labors imposes form on the element, thus producing so many possessions, which temper and buffer its alterity. And yet this work results indirectly from labor. Because the will accomplishes itself in being in order to bring the latter to its term, it ipso facto, and collaterally, produces a surplus of unwanted things within the substrata of its own labor. Laboring activity produces these remainders—which emerge and are consolidated within being, though in a way that is yet unbeknownst to the latter—that constitute the works of the self:

> The hand's rigorously economic movement of seizure and acquisition
> is dissimulated by the traces, "wastes," and "works" this movement
> of acquisition, returning to the interiority of the home, leaves in its
> wake. These works, as city, field, garden, landscape, recommence their
> elemental existence. (159)

If the world of possession reveals a world circumscribed by the self, a world for the self, then the presence of works at once betrays the will exceeding itself. Unbeknownst to it, the will is caught up in an exteriority that reveals it; or, in other words, the movement of interiorization is never exhaustive. Work thus evinces the insidious return to the anonymity of the element, which the self is in no position to prevent. Indeed, as we have seen, the self's recourse in the face of the element consists in labor.

And yet works are the result of labor. This means that if human beings keep the element at bay through labor, our works reveal the reciprocation of the element on the will, through a reversal systematically entailed by the very activity of labor. The more human beings labor, the more our works seem to condemn us to the very anonymity of the element that we purport to suspend precisely by our labor. The grasp of possession does not amount to a total mastery of the element; rather, the activity of attempting to master the element engenders, in spite of itself, those elemental traces of its own activity of interiorization that are works (*oeuvres*), the products of our labor. The activity of mastery evinces a collateral nonmastery, in the form of so many failed by-products resulting from the practical grasp of the will on the element. The exteriorization of the will in the mastery of possession reverses itself, as a result of its own efficacy, in dispossession. The grasp of the will on being, which manifests possession, inversely entails the grasp of being on the will in a work.[13] Our works betray the nonmastery that is automatically entailed by the activity of mastery. In its movement of self-return—that is, in taking up the products of its labor—the hand leaves behind the unwanted by-products of its own activity. The practical intentionality which takes up material in order to give it form is at the same time grasped by that material. This material grasp, integrated within the tissue of being, ipso facto prevents this economic circularity from ever being able to close in on itself without leaving behind some detritus. These remainders are the works of the self: "In undertaking what I willed I realized so many things I did not will: the work rises in the midst of the wastes of labor" (*Totality and Infinity*, 176).

Works are thus in no way the aim of labor and must be understood in terms of what Levinas calls, in reference to psychoanalysis, a parapraxis, or what Lingis translates as an "abortive act;"[14] as Levinas says, "The worker does not hold in his hands all the threads of his own action. He is exteriorized by acts that are already in a sense abortive" (176).[15] The interiorization of the world through possession is thus hindered by works that are diffused in proportion to the increase in the labor of interiorization itself. It is as if the subject is carried off by his or her own activity of mastery, the effects of which he or she is, in the end, no longer able to master.

Any action that targets a goal is thus always overwhelmed by its own production of unwanted effects. Such effects condemn the self to endure the fact that some part of itself is left within the anonymity of being, wherein it cannot achieve exhaustive mastery of either being itself or its own being. There is, therefore, some part of the self that cannot be interiorized, and is not economically recoupable, and thus falls back into anonymity. And yet this anonymity is precisely the anonymity of works. For that reason, it is not an issue of the extinction of the self within material, but rather the fact that the self has an outside that escapes its own will. This irreducible—indeed nonintentional—exteriority of the self puts it in the situation of escaping itself and thus in a position of dependence vis-à-vis that Other[16] whose status is that of the survivor: the historiographer. The works of the laboring self "deliver signs, [but] they have to be deciphered *without his assistance*" (*Totality and Infinity*, 176, emphasis added).

The only means of escaping the alienation of the will, which is reified in the signification that confers another will on it, consists in speaking, which is to say, in departing from economic life. To depart from economic life, in this sense, means to speak, which in turn means to defend one's works, to come to the aid of signs by participating in their interpretation. It is in this way that the act of speaking accomplishes a departure from history; it extirpates the totalizing narrative that envelops the self, in spite of itself, in a

universal, epic adventure in which only the third person can exist, confined
by the muteness of objective reason, within the silence of "the totality of
wars and empires in which one does not speak" (23). Not to speak is thus
to absent oneself from oneself; it is to be in such a way that my affirmation within being does not yet attest to a presence—to be in the mode of
a phenomenon. Where this latter is silent, it is the thing in itself which,
constitutively, speaks.

To exist in the mode of a phenomenon is to be interpreted by one's
works, the products of one's labor, which is to say unbeknownst to oneself.
Thus to absent myself from the Other's interpretation of me is to participate in this totalizing narration whose sense does not come from me, because I am not there to defend, inflect, confirm or deny it: "From . . . work
I am only deduced and am already ill-understood, betrayed rather than
expressed" (176). Economic life, as infra-verbal life, realizes this ontological absence. The mode of being that consists only in jubilation is present
neither to itself nor to the manifestations that emerge from it; it has only
the blurred and equivocal consistency of an appearance without principle:
"a manifestation in the absence of being—a phenomenon" (178).

To exist in the mode of work is to remain absent to oneself; it is to
deliver signs that the Other, without me, in my absence, must interpret
extrinsically, which serves only to increase their ambiguity. As long as the
self does not speak, its works reveal it as a series of apparitions to be interpreted, undefended by any presence. The defense of the self by itself consummates that presence; it is speech; it is the being that absolutely exists in
the position of interlocutor.

Indeed, ontological presence consists in the incessant recovery of my
phenomenality, by which the passage from equivocation to univocality is
accomplished. Here we move from the ambiguous presence of the phenomenon in which I am absent to myself, to the sustained and clear presence of the being in itself (*l'être en soi*), wherein I defend my works to the
Other, which is to say that I respond to my responsibility to the Other: "As
responsible I am brought to my final reality" (178). My presence consists
in nothing less than taking up that act of speech that incessantly recovers
its works, which is precisely to say that it assumes its ethical responsibility
before the Other. There is no ontological presence but the interlocutory,
which is to say the ethical, understood as that which delimits "an order
where all the symbolisms are deciphered by beings that present themselves
absolutely—that express themselves" (178).

To be present within being is to come to the aid of signs, that is, to speak.
The one who does not speak remains absent to those signs that he or she

produces in spite of himself or herself; these signs evince him or her as an absence, revealed to those who survive him or her by the relics that he or she has left behind. The being who is determined exclusively by enjoyment is just as absent from being as the wills of the deceased. In both cases, the existant is not there to defend his or her works, and the difference between the one who exists economically in the mode of phenomena and the one who no longer exists is therefore minuscule. In both cases the existant is absent, and whether he or she exists or no longer exists ultimately amounts to the same, insofar as he or she does not speak, which is to say that he or she does not exist in-himself or in-herself, absolutely, and therefore, for-himself or for-herself, *kath'auto*. It is for this reason that within economic life, where interiority, unbeknown to itself, allows signs of itself to escape, "The Same is not the Absolute; its reality expressed in its work is absent from its work. In its economic existence its reality is not total" (178).

Separation can be consolidated only in interlocution, which reinforces and anchors the first person of the self within being. This consolidation represents the departure from the ambiguity of works understood as un-spoken signs, through expression. In the latter, speech comes to the aid of its own signs, teaching and allowing itself to be taught by the Other, de-fending its works because it has been taught.[17] Speech illuminates a world in which frankness is produced like an absolute event of being, in a social-ity wherein existence affirms itself not as a collection of individuals, but as a plurality of persons who stand face to face. Paradoxically, ethics presents it-self as the sole means of guaranteeing the precarious separation achieved in the atheism of the solitary life. An exclusively egoist life inevitably exposes itself to the risk of every possible incomprehension, of all the equivocation and betrayal that result in the integration of the egoist self into the totality. Its participation in the objective judgment of history is an absence. Absent from being, the one who can either no longer speak or who has not yet spoken leaves the task of giving voice to the works that he or she has left behind to the care of the survivor, the historiographer.

The rupture of participation within economic life is required for the revelation of the idea of the infinite, but, reciprocally, even as the self remains uncoupled from the infinite, its participation is only deferred and in no case annulled. This deferral is required for the revelation of the in-finite, though it is not yet enough to produce that separation from the totality that is only established in the relation with the Other, by the idea of the infinite. It is precisely here that we see just what so radically distin-guishes Levinas's approach from that of Kierkegaard, or even from Rosen-zweig, to whom Levinas remains quite close. Indeed, Levinas's opposition to the totality finds its philosophical ancestor in *The Star of Redemption*, as Stéphan Mosès has demonstrated so well.[18] It is thus not only in contrast to Kierkegaard, but much more immediately to Rosenzweig, that the text of the preface becomes fully intelligible:[19]

> The eschatological vision does not oppose to the experience of totality the protestation of a person in the name of his personal egoism or even of his salvation. Such a proclamation of morality based on the pure subjectivism of the I is refuted by war, the totality it reveals, and the objective necessities. (*Totality and Infinity*, 25)[20]

Following Rosenzweig, Levinas proposes a "defense of subjectivity" but adds that "it will apprehend the subjectivity not at the level of its purely egoist protestation against totality, nor in its anguish before death, but as *founded in the idea of infinity*" (26, emphasis added). To take the idea of infinity as the foundation of subjectivity means that it is in interlocution that subjectivity emerges in itself. This emergence in itself achieves the definitive separation of the self from totalization, and thus in turn from the false dichotomy between the totality and the egoistic assertion that claims to oppose it. Such claims cannot undermine or eliminate participation, and despite that assertion, totalization always recovers its rights over subjectivity in the end.

It is for this reason that we must ultimately deduce the rupture of participation from a movement that already emerges from the infinite itself. The infinite allows a separated existent to emerge within being in order to produce itself by "proximity" (*voisinage*) as infinite. At the inverse of any totalization, what Levinas calls the "paradox of creation" (103) constitutively allows for the being of an existent that is separated from it, in order to produce its very infinition, through the distance within the idea of the infinite that separates the ideatum from the idea. It is thus a question of "the paradox of an Infinity admitting a being outside of itself which it does not encompass, and accomplishing its very infinitude by virtue of this proximity of a separated being" (103). Such a paradox delimits the originary movement of the "contraction" of the infinite. Here Levinas takes up the Kabbalistic notion of *tsimtsum*,[21] in order to give an account of the phenomenon of separation: "Infinity is produced by withstanding the invasion of a totality, in a *contraction* that leaves a place for the separated being" (104, emphasis added).

We must thus deduce separation from the infinite: The infinite allows for the being of an existent spontaneously reticent to live for one other than itself. This reticence fixes a being in its identity, the same as self, even though this reticence does not consolidate that being in its identity, as we will see. This fixation serves as a safeguard, constitutive of the transcendence of desire, for all ecstasy, identification with or participation in the other being (*l'Être Autre*). Indeed, participation would keep us in a framework of immanence, which would obstruct the development of the idea of the infinite, and thus the advent of sociality.

Levinas insists on numerous occasions that the "concrete" human being already possesses the idea of the infinite, which means that sociality is not something that must be conquered or obtained. That the concrete human being already possesses the idea of the infinite means that he or she is always, already in a relation with the Other. Sociality is a fact which Levinas's method of concretization reestablishes as an event, which is to say a return to the situation of atheistic solitude from which ethics can only deploy itself as an event of the encounter with the Other—that is, the ultimate event of being itself.

It may be asked why the concretization of the same, within the self separated from the Other, describes the self as not yet possessing the idea of the infinite,[22] as having to accomplish, on the other side of its separated life, a trajectory that would not have been achieved from the beginning, as if we are not always already held in some relation to the Other.[23] This descriptive isolation takes its signification precisely from the fact that the relation between the same and the other is achieved by way of separation. This means that from a methodological point of view separation is not truly assumed, and thus that the description of the relation is fully developed only to the extent to which such a separation is described for itself as enjoyment and economy. This paradox emerges from the fact that the relation to the Other does not constitute a totalization, and that it does not systematically require the invocation of the other term from which it is separated in order to be described: "If separation had to be described in terms of enjoyment and economy, this is because the sovereignty of man was nowise a simple reverse of the relation with the Other" (*Totality and Infinity*, 180).

The exhaustive delimitation of this separated relation thus comes down to a description for-itself of the immanent life of the same as self, at risk of missing the separation constitutive of the relation between the same and the other. To exist ethically does not amount, in any possible case, to the sacrifice of enjoyment, but rather to the renunciation of that which reduces experience to the egoistic exclusivism of enjoyment. The one who desires is also the one who, constitutively, satisfies his or her sensible needs in so doing. If desire distinguishes itself from need, it is precisely because its goal is no longer to identify the other with the same. However, this rupture in the process of identification, the opening to alterity, requires this identification, and requires a point of departure from which the other remains separate, in order to understand nothing less than the fixed self as the happy self. There is thus no pure altruism that does not transform into its opposite: pure immanentism. In this way, it is fundamental to the development of social life that not everything in human life be social, that we are not always, already turned toward the other.

There is only an elsewhere for the one who lives here; the former is a position assumed from the perspective of a dwelling-place. Even if it is no longer a question of enjoyment in relation to the Other, but rather of a new form of satisfaction that is augmented in proportion to the increasing distance between the desiring subject (*désirant*) and the object desired (*Désiré*), this increase can in no way annul the concreteness of a world that is enjoyed. It is only within such a world, marked by enjoyment and the laborious organization of needs, that the offer, becoming for-another, concretely consummates the idea of the infinite. The offer constitutively supposes the precondition of possession, contested in this way, as only a world experienced as possession can be offered.

In this sense, metaphysics entails a material base—or not. The development of metaphysics remains unthinkable without its anchorage in the system of needs and the social organization of labor that results from it. Materiality is indispensable to the development of the infinite, and its idea. It is always the ponderous being (*l'être besogneux*), the laborer, who desires. The spirit that elevates itself metaphysically is always also bound to a laboring body. This elevation begins here, which is to say that it at once consecrates the here-below in the gift.

In other words, it is constitutive of desiring beings that we find ourselves constantly exposed to the ordeal and the risk of hunger, and thus to the urgency of staving off that hunger through labor. The face addresses itself to the laborer. The spiritual, metaphysics, means that the material world is invested with a signification from which speech resounds. It is in relation to the misery of the Other's hunger that the world, on and within which we labor, assumes a signification, which is to say an orientation, which is itself metaphysical. Metaphysics, thus, does not engage in a departure from the world, but rather the overcoming of the world summoned to sensible immanence. The space "beyond" the world, the domain of metaphysics, concretely coincides with the becoming signification of the world. That signification comes from the face, not from the world, but bears on the world, reveals and exalts the truth of the world labored on and possessed, and thus revealed through its bond to a significant act of speech—which is to say, immediately, to a hunger other than my own. Metaphysics thus signifies nothing other than the advent of a materiality exhaustively assumed in the becoming signification of material possession, in other words, in the advent of a world that is sensed because it is shared—and exclusively under that condition.

Elevation begins here, and departs for an elsewhere that is only truly beyond to the extent that the becoming signification of the here below is accomplished through it. The reception of the face coincides precisely with the advent of a world that is spoken. Metaphysical elevation toward the beyond coincides with a relation to the world that is taught by the Other. The decompartmentalization of the world is the metaphysical event par excellence, as it always coincides with the reception of the face in its exteriority. To see the face is to immediately share the world: "Transcendence is not a vision of the Other, but a primordial donation" (174).

The event of metaphysics—the production of the infinite in the face of the Other—is the realization of a world in which human beings, in our humanity, reign: "Being is a world in which one speaks and of which one speaks. Society is the presence of being" (181). The world finds its ontological consistency only by way of the social situation. There is a world only when it is traversed by sociality. The ontological consistency of that world is founded on the fact that it is inhabited by human beings who possess the idea of justice, which is to say, human beings who in speaking of the world, speak to ourselves. The ontological question entails this surplus of being beyond the totality of the world, which is the signification of the face. There is a world only when it is oriented, and metaphysics consecrates that orientation.

CHAPTER 6

The Metaphysical Context of Intentionality

Phenomena within the Space of Questions and Answers

From the very outset of *Being and Time*, Heidegger insists that the emergence of the question of the sense of being constitutively presupposes the preliminary phenomenon of an as-yet vague and undetermined ("average")[1] comprehension of being. The obscurity of our initial comprehension of being thus motivates the need for clarification, which is to say that it demands an explicit elucidation of being through the formulation of the question of the sense of being. Levinas returns to this thesis numerous times throughout his oeuvre, seeking to draw out all of the consequences of our awakening to the question of being, through the elaboration of what he calls "the question of the Question": "Yet the question about the question is more radical still. Why does research take form as a question? How is it that the 'what?,' already steeped in being so as to open it up the more, becomes a demand and a prayer, a special language inserting into the 'communication' of the given an appeal for help, for aid addressed to another?"[2]

Here Levinas only broadens the Heideggerian question by referring it back to the concrete situation within which any question comes to be posed—essentially and above all in the form of an invocation of the Other: "Even the philosophy that questions the meaning of being does so on the basis of the encounter with the Other";[3] or, as he says in *Totality and Infinity*, "Questioning is not explained by astonishment only, but by the presence of him to whom it is addressed."[4]

An ontological phenomenon is thus inseparable from the elucidation of the concrete situation within which the question of its sense is posed. This means that, for Levinas, we cannot limit ourselves to Heidegger's triple articulation of "that which is asked about" (*Gefragtes*), "that which is questioned" (*Befragtes*), and "that which is to be found out" (*Erfragtes*), in order to bring to light the conditions under which the question of the sense of being can be posed. Rather, it is a question of no longer attempting to identify that existent who is likely to provide the sense of being—*Befragtes* as Dasein, as "the identical subject, allegedly placed in the openness of Being"—in order to elucidate, beneath it, the inscription of the phenomenon in question in "the crux of a diachronic plot (which remains to be determined) between the Same and the other." This kind of diachrony of manifestation does not amount to an "immediate instant of opening and intuition," but is rather identified with the situation of interlocution, the enduring, "silent coming and going from question to response."[5]

The possibility of phenomena, and indeed of every objective manifestation in general, is situated within the gap between questions and answers. For that reason, it must be understood in terms of the primacy of the metaphysical relation of teaching over fundamental ontology, according to the formal relationship of that which conditions to the conditioned object. Further, where impersonal Hegelian reason absorbs the uniqueness of interlocutors into the anonymity of its objective process, the sense of reason that Levinas seeks to deploy emerges from the interlocutory relation of same and other, and inscribes itself within the open space between questions and answers. There is no concrete reason, other than that which is divided by this interval.

For Levinas, the primacy of the metaphysical relation to the Other, understood as a relationship of instruction, entails a rupture with any all-encompassing paradigm. Models such as Husserl's intersubjectivity and Heidegger's *Miteinandersein* make no room for the asymmetry of the Other in relation to the self. In Husserl, the Other is constituted as an alter ego, which is to say as a modification of the ego by an appresentative analogy.

For Heidegger, same and other coexist within an anonymous community rooted in ontology, a community that neutralizes the constitutive asymmetry of the face-to-face encounter and thus suppresses the event of sociality. But for Levinas, the latter can be understood to represent "the ultimate event of being itself" (*Totality and Infinity*, 28) only if, in articulating a relationship between terms, it maintains their separation. Sociality thus respects the asymmetry of the Other and its radical exteriority with regard to the same, in which the authoritative presence of the Other—which is to say its openness to the question—consists.

For Heidegger, to the contrary, "intersubjectivity is a coexistence, a 'we' prior to the 'I' and the other, a neutral intersubjectivity" (68). And yet for Levinas the reduction of the Other, which is constitutive of fundamental and ultimate ontology, entails the suppression of the very principle of the intelligibility of the real. In order to say otherwise, the question of the intelligibility of the world depends on the preliminary elucidation of the masterful presence of the Other (*autrui*), which marks the exteriority of the other (*l'Autre*) to the sphere of identification with the same. This irreducibility issues from the expressive presence of the face, which undoes the form proper to the same, in order to present the other in its absolute alterity. The one who speaks is in-himself or in-herself because he or she signifies himself or herself, which is to say that through his or her discourse he or she remains exterior to and transcends those forms, rooted in the same, that would otherwise characterize him or her. If the intelligibility of the Other were to depend on his or her appropriation by these latter, such an integration would ipso facto entail the dissolution of the expressive presence of the Other within the totalizing silence of immanence.

Any universe governed by a single, totalizing principle can bring about only a world of silence. In such a world, beings conform to a kind of ontological intrigue that, by characterizing them in the third person, at once overwhelms and governs them. Thus, such an existence cannot coincide with the ultimate affirmation of the subject. That affirmation, however, rests on a form of speech that entails the advent of the first person within being and thereby shatters totalization in and through the advent of an existence for itself—which is to say no longer exclusively for itself, but by the idea of the infinite.

The intelligibility of the world, the objective stability of the real, requires the sociality of the discourse that is situated within the gap between the questions and responses that the same and the other exchange. More precisely, the intelligibility of a stabilized world depends on the ongoing possibility of continuing to pose questions to the Other. The masterful position that is constitutive of the Other's presence, consists in its openness to the question. The presence of the Other, which coincides with his or her availability to the question—preceding even the explicit formulation of a response—is constitutive of the ontological fixation of the field of appearances. Openness to the question is the essence of language, and teaching is the fundamental structure of sociality. The development of the idea of the infinite is concretely affirmed through the aptitude of the Other to respond to questions.

The presence of the world rests on the proposition that emerges from the Other; that proposition constitutively opens itself to the question, under pain of losing its very status as proposition. Indeed, such a proposition can be held only between "two points which do not constitute a system, a cosmos, a totality" (96).

And yet the possibility of continuing to pose questions—the discursive situation that consummates sociality—is constitutive of the objective stabilization of phenomena. For Levinas, it is thus no longer an issue of reasoning in terms of things in themselves as the substrata of phenomenality, but rather of considering the face itself as the very "thing in itself" that constitutes the principle of ontology: "The speaking substance confers being upon the object of which it speaks."[6] The Other is the ontological principle of sensible phenomenality because he or she speaks, which is to say that he or she responds to questions and thereby draws attention to the incoherencies of sensible appearance.

The Other fixes the objective consistency of phenomena by thematizing them: "The origin of the truth is found within teaching; the Face is the condition of the truth";[7] "objectivation and thematization, to which objective knowledge accedes, already rest upon teaching";[8] "The Other is the principle of phenomena" (*Totality and Infinity*, 92). And yet the thematization that comes from the Other can never be decoupled from the situation of teaching—or, indeed, of discourse—in which the one who is taught may question the one who teaches.

The objective stability of the world does not belong to the world itself, which is to say the world independent of the interlocution of the same and the other. Rather, that stability emerges from the face as thing in itself, or more precisely from the Other insofar as he or she is able to respond to a question, in the event that doubt arises regarding a claim that he or she has made. The possibility of engaging in ongoing discourse is the essence of discourse itself. Properly speaking, there is no discourse, and thus no intelligibility of the real, without teaching, without the possibility of pursuing the thread of questions and answers, which is to say without a question that necessarily follows from a first response. In other words, there is no discourse without the possibility of a new question, which demands a new response.

All of this means, radically, that any response that does not open up the possibility of a new question is not a proper response and thus teaches nothing. In other words, a response that one cannot question again, which closes off the possibility of a new question, is no response at all. Thus there is no "definitive" response: The interlocutory situation is constitutively open. The response is either masterful or not a response, which is to say it is interlocutory by definition, open to possibilities that give rise to further questions. This is because the content which is taught is inseparable from the one who teaches. In other words, such content is only, properly speaking, actually taught to the extent that the one who teaches, the interlocutor, can answer for what he or she teaches when questioned by the one who is taught: "A proposition is maintained in the outstretched field of questions and answers" (96).

In the masterful relation, the thread of questions and responses does not know the interruption of the last word. The absence of closure, the possibility that a question may interrogate the content taught and thus the one who teaches is constitutive of the "objectivity of the object." And yet the possibility that the thread of questions and responses will stand uninterrupted, which is constitutive of the objective stability of appearances, is itself conditioned by the regime of manifestation by which the other reveals herself to the same.

But how is it possible to maintain the absolute alterity of transcendent being while assuming its manifestation within the same? In other words, how can the other come to present himself or herself to the same without at the same time losing his or her constitutive alterity, his or her transcendence? For Levinas, neither the transcendental apparatus of Husserlian phenomenology (which rests on a noetico-noematic parallelism), nor the ontology of Heidegger (where fundamental ontology coincides with the analysis of Dasein),[9] will allow us to bring together these two needs. In both Husserl and Heidegger, we see a reduction of the other, though the neutralization of his or her transcendence. But it is within the horizon of these two versions of phenomenology that Levinas equally opposes both constituent representation and the unveiling of *Aletheia* to the revelation of the face as expression.

Both intentional representation and the unveiling of being belong to a phenomenological register that is diurnal and thus infra-discursive. Being deploys itself as transcendence in expressing itself. The regime of manifestation proper to expression thus coincides with neither an intentional representation nor an unveiling, but rather consists in the Other's revelation of himself or herself:

> *The absolute experience is not disclosure but revelation*: a coinciding of the expressed with him who expresses, which is the privileged manifestation of the Other, the manifestation of a face over and beyond form. Form—incessantly betraying its own manifestation, congealing into a plastic form, for it is adequate to the same—alienates the exteriority of the other. The face is a living presence; it is expression. (*Totality and Infinity*, 65–66)

To express oneself is to manifest oneself by oneself, *kath'auto*; it is "to signify oneself." The one who expresses himself or herself does not draw his or her intelligibility from the light "borrowed" from intentionality and unveiling, from which the same emerges. Levinas thus readopts the Platonic theme, developed in the *Phaedrus*, of that true discourse that "can come to its own assistance" (71), in opposition to those written discourses which can never do so: "The manifestation of the face is already discourse. He who manifests himself comes, according to Plato's expression, to his own assistance" (66). To come to the aid of one's own manifestation is to speak; it is to guide one's manifestation. To express oneself is thus to undo "the form adequate to the Same so as to present oneself as other" (66). In this way, to express oneself is to present oneself in person: The face speaks, which is to say that it undoes the form that hides, alienates, and suppresses it. As a form of expression, the face ipso facto coincides with presence of the transcendental existent. From there, "the question is possible because the very presence of the master, facing me, cannot be translated into terms of knowledge, because I do not *know* the master, but rather commerce with him."[10] Insofar as the Other presents himself or herself in speech and thus comes to the aid of his or her own expression—and thereby undoes the form that alienates her or him—the Other is ipso facto the one to whom we can address our questions.

To the extent that the Other expresses himself or herself, we are not in a relationship of knowledge, but rather one of exchange. It is only in this way that the motivations behind our questions become pertinent. It only makes sense to pose questions to the Other in light of his or her dissymmetry in relation to me, which is to say his or her masterful position, entailed by the fact that he or she expresses himself or herself, and comes to the aid of the signs that his or her expression dispenses. It is in this way that we must understand "the rectitude of this presence as an openness to questioning."[11]

One who expresses himself or herself reveals himself or herself *kath'auto*, precisely because he or she comes to the aid of the signs that his or her speech articulates. Moreover, and for this reason, this assistance constitutes the very condition of her self-revelation. The one who reveals herself does so as one to whom questions may be posed, and thus by whom "the world is oriented, that is, takes on signification" (*Totality and Infinity*, 98).

Insofar as the Other speaks, and in so doing presents himself or herself with a direct frankness, he or she thereby comes to the aid of his or her own speech. Moreover, it is only in this way that the Other is in a position to respond to questions, as he or she is defined by the possibility of being able to return to and qualify his or her speech. In other words, the fact that the Other speaks, which is to say that he or she comes to the aid of his or her own manifestation, constitutively entails that he or she is in a position to come to the aid of the one to whom he or she speaks: "His speech consists in 'coming to the assistance' of his word—in being present" (69). Contrary to written discourse, which "can neither defend itself nor come to its own support,"[12] the oral discourse by which the Other reveals himself or herself inverts "the inevitable movement that bears the spoken word to the past state of the written word" (*Totality and Infinity*, 69). This means that written discourse organizes signs that speak for the author, who can no longer defend their signification, which is to say that he or she cannot take them back, begin again, or reiterate them. Only the Other, insofar as he or she speaks, in the position of mastery, is in a position to prevent the dissociation of the sign from its originator. The solidarity of the sign and its originator is constitutive of speech as a relation of teaching, of the aid brought to signs, which is the principle of the ontological fixation of appearance.

It is in this sense, by the fact that the one who expresses himself or herself comes to the aid of his or her own expression, that speech "brings what the written word is already deprived of: mastery. Speech, better than a simple sign, is essentially magisterial" (69). Unlike oral discourse, the written word is never in a position to be questioned, because the author is no longer present to bring aid to his or her discourse, which is to say to respond to the questions to which that discourse may give rise: "The written discourse which provokes my questions—that which indicates a real presence behind what is written—cannot hear my questions."[13]

To speak is, therefore, to engage in the inverse of the relationship of written text to its author. For one who produces given signs, it is to endeavor to maintain his or her presence behind the signs that make up a discourse. Levinas thus speaks of "an inexhaustible surplus of attention arising in the ever-recommenced effort of language to clarify its own manifestation" (*Totality and Infinity*, 97). Thus in speech, "The content that is presented to me is inseparable from him who has thought it—which means that the author of the discourse responds to questions" (71). The signified content is thus not an ideal content of signification. That is, it cannot be dissociated from the one who teaches, who can only teach at all to the extent that he or she is in a position to respond to questions regarding the content that his or her discourse articulates. This is precisely what content in a detached state—abstracted in relation to the master who teaches it— is incapable of accomplishing. Thus it is not the "definitive" response that fixes appearance, but the question to come, the field that is always open to interlocution—which is therefore constitutive of sociality.

The Other speaks insofar as he or she is able to continue to speak, which is to say explain himself or herself, and thereby come to the aid of his or her own discourse, in order to prevent any misunderstanding on the part of the interlocutor—precisely what the written word cannot do. This is why Levinas affirms that "to understand speech is to be able to pose a question."[14] Speech constitutively entails that the one to whom it is addressed is able to interrogate that speech, which is to say that the speaker be in a position to respond to what has been said: "Speech consists in explaining oneself with respect to speech; it is a teaching" (*Totality and Infinity*, 98).

For this reason, all speech entails the presence of the speaker. The masterful position of the speaker consists precisely in the effort by which that speaker, insofar as he or she speaks, "never separates himself from the sign he delivers, but takes it up again always while he exposes [it]" (97). What Levinas means here is that the speaker's presence to the signs that he or she issues is essential to speech and signification. If speech constitutively exposes itself to questioning, Levinas reminds us that "questioning is not explained by astonishment only, but by the presence of him to whom it is addressed" (96), or in spite of that person. In other words, self-revelation, *kath'auto*, and teaching amount to one and the same thing. The one who speaks brings aid to the signs that he or she advances, and in so doing reveals himself or herself as the signifier of speech, the master to whom questions may be posed.

This dimension of "the aid that is brought to speech" is not some kind of appendix to speech, as if speech could somehow be deployed without it. The speaker must be able to respond to questions, or, strictly speaking, there is no speech. It is for this reason that Levinas can decisively affirm that the "way the object is posited as a theme [which is offered,] envelops the instance of signifying" (96). The object's appearance is stabilized only through thematization, which is to say by the expression of the signs that invest it in the speech of the master: "The objectivity of the object and its signification come from language" (96). And yet thematization as the ontological fixation of appearances does not merely consist in the regimentation of appearances within signs. More precisely, such regimentation entails the imbrication of the act of signifying with the possibility of repeating that act. Such an act is an act of signification if and only if the one who signifies is in a position of repeating the act, or, in other words, of responding to questions regarding the articulated act. Thus, there is only an act of signification if the one who speaks—the signifier (*le signifiant*)—does not abandon the signs that he or she organizes. Indeed, the solidarity of speaker and the signs he or she deploys is constitutive of the signifying value of the sign.

All of this is to say, again, that the signification that actualizes the act of the speaker/signifier constitutively entails the presence of the master who is able to respond to questions that take issue with the significance of that act of articulation. Once again: Signification is inseparable from interlocution; they cannot be abstractly isolated from one another. In other words, signification is inseparable from the possibility of an interlocutory exchange, initiated by the question. This means that signification does not belong to an ideal register, where its value would be determined once and for all independent of the interlocutory scene of teaching. There is no signification to speak of without the possibility of exchanging questions and answers. This is why signification has no ideal content; it is situated by definition within the *entre-deux*, "the outstretched field" (96) of questions and answers.

This certainly does not mean that there can no be signification that is not dependent on questions, at risk of losing the stability to which all signified content purports. Rather, such stability depends precisely on the fact that the Other brings aid to the signification that he or she advances, which is to say that his or her presence guarantees that to any question that is posed, an answer will be provided. Thus, the link between speech and response is constitutive of speech and signification in general. It is for this reason that Levinas can affirm that the "way the object is posited as a theme offered envelops the instance of signifying" (96). The one who signifies does not represent a factor that is somehow indifferent or exterior to signification, because he or she can only signify what he or she signifies on the condition of his or her magisterial capacity to give aid to the meaning of what he or she is saying, which is to say to respond to questions.

The presence of the master to his or her own speech conditions the possibility of univocal signification, which is to say signification *tout court*.

(This is demonstrated in Levinas's re-writing of Descartes's evil genius, a point to which I return below.) The ontological fixation of the appearance of an object thus depends on the fixation of that appearance in a proposition. That fixation coincides precisely with the presence of the master-teacher (*le Maître*) to the speech that he or she provides: "Thematization manifests the Other because the proposition that posits and offers the world does not float in the air, but promises a response to him who receives this proposition, who directs himself toward the Other because in his proposition he receives *the possibility of questioning*" (96, emphasis added). Put differently, all speech constitutively reveals the speaker. Insofar as linguistic propositions are fundamentally defined by the fact that they propose the world, speech that proposes the world in this way does so only on the condition that the one who receives that speech is promised a response to any doubts that may arise for him or her: "For speech is always a taking up again of what was a simple sign cast forth by it, an ever renewed promise to clarify what was obscure in the utterance" (97).

The signs of the proposition deploy a sense, a series of signifieds, essentially because the intelligibility of the proposition is inseparable from the speaker who provides them. The content of the former is inseparable from the presence of the latter: "The meaningful refers to a signifier" (96). It is for this reason that a proposition is never without the revelation of the face, which is to say of an existent, in person, who speaks in the face-to-face position of the interlocutor, and who thus reveals himself or herself in every act of expression:

> The sign does not signify the signifier as it signifies the signified. The signified is never a complete presence; always a sign in its turn, it does not come in a straightforward frankness. The signifier, he who emits the sign, faces, despite the interposition of the sign, without proposing himself as a theme. He can, to be sure, speak of himself—but then he would announce himself as signified and consequently as a sign in his turn. The Other, the signifier, manifests himself in speech by speaking of the world and not of himself; he manifests himself by proposing the world, by thematizing it. (96)

The Other reveals himself or herself because he or she speaks, which is to say that he or she is in a position to interpret his or her own speech. The Other reveals himself or herself to the extent that his or her revelation coincides with the promise of a response to the eventuality of questions prompted by his or her speech. The face is expressive presence; the signs and works of the face are constantly animated by a presence that deciphers them beyond the intelligible forms with which the self invests them. It is, for that reason, no longer a phenomenon, but rather a thing in itself. And in turn, for this reason, speech ipso facto entails the revelation of the transcendence of the Other. From the moment that I begin to speak, the Other is already here. Through his or her interlocutory presence, because he or she comes to the aid of his or her own speech, he or she teaches and responds to questions, and in so doing stabilizes appearances in unequivocal phenomena. Thus, strictly speaking, without this relationship, there is no speech at all.

And so, all teaching reveals the presence of the one who teaches. This is because to speak of the world, to thematize an appearance, is to ipso facto undo the form that caricatures the teacher, in order to introduce himself or herself by himself or herself (*kath'auto*), independent of the fact that he or she takes himself or herself for the signified of his or her own discourse. In speech, the transcendent being presents himself or herself in person. From the moment that the Other speaks, he or she places the idea of the infinite within me. All speech that teaches me the world, at the same time necessarily teaches me the transcendence of the beings with whom I am in social relation, because it is constitutive of speech that it is maintained and supported. This support engages a presence that constitutively accompanies the intelligibility of the sign, and through that, all intuition of phenomena. Thus to engage in discourse is, necessarily, to receive the idea of the infinite.

The Other guarantees signification, insofar as it can come to its aid. The sign draws its significance from the presence of the speaker, which overcomes the obscurity and equivocation of language. But to speak of the obscurity and equivocation of language entails that there is a level of the deployment of language that falls short of signification and the face. This is the level of the relation that precedes the Cartesian discovery of the idea of the infinite, namely the relation to that "other" who is the evil genius, which precedes the face-to-face encounter.

It is here that we must understand the relationship between appearance and language in much greater depth. As I have sought to show, the objectivity of phenomena results from language, but I must now be even more precise, and underscore the fact that it ultimately results from signification. In reality, it is appearance in general that depends on language, but all appearances are not necessarily ontologically consistent, which is to say that they are not necessarily supported by a univocal significance—that is, a sense signified by the signifier, the Other. There is an equivocal regime of appearance, which indeed presupposes language, but not a bona fide interlocutor, which is to say a signification. Such is the Cartesian exposition of the evil genius, the consequences of which we must explore further.

On the most basic level, Levinas presents a register of appearance which seems to precede speech, a level of pure apparition, which "reveals and conceals" (98). The work of speech would thus be located within the overcoming of the correspondence between revelation and occultation inherent in appearance: "Speech consists in surmounting, in a total frankness ever renewed, the dissimulation inevitable in every apparition" (98). Levinas thus speaks of a state of the world that precedes the relationship of teaching, marked, for that reason, by "the bewitchment and the permanent equivocation of a world in which every apparition is a possible dissimulation" (98). Levinas emphasizes that such a world, where speech does not yet resound, and thus where appearance coincides with dissimulation, is "anarchic" and devoid of all principle. The world of silence is a world within which appearances cannot be oriented and thus reason remain plurivocal and deceptive.

And yet this world that precedes speech is not an absolutely silent world, because "a world so silent could not even present itself as a spectacle" (94). The anarchic world, awaiting a principle, finds its referent in speech, precisely in the reference to a word "that does not come" (93). It is through this negative reference to speech, which refers to a world that awaits a word, a world that lacks sense because it lacks speech, that the anarchic spectacle of appearance already entails a relation to the Other. But such alterity is situated beneath the face as revelation of the infinite. Rewriting one of the central themes of Descartes's *Meditations*, Levinas takes up the figure of manipulative alterity, the evil genius, that Descartes encountered prior to the discovery of the cogito and the infinite. For Levinas, the figure of the evil genius is distinguished from that of the master-teacher by the former's evasive and equivocal speech. The evil genius evades the responsibility of masterful position entailed by all expression, which provides the possibility of the field of questions and responses.

Further, and again, the silence of the anarchic world does not in any way reveal some kind of absolute silence, but rather proceeds from a modality deficient in speech, a speech that deliberately refuses to arrive. Put differently, silence proceeds from a speech that refuses to take responsibility for itself as such, which is to say that it refuses to come to the aid of the signs that it advances. The evil genius speaks, it organizes signs, but it is negligent in their interpretation, and thus in refusing to come to their aid, it refuses itself to speech: "The interlocutor has given a sign, but has declined every interpretation; this is the silence that terrifies" (91).

The evil genius is thus rooted in an alterity that evades presence, specifically the presence proper to the master-teacher whose position it occupies, as "the interpretative key in the sign to be interpreted, [which] is precisely the presence of the other in the proposition, the presence of him who can come to the assistance of his discourse, the teaching quality of all speech" (96). Silence is thus saturated with signs but not with speech and thus cannot articulate any signification capable of assigning appearance to univocal signs. The sign that lacks the presence of the speaker, its originator and interpreter in the figure of the master-teacher, remains condemned by the regime of appearance to plurivocity. Because it dispenses signs, the evil genius does indeed open up the world, but it does so in the mode of an anarchic spectacle, without principle because, strictly speaking, without speech. Silence is thus not the converse of speech, but rather a form of speech that is deliberately vexed by the deceptive malevolence of the one who deploys the signs of language in service of a refusal to speak: "the word never uttered" (94), "the inverse of language" (91). "Silence is not a simple absence of speech; speech lies in the depths of silence like a laughter perfidiously held back" (91).

Without the speech proper to teaching, capable of responding to questions, "thought would strike nothing substantial" (90). This means that prior to the relationship of teaching, the world of phenomena, still lacking a principle, is constantly menaced by the possibility of devolving into so many contradictory apparitions, thus rupturing the objective continuity of a thing that presents itself in outline from one moment to the next. Such a rupture is always possible, because no master is present to teach the appearance, by thematizing it in a proposition. For that reason, the pressure to re-qualify the identity of the object weighs heavily as a permanent menace. The impossibility of posing a question is constitutive of the relation to the evil genius insofar as it evades the interpretation of the signs that it advances. This situation entails the constant menace, impossible to remove, of an ever-possible degradation of phenomenality. That potential corresponds to the deception of the evil genius and to the inclination that characterizes the one who refuses to accept speech as that which one pronounces and interprets at the same time. With the evil genius, speech is deliberately halted in the midst of its articulation and thus cannot provide any stable content, which is to say pedagogical content.

The consistency of the world is assured by the Other, who brings aid to his or her own manifestation in expressing himself or herself, and is thus constitutively in a position to respond to questions, and thereby to grant to the object of perception the selfhood that it would otherwise lack. This lack entails the anarchy of the spectacle, the renewal of that ambiguity that is the result of the absence of the speaker to his or her own speech. However, that anarchy is not the chaos of appearance, but rather consists in the impossibility of obtaining a guarantee regarding the identity of the phenomena in question. Such would be the sense of a transcendental theory of impressions that lack the support of a relationship of teaching:

> Husserl, who nonetheless admitted the possibility of an autopresentation of things, found this equivocation again in the *essential* incompletion of that autopresentation, and in the always possible break-up of the "synthesis" that sums up the sequence of its "aspects." (90–91)

It is nothing less than the "mocking intention" (91) that takes the place of speech as a principle and that disinvests signs in order to neglect presence, which is to say, to avoid questions. In this vitiated relationship, the Other "dissimulates his face, that is, declines the assistance he would have to bring to the signs he delivers, and which he delivers, consequently, in equivocation" (93). Language is constitutive of appearance, but only speech, the true form of language, constitutes appearance in its objective continuity. In this way, genuine speech entails the presence of the one who reveals himself or herself through that speech. Further, the masterful presence of the Other opens up the interlocutory extension of questions and responses, and in so doing constitutes the principle of appearance, of the world in its ontological stability.

Here, however, two issues no doubt arise. First and foremost, the Other reveals himself or herself through discourse, which is to say that in speaking of the world and not specifically of himself or herself in the themes of his or her speech. To the extent that the one who speaks brings aid to his or her speech, or does not speak at all, all speech entails the presence of the interlocutor, which is to say the revelation of the interlocutor, regardless of the objective content of the discourse in question. Without the revelation of the Other as principle and presence—that is, as the existent to whom questions can be addressed—discourse can never result in the intelligibility of the signified, because the stability of the latter depends on the assistance of the Other. To understand any discourse, regardless of its content, is therefore ipso facto to be in relation with the Other. To purport to understand without a relation to the Other having been established, without the revelation of the Other through his or her speech, is to remain within the equivocation of signs. Such pure indexes or works without principle call for the interpretation of the survivor, the historiographer—outside of interlocution.

To speak is to speak of, and therefore to reveal, oneself. All of Levinas's reasoning leads toward this, the constitutive contemporaneity of the intentionality of the Other's discourse and the revelation of the interlocutor. Furthermore, if it is true that the first word of discourse as revelation of the face comprises the commandment "Thou Shalt Not Kill," and insofar as that commandment need never be explicitly formulated as such, it is the very essence of all discourse, regardless of content. In other words, interlocution, the relationship of teaching is not simply one situation among others sustained by the same and the other. Rather, it differs because of this commandment, which comes before all else.

It is for this reason, then, that interlocution, the masterful relation in which the Other speaks and the self poses questions, is always already ethical in itself. As such, teaching does not derive from ethics, but rather consummates it. This is why ethics is the metaphysical condition of phenomenological intentionality. Intentionality has a context; intuition supposes the nocturnal event—which its phenomenological primacy conceals—of the revelation of the Other. That revelation concretely supports the play of lights and the noetico-noematic structure of intuition itself. Intentionality supposes interlocution; discourse is its very foundation. Thus, "All knowledge consists in *a reception*, so inseparable from its origin that the master *must speak to me in order for me to think at all.*"[15]

The effacement of the event of revelation, which undergirds the theoretical gaze, is explained by the propensity of the latter to exclude everything that cannot be reduced to its illumination, above all the metaphysical event that conditions it. Nocturnal events of metaphysics are masked by the light of the gaze, understood as clarity and evidence. And yet these events are the condition of possibility of such a gaze and require a method of deduction no longer founded on phenomenological intuition, a method that instead consists in the break or rupture of the noetico-noematic structure of the play of lights.[16] The primacy of the gaze obscures its condition, which as condition remains inassimilable to that which it conditions, which is to say that it cannot itself proceed from a look or a glance. There is thus no sense in measuring the excessiveness of the infinite from the perspective of intentionality in order to understand the former as that which escapes the latter. The excess of the infinite, its true exteriority, represents the passage into a register that renders the notion of intentionality possible. For that reason, the relation to the Other—defined as that which resists intentionality—cannot find the source of its own intelligibility within a negative intentionality without committing an absurdity. It would be to maintain intentionality as the measure of all things, when it is instead a question of thinking a level from which intentionality becomes an operating concept:

> The sense of our whole effort lies in affirming not that the Other forever escapes knowing, *but that there is no meaning in speaking here of knowledge or ignorance*, for justice, *the preeminent transcendence* and the *condition* for knowing, is nowise, as one would like, a noesis correlative of a noema. (*Totality and Infinity*, 89, emphasis added)

It is for this reason that we must anticipate a clumsy misinterpretation of the concept of "religion" evoked within *Totality and Infinity*, as the opposite of what Levinas calls "totalization." For Levinas, "religion" is "the bond that is established between the same and the other without constituting a totality" (40). Religion here is in no way the contrary of reason, but is rather the proper understanding of reason itself. In other words, totalization does not have a monopoly on rationality.

The totalizing form of reason, which assimilates the same and the other in a universal historic process, leads directly to the death of interlocution through the repression of the infinite. Reason properly understood finds itself fundamentally shared by the same and the other, traversed by the space of questions and answers. As plurality, reason concretely produces itself as teaching:

> The sociality of intellection must be something other than pantheism or monadology. It is neither a fusion of individual beings within a reason that accomplishes their (true) individuality, nor isolation within a harmony pre-established by a God who dominates them, and at the heart of which the monads constitute an ensemble. It exists rather within the possibility for individuals to be *close* to one another—which is to say, for Reason *to be other for a reason*. To say that reason does not accomplish its social existence through its internal accord with itself, *but rather in its accord with another reason*, is to admit that something other than evidence dominates rationality itself, and that thought immersed in *teaching* is not merely maieutic. Teaching entails reason as *you* [*raison comme tu*]. Language is only the admission of the distinction between "I" and "you," neither on the model of affectivity, nor solely as a function of our animality, *but within the framework of reason itself*. Transmission *from reason to reason* exists.[17]

Levinas's insistence on pedagogy could indeed be understood to support the idea that he could abandon all of the demands of reason to the benefit of an authoritarian model in which mastery entails submission and the abdication of consciousnesses. My goal, however, is to show just how the primacy of teaching aims at a redefinition of reason, which would allow us to pass from totalizing monism to interlocutory plurality. This means that the master-student relationship is in direct opposition to the subjection of a servant to a master, the model of a relationship that knows only a unilateral form of reason.

It is possible, certainly, to read the relationship of teaching as one of domination, in which one subject, possessing a certain knowledge, exercises that dominance over another, who lacks it. Such a relation would necessarily rest on a kind of truncated reason. But even here we must be cautious: It is not because the Other possesses some knowledge that I lack that the Other has the status of master. The significance of teaching is not a question of content, but rather of form.

The Other is my master insofar as he or she is other—not because he or she possesses some knowledge greater than my own. In other words, even some ignorance on his or her part does not negate the Other's position of mastery. Mastery is, simply put, constitutive of the alterity of the Other. The Other does not provide some supplementary content, but rather provides the stability necessary for the intelligibility of any content. Nor is that provision itself a content, but rather the principle by which intentionality applies to any content. To be in such a position does not in principle amount to greater knowledge, but does entail that the Other constitutively speaks, which is to say that the Other gives sense to that speech by coming to its aid in the field of questions and answers: "The master furnishes us with a principle. That which allows us to see, is given to us in words. It is not that the other 'knows more than me.' The master does not deliver us a surplus of content, *but rather provides us a point of departure*."[18]

This relationship to the principle of all intentional content is not itself a form of intentional content; it is rather the work of justice that constitutively undergirds the light of intuition:

> The intentionality proper to the intellection of words consists in
> receiving, in learning—beyond any comprehension—something *more*
> than the perception of light. And yet, it is not a new content. In under-
> standing a word, I fully assimilate its content as if it originated with
> me. . . . This fact of having an origin is not a content given to vision.
> However, within the idea, it opens a profound dimension to which
> consciousness can do nothing, but is not a form of weakness, placed in
> a strange relation to the notion of power.[19]

Thus the relationship of teaching does not provide some kind of supplementary content, but rather a principle, an origin, from which all the content of thought is constituted, and by which the latter can become mine—which is to say my idea, and my thought.

Signification and Appearance

According to Levinas, it is in Heidegger that we find the first explication of the relationship that links objective appearance to signification. Without directly citing Heidegger, Levinas summarizes the passage from the ontological regime of readiness-to-hand (*Zuhandenheit*) to that of presence-at-hand (*Vorhandenheit*), from circumspect preoccupation to the contemplation of the existent:

> Once the indissoluble bond that connects apparition with signification was understood, an effort was made to render the apparition posterior to signification by situating it within the finality of our practical behavior. What only appears, "pure objectivity," the "nothing but objective" would be only a residue of this practical finality from which it would derive its meaning. Whence the priority of care over contemplation. (*Totality and Infinity*, 94)

Taken within the surrounding world (*Umwelt*), Dasein's access to worldly beings is articulated in the form of a circumspect gaze (*Umsicht*). The theoretical view comes to replace the latter following a modification of the ontological comprehension of Dasein. The latter consists in dis-inscribing the existent from its place within the system of equipment from which it draws its intelligibility as existent—as a capacity for action that aims for the realization of a practical finality. This modification of the ontological comprehension leads to the objectivation of the existent, to its explicit appearance through the act of depriving it of its worldhood (*Entweltlichung*).[20]

From the reconstruction of this process of ontological mutation, Levinas contests, on the one hand, the idea that the intelligibility of the existent can find its principle in the practical finality on which, as a malleable existent, he or she relies. On the other hand, he also contests the idea that contemplative consciousness can result from "a simple suspension of action . . . to apperceive the tool as a thing" (*Totality and Infinity*, 94). The source of signification can come only from the face to face. And yet fundamental ontology, by the ontological restriction that it entails,[21] prohibits us from thinking the very event of sociality. In order to support his demonstration,

Levinas begins by recalling Heidegger's argument that it is Dasein that constitutes the ultimate finality of the system of references that structure the framework of "equipmentality":

> Qua practical, signification refers ultimately to the being that exists in view of this very existence. It is thus derived from a term that is of itself an end. Thus he who comprehends the signification is indispensable for the series in which the things acquire a meaning, as the end of the series. (*Totality and Infinity*, 94)

That the finality of the network of equipment is nothing other than Dasein itself means that, from Levinas's point of view, it is enjoyment that constitutes the outcome of the system of returns, from which every existent constitutively draws his or her worldly significance: "The reference that signification implies would terminate where the reference is made from self to self—in enjoyment" (94).

Once this outcome is realized, the signification of the existent as a means oriented toward some end is annulled. And yet, as we have seen, the outcome is systematically achieved from the commencement of any activity that targets some end. Indeed, the manipulation of a tool is already its own end, which is to say that it is satisfaction or suffering—in brief, it is enjoyment: "The enjoyment of a thing, be it a tool, does not consist simply in bringing this thing to the usage for which it is fabricated—the pen to the writing, the hammer to the nail to be driven in—but also in suffering or rejoicing over this operation" (133). If signification depends on the return of a worldly existent to its own finality, the finality attained in enjoyment ipso facto entails the annihilation of that signification: "The outcome is the point at which every signification is precisely lost. . . . The means themselves lose their signification in the outcome" (94–95). It is for this reason that in such an ontological framework, signification can be consistently maintained only to the extent that Dasein is itself maintained in a state of perpetual dissatisfaction: "Things begin to take on signification in the care of the being that is still 'on the way.' . . . The intelligible would result from the non-satisfaction, the provisional indigence of this being, its remaining short of its accomplishment" (95). The idea that it is the suspension of its operative function within the surrounding world (*Umwelt*) which makes a tool the object of an explicit appearance, emerges here: "Consciousness itself has been derived from this breach" (95).

Such a thesis is credible only if more value is accorded to potential than to the act, which, however, in all ontological coherence, actualizes that which is potential (*dunamis*): "The act is more than the potency" (95).

In order to avoid falling into this inversion of values, it must be understood that sense can be established only by a modification of the state of enjoyment.

However, this modification does not correspond to a frustration of the self, nor does it suspend the operativity of equipment-existents (*étants-ustensiles*), but rather calls possession into question. The first state remains inscribed within the horizon of enjoyment, and thus of selfhood, wherein to question the self is to summon the Other, and therefore entails discourse. In this way, existents do not draw their meaning from serving as means to some end, "but from an event for which the process of finality cannot serve as the prototype" (95). As we have seen, this event is nothing other than the establishment of language within the face-to-face encounter, the source of the intelligibility of all worldly existents. This is why the meaning of an existent does not issue from finality, and objectivity does not proceed from an ontologically mutated signification:

> Objectivity, where being is proposed to consciousness, is not a residue of finality. . . . Objectivity is not what remains of an implement or a food [*nourriture*] when separated from the world in which their being comes into play. It is *posited* in a discourse, in a *conversation* [*entre-tien*] which *proposes* the world. This *proposition* is held between [*se tient entre*] two points which do not constitute a system, a cosmos, a totality. (95–96)

Finality, and the suspense of finality, disallows the explication of the advent of objectivizing consciousness. The intelligibility of worldly beings is fixed by discourse. The meaning of the system of equipment itself rests on the nocturnal event of the revelation of an irreducible being. Ontological sense thus requires the fully mature elucidation of the ultimate event of being—which consummates sociality—and only from which the question of the sense of being may be posed. It thus finds the intelligibility that it requires within a discourse that questions the Other.

The De-compartmentalization of the World

The primacy of teaching, the idea that there is only a world that is taught, means that there will never be an exhaustive appropriation of the goods of the world. A world in which one speaks, where sociality is produced within being, is a world in which the privative ambition of all possession is incessantly called into question. The social situation, in which human beings come face to face and speak to one another, encircles the world, thus causing the goods of the world to circulate between the same and the other. No privative monopoly could ever silence the exchange by which the world is deployed—and thereby desegregated—through the ceaseless communalization that leads to the abolition of exclusive property necessarily entailed by the entry into language: "To speak is to make the world common, to create commonplaces. Language does not refer to the generality of concepts, but lays the foundations for a possession in common. *It abolishes the inalienable property of enjoyment*" (76, emphasis added).

The communalization of the goods of the world is realized by the social situation and coincides with possession itself becoming something that is *for-the-Other*. Here the ontological format of reality is broadened by the presence of the Other and by the ethical interpellation that follows from it. This enlargement is the work of language, confirmed—rather than denied—by the refusal of the gift. But we must be prudent: There is certainly no question of claiming that with the ethical one could pass from the world possessed by the ego to a world instead possessed by the Other. To do so would be to take up a pre-ethical conception of language. Language, as the work of sociality, ruptures the restrictive form of property; the former is the incessant contestation of the latter. Where human beings speak—and human beings speak in order to survive—property is contested in its very principle. Ethics is situated within the horizon of the communalization of "the goods of this world" (76). The work of sociality, inseparable from ethics, coincides with the communalization of the world, such that the gift of the world to the Other coincides with "the abolition of inalienable property" (76). Community is intrinsic to the advent of language and sociality: Where human beings speak, the world is shared.

In a world where society is produced in being, exclusive appropriation can only work against the Other. It therefore affirms itself as a vexed way of accepting the presence of the Other and is therefore already discourse. Thus, again, privative egoism makes sense only within the horizon of sociality, and it is not in its power to ensure that there is no Other. The privative monopolization of the goods of the world thus paradoxically constitutes an inadequate form of a world whose fundamental intelligibility comes from the Other; that is, from the sociality and community of the goods of the world correlated with the Other. In the same way that a dissymmetry exists between the idea of consciousness and the idea of the infinite, there is a dissymmetry between the community of the goods of the world and those goods as forms of private property. The latter is not the mere contrary of the former, rather, private property entails the community of goods as its very condition. Appropriation can therefore never exhaust the fact that human beings speak, which is to say the communalization of the world. The idea of private property results from the utopia of a world without interlocution and without faces, a world in which speech is amputated from any social significance, and is thus reduced to silence.

Egoistic or privative possession is impotent regarding the becoming-common of the world. Just as all forms of opposition to the Other (private and exclusive appropriation, egoism, war, murder) paradoxically already reveal, in spite of themselves, the transcendence of the Other and the community of the goods of the world that follows from it. The acceptance and refusal of transcendence are not contrary terms here; they do not represent a pair of alternatives. The refusal of the Other always proceeds from a modality of discourse. It thus presupposes an already realized form of that which it pretends to deny, because egoism has sense only within the horizon of an already rejected private property, originating in the insurmountable presence of the Other, which no war can ever abolish.

Such is the asymmetrical impact of sociality as the development of the idea of the infinite. The universe of possessive individualism paradoxically constitutes a world in which the very form of private property is already overcome. Possessive individualism remains inadequate to its own truth, because it not only entails a de-totalized communism of the goods of the world but also lacks the power to abolish that implication. Indeed, such communism is constitutive of the very concept of the world. Far from being some mere opposition to the possessive vision of the world, it overrides the very notion of exclusive property. No appropriation can ever overcome the insurmountable fact of language, which is to say always already the ethical absolution of the exclusive ownership of the material goods of the world. Exclusive appropriation cannot suspend the fact of language; it can only contradictorily assume precisely what it purports to contest in war, namely the insurmountably primacy of sociality—the presence of the idea of the infinite within us.

It is the incessant movement of reality toward becoming a world—that is, common goods—through the de-totalization of that reality, which discourse accomplishes as the eschatological advent of human sociality. To possess the idea of the infinite, which social reason concretely articulates, as a matter of principle entails the absurdity of the pretention to exclusively and exhaustively appropriate the goods traversed by the interlocution between the same and the other, which is to say of the world itself. The social relation understood as a relation of teaching has nothing to do with a hierarchical relation of domination; it does not amount to a Kojèvean dialectic of master and slave as a duplication of the conflicted relationship between the bourgeoisie and the proletariat. The master-teacher does not possess the world. Rather, by his or her masterful presence, the Other de-compartmentalizes the world and liberates its goods from any privative form. In a world in which the master-teacher is absent, where speech, in its social signification cannot hold, and where the idea of the infinite is restrained, the domination of human beings over one another flourishes. The social relation, wherein the Other occupies the position of the master-teacher who teaches, opposes the tendency toward exclusive appropriation, and thus delivers the world from it. The dissymmetry of the Other remains a formal lever by which the world emerges from a single point-source that, only by its openness to the question, stabilizes appearances in an objective world.

It follows from all of this that an objective world is a world that is taught, which is to say a world that is constitutively inappropriable. Indeed, the latter term is definitional of the very concept of "world."[22]

The Eye and the Gaze

It would be irresponsible to fail to give full weight to the critical scope of the many passages in *Totality and Infinity* devoted to the Sartrean theory of "being-for-others." Indeed, so many of the analyses developed in *Totality and Infinity* can be understood only in relation to the theses of *Being and Nothingness*, and we are thus forced to admit that Levinas is in no way loath to reject the Sartrean lexicon. To the contrary, Levinas's analyses of sensible interiority rewrite the Sartrean "for-itself" by reorienting it from the perspective of an assumed egoism.[23] Consequently, the passage from the "for itself" to the "for another" never completely assumes the same signification from one author to the other.[24] Moreover, Levinas's relationship to Sartre is even more ambiguous, as it is not apparent on the surface. And yet Levinas, in so many ways, remains a paradoxical inheritor of Sartre.

From this perspective, it is possible to see just how *Totality and Infinity* proposes an alternative philosophical construction to that of *Being and Nothingness*. We can emphasize that in Levinas, following Sartre, the encounter with the Other is described as an expansion of the cogito.[25] That expansion is itself indebted to another point of convergence between the two authors. The Other (*Autrui*) for both thinkers cannot be the object of a phenomenological reduction. As the very condition of objective sense for Levinas, the Other cannot constitutively fall within the constituent sense that issues from transcendental consciousness. Because the Other thematizes the world in speaking, it is the metaphysical principle of the presence to intuition of objects grasped by intentional consciousness. To be transcendent, or to be in itself,[26] is to speak. To speak of the world simultaneously consists in revealing oneself and signifying oneself.

The one who speaks thus does not draw his or her sense from the constituent acts of transcendental consciousness, because it is the self's signification of itself (*kath'auto*) in the face that renders such acts possible.[27] For Sartre, just as for Levinas, the inclusion of the Other within the transcendental reduction simply amounts to the renunciation of any consequent description of the alterity of the Other. For both authors, the Other cannot undergo the phenomenological reduction because the Other does not appear within the objective framework of the world.

For Levinas just as for Sartre, if the Other is not an object in the world, it is because the Other is not of the world: "By the Other's look I effect the concrete proof that there is a 'beyond the world.'"[28] If, for Levinas, the Other transcends the world, it is essentially because the Other addresses itself to me, reveals itself as a face, which is to say, in a word—a word whose meaning is "without a context" (*Totality and Infinity*, 23). If it is true that "We *encounter* the Other; we do not constitute him,"[29] then the modalities of such an encounter differ from one to the next. For Sartre, the irreducibility of the Other does not come first and foremost from language as it does for Levinas; rather, it comes from the gaze (*regard*), which is to say that the Other does not initially speak to me but rather looks at me. And yet it is very much this gaze, constitutive of the Other in its alterity, that one cannot, for that reason, phenomenologically reduce:

> [The] Other is given to me as a concrete evident presence which I can in no way derive from myself and which can in no way be placed in doubt nor made the object of a phenomenological reduction or of any other ["epoché"]. . . . The presence to me *of* the Other-as-a-look is therefore neither a knowledge nor a projection of my being nor a form of unification nor a category. It *is* and *I can not derive it from me.* At the same time I can not make it fall beneath the stroke of the phenomenological [epoché]. The latter indeed has for its goal putting the world within brackets so as to reveal transcendental consciousness in its absolute reality. . . . But in the case which concerns us the *Other* can not be put out of consideration since as a look-looking *he definitely does not belong to the world.*[30]

The existence of the Other thus presents itself to consciousness as a "contingent and irreducible *fact*,"[31] which cannot be placed under the phenomenological reduction to the extent that it is "the fact of the presence of a strange freedom,"[32] a "*factual necessity*";[33] in other words, "The fact of the Other is incontestable and touches me to the heart."[34] The gaze, for Sartre, will not allow itself to be reduced to the category of the object, because the eyes of the Other manifest a vigilant gaze, always the presence in fact of another freedom that does not appear to the world that is bounded by the horizon of my possibilities: "The Other is in no way given to us as an object. The objectivation of the Other would be the collapse of his being-as-a-look. Furthermore as we have seen, the Other's look is the disappearance of the Other's eyes as objects which manifest the look. . . . In the phenomenon of the look, the Other is on principle that which can not be an object."[35]

For Levinas, in contrast, the irreducibility of the gaze comes from the fact that the eye destroys its own objectification in that it is, already, speech: "The eye does not shine, it speaks" (*Totality and Infinity*, 66). In this sense, if the Other looks at me, and if this gaze is in fact originally speech, it is precisely the absence of reciprocity that appears in the gaze of the other: "The Other measures me with a gaze incomparable to the gaze by which I discover him" (86).

For Sartre, my freedom under the gaze of the Other becomes "transcended transcendence," which is to say that it is objectified and not revealed to itself—this being only the fact that another freedom exists, that there is another origin of the world: "It is in and through the revelation of my being-as-object for the Other that I must be able to apprehend the presence of his being-as-subject."[36] It is in this sense that for our two Others, though following opposing connotations, the presence of the Other constitutes a principle of the dispossession of the world.

Further, for Sartre, the Other emerges as another principle of the structure of experience, another origin. The objects of the world present themselves as an ensemble of means serving the ends that I pursue within the world. It is in relation to a goal that I target in the world that the world is ordered into a regulated system of equipment. And yet I am deprived of such organization as soon as another freedom appears, which is to say from the moment that the system is reorganized according to ends that are not my own: "With the Other's look a new organization of complexes comes to superpose itself on the first. . . . The alienation of myself, which is the act of being-looked-at, involves the alienation of 'the world which I organize.'"[37]

This theme of the dispossession of the world, as it follows from the encounter with the other, is also very much present in Levinas, for whom the seizure of things in language constitutes a "primordial dispossession" (*Totality and Infinity*, 173). The difference is that, unlike Sartre, Levinas does not understand this dispossession as a form of alienation from the world. The relation to the Other, through its immediately interlocutory character, effaces the boundaries of a contradictory world—a world that is possessed, and thus remains subjective and relative. Through its thematizing function, speech objectively fixes the universe of possessed things. For Sartre, the gaze serves as a factor in the disintegration of the world. For Levinas, however, the interlocutory presence of the Other does not bring about our alienation from the world, nor does it take us to possible worlds that will always escape us, but rather it entails the real becoming an objective world, which is to say the incessant effacement of the privative dimension of possession. The boundaries of possession are eliminated through the language by which the self relates to a world of objects, whose universality emerges from the fact that, thanks to the ethical dimension of language, they are immediately for the Other as well. Indeed, this elimination is always already realized for the concrete human being who possesses the idea of the infinite— which is to say, the one who lives in the society of others. Here, where one speaks, the world is ipso facto a world offered up. It is therefore within the ethical situation in which beings speak to one another, and thus come to the aid of their own speech—which is to say, in which they teach—that appearances are stabilized into a world.

Such a situation constantly calls into question the exclusive possession of things obtained through labor, and that questioning itself already announces the advent of a common world. The objectification of the world coincides with an openness to the question, which at once calls the world into question and a makes it common through language.[38] The theoretical gaze thus depends on the ethical situation of interlocution. An objective world is a world in which the ethical resonates, in which the Other is welcomed. It is for this reason that "To see the [Other] [*autrui*] is to speak of the world" (*Totality and Infinity*, 174).[39] To see the face does not amount to objectively seizing it, but rather to come into a relationship with the very condition of the objectivity of things; it is thus to speak, which is to say, to be taught. The face speaks and signifies itself in speaking of the world—not, therefore, by essentially constituting itself as the subject of its own discourse. The manifestation of the face already marks the entry into discourse, because the face, before any empirical act of language, speaks, which is to say it produces the Other in its irreducible alterity. And yet this situation, in which the Other and I speak together of the world (which is to say, in which I am ipso facto taught by the Other) immediately constitutes the very content of the ethical. Indeed, it is in speaking of the world with the Other that my powers are called into question.

It is for this reason that the objective world does not in any way result from some kind of monadic intersubjectivity that would evoke an identical consciousness between two people. Such a situation would preclude the development of the idea of the infinite, which is to say the entrance into a discourse that does not reproduce the silence of phenomenological egoism or fundamental ontology. To enter into discourse is to welcome the face, and together they open up a new ontological scheme for the world.

The discursive situation, as the face-to-face encounter, thus opens up a world in which nourishment is no longer the exclusive good of the self, which is to say, an objective world. An objective world is not a world in which enjoyment disappears, where the subject must sacrifice what he or she possesses and is thus condemned to absolute indigence to exclusive benefit of the other. Such sacrificial altruism would ipso facto entail the abolition of the separation that is constitutive of the idea of the infinite. Rather, the objective world is a world in which enjoyment is not exclusive, in which the goodness of the world is shared, which is to say, a world in which by the sole fact of language, our possessions become gifts for the Other.

And yet the gift presupposes possession—as the mode by which separation is accomplished—on which interlocutory language exercises its contesting grasp, an event that corresponds to the development of ethics as such. It is for this reason the universe of the gift delineated by sociality can never depart from the indigence of the self, nor can it ever result in it. The gift is not a privation of the world for the self, but rather the becoming-signification, and thus the justification, of past possession. It thus justifies that a being possesses in order to give, inscribing his or her existence in labor, fabrication, and rendering the elements into things. The gift fundamentally summons the possession that it contests.[40]

Privative possession is incessantly contested by the fact of language, because we speak. No good within the world is ever exhaustively appropriable, no fragment can ever be truly privatized, precisely because the relation to the world is never accomplished by a singular, isolated subject, but rather through a subjectivity already held within the embrace of the relation to the Other. The world thus never stands in opposition to the self, but is rather the *entre-deux* of the social relation. There is no solitary relation to the world as world. Rather, to relate to the world is already to stand in relation to the Other, to have already taken up the clandestine events of being.

The world in common is a world in which possession never attains the exhaustive stage of exclusive appropriation, because the Other is always already speaking, and addressing that speech to me. An indigent being (*être*) is incapable of giving. The one who receives the idea of the infinite in the concrete form of a face, naked and indigent, is none other than the one who understands the happiness of the sensible satisfaction of needs. The idea of the infinite as it is addressed to me by the face is concretely developed from a separated ego, which is to say a Dasein who constitutively knows the test of hunger—and who, as such, is no longer (as in Heidegger) in any way reducible to a single ontological existentiality.

The reception of the face does not, therefore, in any way entail the disincarnation of human beings, but rather coincides with a metaphysics concretely deployed as ethics. Indeed, the latter corresponds with a metaphysics that undergirds the advent of a world in common, a world in which the ontologically definitive status of the nourishing character of things cannot be found within an exclusive appropriation. If "of great importance is the mouthful of food," it is because, as Levinas puts it, "The Other's hunger—be it of the flesh, or of bread—is sacred."[41] Nourishment does not merely sate my own hunger or satisfy my own thirst, but rather it already, in so doing, welcomes the Other, which is to say that it sates the hunger and quenches the thirst of the Other as well.

Ethics is a concretized metaphysics, which is to say a metaphysics in constant reference to the sensible, terrestrial condition of human beings, and where the relation to what is beyond the world—articulated by the idea of the infinite—requires a world of possessions that can be offered: "Language accomplishes the primordial putting in common—which refers to possession and presupposes economy" (*Totality and Infinity*, 173). The gift of the world, offered to the Other, consummates sociality: "Transcendence is not a vision of the Other, but a primordial donation" (174).

In this sense, far from abstractly revealing the Other, language always uncovers the alterity of a being that is naked and destitute. Language undoes all of the objective forms that emerge from the same, and which come to alienate the Other in his or her alterity, which is to say covers up his or her misery. The exposition of the latter coincides with the full revelation of the Other in its original condition of nakedness and indigence. The candor of the face is at the same time uncovered in its nudity, wherein the Other presents himself or herself as absolutely other, which is to say always in a state of need and distress. The face thus speaks—that is, it presents itself in all of its naked misery—to a being who, because he or she is separated, knows the hardship of need. Only such a being, a being solicited by the hunger and the distress of the other, is in a position to receive the idea of the infinite.

In this sense, there is yet another an affinity to be found between Sartre and Levinas in terms of the shame that we inflict on the Other. In Levinas, we find it specifically in the occurrence of the shame of the one who persists in wishing to possess things to the detriment of the Other: "The welcoming of the Other is ipso facto the consciousness of my own injustice—the shame that freedom feels for itself" (86). With rather transparent Sartrean connotations, Levinas writes, "My arbitrary freedom reads its shame in the eyes that look at me" (252).

Nevertheless, the paradox means that the separated self can only experience the shame of possessing to the detriment of the Other to the extent that the former's egoist disposition appears to him or her retroactively as an indisposition vis-à-vis the Other. Our deafness to the Other is entailed by enjoyment, but it is not an act against the Other, but rather occurs in ignorance of the Other: "Not against the Others, not 'as for me . . .'—but entirely deaf to the Other, outside of all communication and all refusal to communicate—without ears, like a hungry stomach" (134).

It is only when I finally see the face, when my egoism stands thus accused, that my powers are retroactively understood as instruments of violence against the Other. As we will see, it is not simply that murder is the product of egoism, but rather that it already entails a modification of egoism. In reality, both war and murder emerge from a paradoxical modality of discourse. This is why shame always consists in the identification of a vague desire to kill, which is not inherent in egoism as such, but to the possibility of my egoism being seized by a situation already invested by discourse. Far from opposing him on this point, Levinas agrees with Sartre here that the presence of the Other means that "I have my foundation outside myself."[42]

However, the event that accomplishes this decentralization of the self is not a form of alienation. Rather, for Levinas it precisely coincides with the act of speech, with my apology to the Other. As paradoxical as this appears, discourse—for example, in an apology—as it is conceived when it departs the self and makes its way toward the Other, corresponds to the awakening of a movement that no longer draws its principle from the self.

But a question that must be posed emerges here. What exactly justifies the fact that the face presents itself in misery and hunger to me, if the face is in fact already speech—which is to say, the communalization of the goods of the world? That the revelation of the Other's hunger entails the consequence that the world begins, from this point on, to possess a sense in relation to the Other—a relation constitutive of his or her objective signification. In other words, it is from the moment that the face presents itself as misery and hunger that I am divested of the world, no matter what my efforts, in a kind of bad faith, to refuse this state by defying the Other in refusing to exercise my responsibility toward her or him. Indeed, to refuse to exercise my responsibility actually attests to the renewed presence of a world that already evades my exclusive possession, a world that is meaningful and against which I am powerless.

Moreover, the revelation does not proceed from my powers: Metaphysical Being is present whether I wish it or not, prior to any initiative or decision of subjectivity. Even in war, the idea of the infinite is assumed, though in a repressive manner[43]—a repression that attests, however, to its ineluctable advent. To not assume dispossession in entering into conflict with the Other is to already recognize the Other despite oneself; it is to assume, in the mode of denial, the entry into discourse and the reshaping of the world that it entails.

Discourse inscribes us within the horizon of a world already held in common, whether we want it to or not. We do not decide on the presence of the face, as it is already anterior to all decision; its presence exceeds the ego's powers of constitution. Thus the world is not, empirically, divided, but rather constitutively shareable, which is to say that it is a world beyond my possession, an objective, spoken world, a world that is taught.

To refuse the gift is to already suppose the gift as a measure of the world and thus to welcome the face. The suffering of the Other thus coincides with the making-common of the world or, in other words, the inscription of the latter within a hunger that exceeds that of the subject. Without this materialism of needs, and of the world as possessions, offered to enjoyment and given to the Other in my responsibility to his or her naked misery— his or her face—the phenomenon of objectivity remains incomprehensible. The nudity of the face, its distress, paradoxically coincides with its position of mastery and pedagogy, from which the objectivity of the world ensues.

In this sense, openness to the face is not something that I decide on. Rather it comes, as in Descartes, from the other who places this idea within us. Before I can even decide to refuse or reject it, and independent of that fact, the face is there.

Alienation and Freedom

For Levinas, the subject is only fully himself or herself through the relation to the Other, where the face-to-face perfects the subjectivation (*assujettissment*) of the self. To be a subject in the fullest sense is to respond to the

Other, which is to say to address the world to the Other in allowing him or her to teach me. Thus my subjectivity paradoxically depends on a principle that is not within me, but rather is situated outside of me. Levinas however, unlike Sartre, does not view this dependence as a factor in the alienation of the for-itself.

To the contrary, insofar as the subject is a principle unto himself or herself, he or she is not a subject in the full sense. Levinas reverses the Sartrean schema: Although the self remains the center from which the world is organized, here it is ceaselessly menaced by the possibility of finding itself stripped of itself by its own works. Inversely, it is in assuming a principle for itself that is outside of itself, which is to say in speaking, that the self emerges fully in being. The face-to-face only rescues subjectivity from the anonymity to which egoism condemns it. In such a life, the self is expressed by the works that, unbeknownst to itself, signify it. This other who interprets the subject by his or her works, and not by his or her speech is, as we have seen, the historiographer.

It can be said then, following Sartre, that there is one sense in which the Other is the origin of my objective alienation, or what Levinas calls my third-person inscription in the course of universal history, though only within the situation of commerce. Here, the Other occupies the position of the historiographer, the interpreter of the will of the deceased or absent, through the works of the subject who does not or can no longer speak. But this position is not originary. The Other is not the origin of the alienation of my liberty, as such alienation results from a situation derived from discourse. If, therefore, in the face to face, the self finds a principle outside of itself, that principle constitutes a factor of disalienation. The face to face accomplishes my subjectivation, it renders me a subject in my being, by consolidating the position of an "I," which is only truly a first person when I speak, which is to say, when I respond to my responsibility to the Other or, in still other words, when I defend my works by bringing aid to them.

Thus the Other does not abolish my freedom, but rather consolidates it by justifying it. When the Other calls my freedom into question, he or she does not bring about, as for Sartre, the alienation of that freedom. Rather, the Other targets my freedom in order to invest it with a sense, which is to say to deliver it from the arbitrariness that characterizes it on the level of its spontaneous deployment. Far from alienation, the passage from the for-itself to the for-the-Other invests my freedom with a sense that it lacks on its own: "The Other does not limit the freedom of the same; calling it to responsibility, *it founds it and justifies it*" (*Totality and Infinity*, 197, emphasis added). Indeed, "in expression the being that imposes itself does not limit but promotes my freedom, by arousing my goodness" (200). Moreover, it is by revisiting the Sartrean notion of the "situation" that Levinas considers rethinking the critical anteriority of the Other to the self, namely the revelation of the imperfection of my finite liberty, the arbitrary injustice in which, left to its own devices, a freedom that lacks any external foundation—in the infinite—results.[44]

An unjustified freedom, a freedom that experiences the relation to the Other in terms of exile and alienation, is a freedom that fails to assume the critical priority of the Other over the self. The originary experience of shame does not lead to the alienation of my freedom in an objective nature, as in Sartre, but rather originates in my awareness of the arbitrariness of my freedom left to itself when it is not called into question by the Other. Only the Other gives meaning to my freedom, as the latter finds its ontological meaning in serving the Other: "The 'for itself' . . . by itself [is] only freedom, that is, arbitrary and unjustified, and in this sense detestable; it is I, egoism" (*Totality and Infinity*, 88).

In this way, the meaning of desire changes completely from Sartre to Levinas. The lack that originally affects the for-itself as desire in Sartre[45] instead betrays the structure of need for Levinas. To lack something is to still inscribe oneself within a logic of completion, which reduces the relation of same and other to a totalization, and to thus destroy the possibility of a discursive situation that does not reestablish the silence of totality— namely, the advent of ethics as sociality, or the idea of the infinite. Desire, however, can emerge only in one who no longer lacks for anything. Because such a subject is already happy in being, thanks to the satisfaction of all of his or her sensible needs, he or she can open to an experience that is irreducible to the satisfaction of a lack. The distance that continues to grow between the same and the other is the inverse of need, and is precisely what is desired in desire.[46] The situation of desire is interlocution, wherein the other widens the distance and remains exterior to the same, which is to say that it "infinitizes" itself through discourse.

To desire, in this sense, does not mean addressing oneself to an evanescent or elusive being, because the being who widens the distance between us still faces me as the presence of a face. Discourse thus constitutes a unique situation, wherein the same is at once in relation with and separate from the Other, but does not affirm itself as an egoistic self. This paradox falls within the singular bond between the same and the Other, which does not form a totality, and which, as such, marks the advent in being of desire, in opposition to need. The relationship between the same and the Other thus never forms a totality, and coincides with both desire and discourse. It is in this sense that desire, as transcendence, can no longer be defined as a negativity, because "the negator and the negated are posited together, form a system, that is, a totality" (*Totality and Infinity*, 41).

For Levinas, it is a question of thinking a metaphysical concept of transcendence that would disallow the Hegelian primacy of negativity. On this point, we cannot ignore the evident influence of Kojève's analyses, in the early lectures attended by the young Levinas. Without explicitly referring to the situation of the slave in Hegel and Kojève, as well as to the assimilation of labor to transformative negativity from the positive given,[47] Levinas cannot maintain that "labor transforms the world, but is sustained by the world it transforms" (*Totality and Infinity*, 40). On Kojève's reading of Hegel, the slave's labor denies the natural world by transforming it for the sake of the enjoyment of the master: "In his work, he [man] trans-forms things and trans-forms himself at the same time: he forms the things and the World by transforming himself."[48]

And yet even if Levinas does not contest the idea of a negative power operating in labor, he still refuses to assimilate that concept to that of desire. In this way, *Totality and Infinity* assigns labor to the immanence of need. Here the negativity of the slave cannot be understood to in any way correspond to desire, as the latter constitutively describes a transcendent movement. It is in this sense that the thesis that negativity remains a movement immanent to the same—which is to say a totalizing movement, in that the negator and the negated "form a system"—does indeed echo Kojève's metaphor of the golden ring.

For Kojève, human beings transcend the naturally given by our transformative, and negative, labor. However, this transcendence remains ambiguous, which he demonstrates with the metaphor of the gold ring: The gold represents nature, the hole represents human beings as negativity, and the ring that they form together represents *Geist*. The metaphor is meant to demonstrate that the gold can exist without the hole, which refers to the temporal priority of nature over humanity, such that human negativity affirms itself within the horizon of a world on which it is constitutively dependent: "The hole is a nothingness that subsists (as the presence of an absence) thanks to the gold which surrounds it. Likewise, Man who *is* Action could be a *nothingness that 'nihilates' in being, thanks to the being which it 'negates.'*"[49] In this sense, it is certainly true that the negation of being is dependent on the being that it denies, and that is why, for Levinas, they cannot fail to form a totality.

It is also for this reason that Levinas must necessarily deny a transcendental status to desire in the Sartrean sense of a lack. The negativity of the for-itself,[50] constitutive of its transcendence for Sartre, is thus revealed to participate in the immanence of totalization. This is what, from an orthodox Sartrean point of view, could be criticized, because for Sartre the for-itself ceaselessly fails to accomplish the synthesis of the for-itself and the in-itself: "This totality can not be given by nature, since it combines in itself the incompatible characteristics of the in-itself and the for-itself. . . . Thus human reality arises as such in the presence of its own totality or self as a lack of that totality."[51]

Levinas contests the idea that negativity can in any way permit the accomplishment of a transcendental movement: "Negativity is incapable of transcendence" (*Totality and Infinity*, 41). All of Levinas's argumentation tends toward demonstrating that there can be no transcendence but for metaphysical transcendence. For that reason, the movement away from the self, which attempts to accomplish the existence of the for-itself as the nihilation of the in-itself, remains enclosed within the immanence of totalization, in that "the negator and the negated are posited together, form a system, that is, a totality" (41)—and inevitably so.

The infinite alterity of the other does not depend on the finite; there is no question of an infinite constructed from the mere negation of the finite: "The negation of [the] imperfections [of the here below] does not suffice for the conception of this alterity" (41). Levinas opposes the representation of the infinite from the negation of the finite because such a representation still depends on the experience of the finite. In order to think the infinite as transcendence, we must transgress the finite in a way that is equivalent to what Husserl called "a passage to the limit" in his *Crisis*. As Levinas puts it, "Perfection exceeds conception, overflows the concept; it designates distance: the idealization that makes it possible is *a passage to the limit*, that is, a transcendence, a passage to the other absolutely other" (41, emphasis added).

Only an act equivalent to a "passage to the limit" could introduce a radical discontinuity with what precedes it and thus radically break with the horizon of the finite world. Such a model thus avoids constructing an infinite derived from the finite, in order to open up to the transcendence of the other qua other, which is to say an infinite that would not amount to an infinite-finite, produced by the negation of the finite.

In this context, Levinas refers to "the common plane of the *yes* and the *no* at which negativity operates" (41), which is itself an allusion to Koyré's famous 1934 article "Hegel à Iena." There Koyré comments on the dialectical participation of the *no* in the speculative affirmation of the *yes* in Hegel. It is thus a question for Koyré of demonstrating the positive value of the negative, of "the *no* insofar as it opposes the *yes*; of the *no* which, alone, confers the sense of affirmation and position on the *yes* that it overcomes."[52]

It is precisely this dialectical participation of the *no* in the *yes* that Levinas critiques: That the *no* does not inscribe *any* discontinuity in relation to the *yes* attests to the participation of the *no* in totalization, which is to say in the immanence of the same. Contra totalization, Levinas thus rehabilitates the idea of the infinite as a nontotalizing relationship to the infinite— or the production of the infinite. Such a relation is situated "prior to the negative or affirmative proposition; it first institutes language, where neither the no nor the yes is the first word" (*Totality and Infinity*, 42).

CHAPTER 7

Being toward Infinity

The night is long that never finds the day.

—SHAKESPEARE, *Macbeth*

The Eschatological Infinite

For Levinas, it is a concretized form of Descartes's idea of the infinite that is revealed in the relation to the face, in a manner not of reasoning but of the ethical ordeal of the finite in relation to the infinite that calls it into question. This notion of the infinite is not constituted by the self. The self can neither give the infinite to itself nor, we must recall, refuse it. The idea of the infinite assumes that the infinite organizes and initiates the idea that we possess; that is, it is the infinite that reveals itself to us, and not the self that constitutes the infinite.

For Heidegger, and Kant before him, the relation to finitude does not entail the precondition of the idea of the infinite. Indeed, for Kant, the infinite is understood as the ideal of reason, which relates to the finite as its indefinite prolongation:

> The finite is here no longer conceived by relation to the infinite; quite the contrary, the infinite presupposes the finite, which it amplifies infi-nitely (although this passage to the limit or this projection implicates in

an unacknowledged form the idea of infinity, with all the consequences Descartes drew from it, and which are presupposed in this idea of projection). The Kantian finitude is described positively by sensibility, as the Heideggerian finitude by the being for death. This infinity referring to the finite marks the most anti-Cartesian point of Kantian philosophy as, later, of Heideggerian philosophy.[1]

The infinite is here understood in terms of an indefiniteness of the finite, and thus no longer in the Cartesian sense of a positive infinity.

From Levinas's perspective, Heidegger marks the apogee of an understanding of the finite that ceases to refer to the infinite. The ordeal of finitude is thus experienced as thrownness, as the ordeal of what Levinas calls a birth "non-chosen and impossible to choose (the great drama of contemporary thought)" (*Totality and Infinity*, 223). My awareness of the finitude of my freedom does not coincide in any way with the experience of the ordeal of my powers. And yet for Levinas, following Descartes, consciousness of my finitude rests on the realization of my imperfection, which is to say that it understands the idea of the infinite as the idea of the perfect.

Consequently, the realization of my finitude does not amount to the realization of the limits of my freedom, but rather a moral justification of my freedom in front of the Other. Such an ordeal does not amount to a denial of human powers, but instead breaks fully with the philosophy of power to which existentialism limits itself. Although the powers of the thrown human being are visibly limited, the drama of concretely tested finitude never calls this freedom or these powers into question, regardless of how limited they are. When the Other calls my freedom into question, it does not limit my freedom, because the Other calls my freedom into question in order to invest it with a sense, that is, to deliver it from the arbitrariness that characterizes it on the level of its spontaneous deployment.

The approaches of both Heidegger and Sartre are characterized by a lack of any reference to the infinite, and both therefore describe an ontology in which the same does not refer to the other in order to think itself. In such an ontology, there is no place for the ontological event by which the other reveals itself by calling the same into question—the idea of the infinite. Existentialism leaves absolutely no ontological space for a situation in which the same is in society with the Other, which is to say that it leaves no space for an ultimate event of being. As we have seen, in order for such an exceptional event to occur, the same must be joyful (*jouissant*), that is, and as I have attempted to show, never altruistic on its own, nor spontaneously. Such a disposition on the part of the same conditions the advent of a world fabricated of possessions thanks to which the demands of responsibility remain tied to being—never independent of determined material conditions. Contra existentialism, we must return materiality to egoism, precisely in order to be able to think the primacy of justice over freedom.

Hegel, for his part, and only up to a certain point, does join Descartes in defending "the positivity of the Infinite." However, for Hegel, unlike for Descartes, the infinite cannot truly produce itself, because the former's conception of the infinite excludes "all multiplicity" and "every plurality" constitutive of the relationship between the same and the other. There is no place in Hegel for the finite vis-à-vis the infinite, or for the face to face through which the infinite is produced. This is because such a production, to the extent that the distance between the infinite and the separated self is constitutive of the infinite itself, supposes the emergence of the separated self, independent of the "All" that envelops it. The idea of the infinite thus entails that the infinite does not comprehend the finite. Here, we will indeed require "the paradox of an Infinity admitting a being outside of itself which it does not encompass" (103).

The idea of the infinite maintains the separation of the ego and the infinite, a separation that is constitutive of the very infinitation of the infinite. For Hegel to the contrary, the "relation of a particular with infinity would be equivalent to the entry of this particular into the sovereignty of a State" (196). Hegel's philosophy thus excludes the possibility of the face-to-face encounter as an interlocutory relation: The finite cannot face the infinite because it is included within the infinite. The epiphany of the face as the originary mode of ethics is unthinkable in a philosophy for which the infinite coincides with the totality. For Levinas, to quite the contrary, the other is defined by its absolute alterity, which is to say by its exteriority to any system. Here the passage from subjective to objective Spirit cannot, therefore, represent a higher degree of rational accomplishment for the subject. This passage consecrates the dissolution of the will within universal reason. This "identification of will and reason," is what Levinas calls "the ultimate intention of idealism" (217).

That "ultimate intention" targets "the submission of the subjective will to the universal laws which reduce the will to its objective signification" (242). However, and this is something to which I return, the institutions of the state represent one of the paths by which the self can seek to avoid the threat of murder, of which the Other, by its transcendence, may be the vehicle. Exposed to the menace of death—which transcendence does indeed entail—the will can seek out sanctuary within political institutions and thus sacrifice the particularity of the self. The identification of the will with objective reason remains legitimate as long as it opposes, in the manner of Rosenzweig,[2] the egoistic protestation of the individual. Indeed, the latter maintains the exercise of the will in an arbitrariness justifying its "subsumption" by reason: "The protestation against the identification of the will with reason does not indulge in arbitrariness, which, by its absurdity and immorality, would immediately justify this identification" (*Totality and Infinity*, 218).

For Hegel, according to Levinas, the first-person affirmation of the subject would represent "the aftereffect of its animality" (242), just as much as an illusion of subjective conscience. Levinas reminds us, to the contrary, that the subject's illusion regarding his or her situation of dependence has, as such, an ontological impact, namely, the event of separation, which Hegelian logic refuses and "relegates to the subjective or the imaginary" (217). Illusion is thus never reducible to a participation that ignores itself. Interior life is not only an illusion of consciousness:

> We seek to present the inner life not as an epiphenomenon and an appearance, but as an *event* of being, as the openness of a dimension indispensable, in the economy of being, for the production of infinity. The power for illusion is not a simple aberration of thought, but a movement *in being itself. It has an ontological import.* (240, emphasis added)

Totalization describes a universe in which no ontological place is left for the activity of interlocution and thus coincides with the irrepressible accomplishment of impersonal reason. The totalization of the state dissolves the plurality that the situation of interlocution—that is, ethics—constitutively requires. Indeed, the absolute grasp that totality exercises over being entails the depersonalization of subjects in their participation in the state, understood as both anonymous community and impersonal totality. In this understanding of inclusion, the self does not exist from itself and for itself; rather, it has no existence other than the ideal relative to the All that encompasses it. In the "universal State . . . multiplicity is reabsorbed and discourse comes to an end, for lack of interlocutors" (217).

The tyranny of the state performs its inaugural act of violence in forbidding the personal existence of the "I" (*le* "*Je*") or, in other words, in excluding the possibility of apology within the discourse that the same addresses to the other:

> The invisible, ordered into a totality, offends subjectivity, since, by essence, the judgment of history consists in translating every apology into

visible arguments, and in drying up the inexhaustible source of the singularity from which they proceed and against which no argument can prevail. For there can be no place for singularity in a totality. (243–44)

Indeed, "The renunciation of one's partiality as an individual is imposed as though by a tyranny" (252–53).

Absolute idealism thus describes a "world without multiplicity" in which "language loses all social signification" (217). Such a world operates to the benefit of an anonymous universality in which, unable to speak in the first person, individuals are traversed by an impersonal logos that "already sustains their effective reality" (217). Within absolute idealism, the will of the self confounds itself with the rational order that circumscribes it. Because separation remains illusory and ontologically sterile within it, no apology can be born within historical reason. The "ruse of reason" consists in discovering that behind every first-person action, understood to be voluntary, is the third-person accomplishment of an anonymous rationality that deploys itself unbeknownst to the subject; it is "the presence, behind [me], of a foreign principle" (272).

Eschatology, to the contrary, breaks with such a uniform conception of being, and thereby, historically, breaks from the grip of totalization over ontology. *Totality and Infinity* gives an account of a completely new situation of being. By parting ways with—and indeed surpassing—Descartes,[3] the deployment of ontology is here identified with the idea of the infinite, and thus with plurality, or society, beyond any totalizing monism.

The *"Ethical Resistance"* of the Face

The face presents an "ethical resistance" (*Totality and Infinity*, 199) to our powers. This resistance is not another power or a force that opposes my powers. Indeed, I have no power at all over the face, not because it opposes me with a greater power, but because it transcends the register of power in general. In other words, the face does not confront me with its own "counterpower," but rather suspends my powers: "The expression the face introduces into the world does not defy the feebleness of my powers, but my ability for power [*mon pouvoir de pouvoir*]" (198). However, Levinas immediately affirms that the face is "still in a sense exposed to powers" (198). But what may seem a contradiction here is in fact nothing of the sort: The face defies human powers by its transcendence, which, insofar as it is deployed by language, unmasks the face, disposing of the sensible form that had seized it. By transcending sensible form in this way, the epiphany of the face is the middle path between the sensible and what is beyond the sensible, between the form that caricatures it and what is beyond that form. It is by this incessant overcoming that the face defies my "power of power," precisely in offering itself to my powers in order contest them—that is, in liberating itself from the form that they impose on it.

Indeed, the face begins by articulating itself within the sensible in a form that the frankness of its expressive presence ceaselessly unravels, in order to manifest the Other, *kath'auto*, as absolutely other. The expression of the face can only undo the sensible insofar as it begins by revealing itself within the sensible. Transcendence "opens in the sensible appearance of the face" (198). The sensible moment of the face, the moment that "caricatures" the face, exposes it to human powers. Here Levinas speaks of the "mutation" of the face: first offered to the powers of the self in its sensible dimension, before announcing its absolute—ethical—resistance to the grasp of those powers.

"The face expresses itself in the sensible," and in that way it offers itself to the powers of the self by provoking their will to possession. First inscribed within the sensible, the face arouses these powers, but that solicitation changes in nature as the face undoes the sensible form within which it first appears. The modality of possession that begins with the provocation of the face is modified by the ethical depth of the face. As the latter dismantles the sensible domain within which it initially appears, it is no longer merely something that the powers of the self seek to possess, but rather that which they seek to annihilate through murder. Here we pass from the register of labor as partial negation to that of murder as total negation.

In the economic context, the negation of the non-self in possession can only ever bring about a partial negation of the non-self in appropriation. Labor and possession can never bring about the full negation of the sensible exterior; rather, it is a question of transforming an element into possessed things or, in other words, to partially deny that which is not-me. Such partial negation consists in reducing what is not-me to the form of the same, to the measure of the same, to comprehension as a way of grasping the element.

And yet it is precisely because the face presents itself within the sensible, subjected to the powers of the same while defying its identification with the form that the same attempts to impose on it, that the face can be the object of a desire for total negation in murder: "Murder still aims at a sensible datum, and yet it finds itself before a datum whose being can not be *suspended* by an appropriation. It finds itself before a datum absolutely nonneutralizable" (198). To speak—and the face speaks—is from this point to pronounce the interdiction against murder and to oppose an "ethical resistance" to human powers, which is to say, to establish sociality. However, the possibility of murder does not refer to a spontaneous emanation of such powers on their own, but always already to powers confronted by the transcendence of the face. I can only desire to exercise my powers in the modality of murder when confronted by the face, and only insofar as it at once invokes those powers and constitutively eludes their grasp.

In other words, power exercises itself by labor and possession over everything that opposes it through forms of surmountable resistance. At the same time, power exercises itself over everything that is constitutively resistant to any form of possession or grasping—that is, the face—through murder. Murder thus "exercises a power over what escapes power" (198). It is because the element is a non-self, which the self can identify with the form of its identity, that the question of murder cannot be absolutely posed in the economic context—the identification of the other with the same, aimed at turning the elemental world into the abode of the self, the place where it is at home.

The transcendence of the face reveals a form of resistance other than that of power, the resistance of the fully other. It is absolutely beyond the register of power, and as such, it is paradoxically because it is the sole entity that can present its irreducibility to the sensible within the sensible itself—which "opens in the sensible appearance" (198) something beyond the sensible—that it becomes the object of a nihilating will. The question of murder makes sense only in relation to the transcendent being expressed by the face. This means, then, that the one who seeks to kill has already received the transcendence of the Other, because one only wishes to destroy the Other if and only if such transcendence has already been revealed: "The Other is the sole being I can wish to kill" (198).

This means, paradoxically, that the prohibition against killing only makes sense to the extent that the transcendence of the Other opens up the possibility of murder at the same time that it prohibits murder, by rendering it impossible through the "ethical resistance" of the face, which "paralyzes my powers." The face invokes my powers of nihilation at the same time that it indicts them. The face immediately prevents, and thus prohibits, precisely what it evokes in paralyzing my "power of powers." It indicts the very power to kill that its own transcendence evokes. I can kill only the one whom I can wish to kill, and yet I can only wish to kill the one who forbids me to kill, the Other. It is in this way that the prohibition against murder inaugurates sociality.

The constraint that the face places on me suspends the ability to kill only insofar as the incitation to murder is opened up by the absolute transcendence of the face. I can kill only the one who prohibits me from killing, which is to say the face in its originary speech, the Other insofar as it is the transcendent being. In other words, the negation of the Other in murder confirms its transcendence. I can kill only a being that I have recognized as transcending my powers. If I can empirically kill the Other, it is not in my power to fail to recognize the Other in its transcendence, as the murder itself attests to this recognition. It is precisely in this sense that "murder exercises a power over what escapes power" (198). To resort to murder in order to annihilate the Other confirms the impossibility of abolishing the transcendence of the Other—which is again the event of sociality—because in its desire to destroy the Other, murder attests to the event of discourse over which I have no grasp because the desire to kill must already suppose it. Empirical murder paradoxically attests to the fact that we have already entered the ethical register. No empirical murder can suspend the "ethical resistance" of the face, because the former in fact proceeds from the latter; indeed, I can desire to kill only a being who confronts me with this ethical resistance.

The entry into discourse cannot be decided on, and it is in this sense that war does not reveal something contrary to discourse, but rather a deficient modality of discourse. We cannot prevent discourse from resounding within being. War itself confirms discourse—the ethical resistance of the face—and only has a sense thanks to its inability to abolish the horizon of peace that it always already supposes. Indeed, the possibility of the total negation of the Other only makes sense as a relation to the epiphany of its face. I can only seek to completely annihilate something that lies absolutely outside my reach. This is the sense in which the one who forbids me from killing opposes me with a resistance that is not physical, but is already moral: "The force of the Other is already and henceforth moral" (225).

It is for this reason that war does not have the last word on the relation to the Other, because it supposes a more originary relationship, which it in fact reveals: "War presupposes peace, the antecedent and non-allergic presence of the Other; it does not represent the first event of the encounter" (199). War is a way of failing to understand that we are already in every way in society with the Other, including even those moments when we wish to destroy the Other. In other words, the advent of the social produces itself like an ultimate event on which we can exercise no grasp. Murder, as the physical exercise of a nihilating power, paradoxically realizes our weakness before the "ethical resistance" of the face. Indeed, without that resistance, the murderous will to annihilation would itself be unintelligible.

War and the Face

One of the most interesting consequences of *Totality and Infinity* is that it does not simply stop at a description of the face as resistance to murder, but poses the strength of the unpredictability of the Other within the confrontation as a corollary of the very prohibition that it expresses. That the Other does not present me simply with physical resistance, but with a moral resistance, means that within the context of a confrontation between us, the Other's actions remain radically unpredictable to me.

However, Levinas does not reduce morality to the mere paralysis of power. The moral, by its very asymmetry, is accomplished in a mode that is derived and nonoriginal, as the threat of conflict in events that we are completely unable to foresee. The situation of war is not the simple contrary of morality, as war in fact proceeds from morality. Discourse, the transcendence of the Other, deploys itself in a nonoriginary mode as war: "Discourse subtends war itself" (225). In this sense, war does not exhaust discourse. Far from being its simple contrary, conflict inscribes itself within the horizon of peace, which the events of war come to disrupt. The exhaustive description of the event of the epiphany of the face cannot ignore the situation of war. The transcendence of the Other also entails its unpredictability, which is to say the possibility of murder understood as something that can come from the Other.

The Other, insofar as it does not oppose me with a greater force, but instead with its transcendence, its "ethical resistance," immediately opposes me with the unpredictability of its reaction. The origins of this unpredictability, the possibility of my own murder at the hands of the Other, are found within his or her transcendence, such that "the Other, in the hands of forces that break him, exposed to powers, remains unforeseeable, that is, transcendent" (225).

By virtue of the exceptional character of the ethical relation as metaphysical relation, the relation between the two terms does not form a totality, and each one absolves itself of the relation. Indeed, Levinas emphasizes that far from extending the classic philosophical aspiration toward unity, unification, synthesis, and totalization, "the metaphysical relation realizes a multiple existing [*un exister multiple*]—a pluralism" (220). Such a pluralism is completely distinct from any "numerical multiplicity," which "remains defenseless against totalization" (220). In order for such a "pluralism" to be produced, the subject must maintain a distance from that which it thinks; it must not absorb that with which it is in relation; it is what Levinas calls "the impossibility of conjoining the [self] and the non-[self] in a whole" (221).

The section of *Totality and Infinity* titled "The Ethical Relation and Time" examines the relations between the same and the other which entail their multiplicity. The impossibility of their totalization does not result in their isolation from each other, but rather organizes a series of relations that are the result of the transcendence of each of these terms: "They affirm themselves as transcending the totality, each identifying itself not by its place in the whole, but by its *self*" (222). This latter phrase could give rise to some confusion. In reality, there is no symmetry in the transcendence of each of these terms in relation to the totality: The "transcendence of the Other with regard to me which, being infinite, does not have the same signification as my transcendence with regard to [it]" (225).

Such relations are beyond totalization and result from the plurality of same and other. They take the form of war and commerce, which are the nonoriginary modalities of the relationship of the same to the transcendence of the Other. The latter does not immediately evoke the goodness of the same toward the Other, but rather engenders a series of relationships that can be understood only in light of the impossibility of joining the same and the other within a common totality.[4] This means that "War and commerce presuppose the face and the transcendence of the being appearing in the face" (*Totality and Infinity*, 222). Thus, in turn, war does not represent the "originary form" of the multiplicity of same and other: "The primordial form of this multiplicity is not, however, produced as war, nor as commerce" (222).

The unpredictability of the Other, the fact that he or she cannot be integrated into the calculations and totalizing aspirations of the self, is an aspect of his or her transcendence. In war, "no logistics guarantees victory" (223). And yet the antagonism born from the plurality of the same and the Other, of the multiplicity of terms, is not their inclusion within a totality. That is, it is not a suppression of their plurality, which is the origin of peace: "Totality absorbs the multiplicity of beings, which peace implies" (222). Peace requires this multiplicity; indeed, this is why "only beings capable of war can rise to peace. War, like peace, presupposes beings structured in ways other than as parts of a totality" (222). The opposition of the same and the other in war is not a logical opposition, of the sort that would be ultimately recoupable within a totalized unity, synthetic and common.

War itself presupposes beings who are exterior to the totality, separated beings, that is, beings capable of peace.

As discourse, peace supposes plurality, which is to say that each term situates itself beyond totalization. When menaced by violent death, peace, as the original form of discourse, can invert itself, just as soon as each term in the relationship is in a position to resist the calculations and anticipations of the adversary: "The possibility, retained by the adversary, of thwarting the best laid calculations expresses the separation, the breach of totality, across which the adversaries approach one another" (222–23).

War does not refer to the limitation of multiple beings, because this limitation has a sense only from the perspective of a totality in which the differing parties signify something to one another. Here, in a way that differs from Levinas's claims in the preface, there is no place within the totality for the development of violence. And yet the concept of limitation—the limitation of one part by another—can be understood only through that of totalization, as it is inadequate to the task of understanding the phenomenon of war: "Limitation is not of itself violence" (222). At the same time, Levinas rejects the explication that understands the relation between the same and the other in terms of the limitation of the freedom of each, supposedly divided into one part that is free and one that is not. This notion of finite liberty is contradictory, to the extent that one cannot see how the part that is free could depend on exterior causes without denouncing itself as unfree. Furthermore, Levinas criticizes the very model of limitation, as we cannot conceive of the relation between warring terms as the limitation of a supposedly originary independence.

I do not begin as a fully independent being, who then enters into a relationship with the Other, which in turn limits the substance of my free being. Such a schema of limitation either supposes the primacy of totality or contradicts itself. It is not by the limitation of my freedom, but by my temporal existence that I am at once independent of the Other and exposed to the violence of the Other.

Everything begins with my first exposure to the unpredictable violence of the Other. I am not independent of, and therefore limited by, the Other. Rather, I am first and foremost dependent on the other, which is to say exposed to the violence of the Other. Here the relationship to my own death escapes my powers, because it comes to me by the transcendence of the Other and thus may arrive at any moment. The unpredictability of the Other coincides with the unpredictable character of the event of my own death, the radically unforeseeable nature of the instant of my death.

The event of death does not, therefore, fall within the category of a possibility of Dasein, but rather of my exposure to the "mysterious" violence
that originates with the transcendence of the Other. In such a context, my
independence coincides with the adjournment of my exposure to the "inevitable" violence of death inflicted by the Other.

This independence refers less to my limited freedom—because in the
face of violence my freedom is above all nothing—than it does to the temporality of my finite being and the ambiguity of my being as consciousness.
As Levinas has said, "To be conscious is to have time" (237), which is to
say that it is to have the capacity to defer the violence of the Other, that
violence to which I am always, but not fatally, exposed: "Consciousness
is resistance to violence, because it leaves the time necessary to forestall
it" (237).

This is why temporal being does not signify "being-toward-death" for
Levinas as it does for Heidegger. Rather, it designates, first and above all, a
kind of being-against-death: "Time is precisely the fact that the whole existence of the mortal being—exposed to violence—is not being for death,
but the 'not yet' which is a way of being against death, a retreat before
death in the very midst of its inexorable approach" (224).

Temporality attests to the ambiguity of being, neither purely and originally independent, nor entirely passive, completely, and fatally condemned
to the mysterious violence that emanates from the transcendence of the
Other. War creates a relationship between beings who are characterized
by this ambiguity, a relationship that proceeds from time, that is, from
their existence as conscious beings. In other words, such beings still have
enough time before the inevitable event of death that they are capable of
fighting. Confrontation is only possible between temporal beings, beings
who, in conflict, defer their own exposure to the violence of death. Beings
are mortal and exposed to the violence of the Other, but we are temporal
as well. And temporality is not, as Heidegger understands it, what defines
Dasein as being-toward-death; rather, and to the contrary, it is what turns
beings away from death.

Mortal beings are exposed to death to the extent that we are given over
to violence, but we are opposed to death thanks to time, by which the event
of death is deferred. Levinas thus departs from Heidegger and affirms that
"to be temporal is both to be for death and to still have time, to be against
death" (235). It is in this way that the disquiet of standing before nothingness does not amount to a relationship to death. This disquiet, as the trial
of nothingness, cannot be dissociated from that of the event of my murder
at the hands of the Other. The relation to death does not drive away the

Other; it is never a question of an ordeal of existential solitude. The fear of death proceeds from a "mysterious" violence that issues from the transcendence of the Other: "The solitude of death does not make the Other vanish" (234). In this sense, because it is impossible to anticipate it, death "approaches without being able to be assumed" (235). Death is not "the possibility of impossibility," but rather "the impossibility of every possibility" (235).

The consciousness of my death thus coincides with the consciousness of the unpredictable hostility of the Other: "Thus the fear for my being which is my relation with death is not the fear of nothingness, but the fear of violence—and thus it extends into fear of the Other, of the absolutely unforeseeable" (235).[5] Unlike Heidegger, Levinas argues that "in the being for death of fear I am not faced with nothingness, but faced with what is *against me*" (234). Indeed, the relationship to death is not one of anxiety regarding nothingness, but fear of the Other. Put differently, the relationship to death represents a modality of the face to face; it coincides with a relationship to the transcendence of the Other oriented against me. I am not so much afraid of death as I am, first and foremost, of being killed; or, in other words, the fear of the former cannot be dissociated from the fear of the latter.

The death that I fear is fundamentally the death that the Other is able to inflict on me, and which remains unforeseeable, again because it issues from the transcendence of the Other and thus stands beyond my powers of calculation and anticipation. Death does not fall within the register of my possibilities; it comes from the transcendence of the face, and is for that reason radically unforeseeable. I cannot anticipate my own death, that event whose maturation I cannot forestall. All fear of death is first and fundamentally a fear of being killed by the Other.

It is in this way that we can come to understand why freedom is not primary, but rather the degree zero of choice which is primary. Death does not come from outside to contest my freedom; rather, the latter emerges as the deferral of the fatal event to which the transcendence of the Other exposes me, and which my temporal existence accomplishes. To be conscious is to be certain of a death that I cannot anticipate, certain that it will strike me without warning, and to be at the very same time capable of struggling to postpone the instant of my death. In struggle, "my skill postpones the inevitable" (224); indeed, "war can be produced only when a being postponing its death is exposed to violence" (225).

The Other's transcendence renders him or her unpredictable; it frustrates all of my calculations and in so doing exposes me to the violence of an unforeseeable death. But at the same time, by that very transcendence, by his or her withdrawal beyond my powers, the Other opens the dimension of time: "the other who, as infinity, opens time" (225). "The face arrests totalization. The welcoming of alterity hence conditions consciousness and time" (281).[6] It is thanks to the time that is imparted to them that adversaries can escape one another: By its transcendence, the Other escapes me. But at the same time, through the distension of time that such transcendence opens up, the transcendence of the face allows me to delay my own death by struggling against the very one who escapes. The Other menaces me by his or her transcendence, but that menace is never absolute.

In opening the dimension of time, alterity also opens the possibility of war as the ability to struggle against, which is to say postpone, the final, fatal blow, through my skill and dexterity in combat: "My skill postpones the inevitable" (*Totality and Infinity*, 224). This ability to skillfully avoid the fatal blow, by the suppleness of the body, delimits the horizon of war, wherein beings seek to save themselves. In other words, this is the space in which each one of us postpones our inevitable deaths: "War can be produced only when a being postponing its death is exposed to violence" (225).

War presupposes discourse, and thus the constitutive possibility of reversing of war and returning to peace. Although war can open us to transcendence, it does so in a mode that is not originary: "The primordial form of this multiplicity is not, however, produced as war, nor as commerce. War and commerce presuppose the face and the transcendence of the being appearing in the face" (222). If I am exposed to the hostile will of the Other, from which the relationship to my own inevitable death is inseparable, the fact remains that this will is still the will of the Other. Consequently, the menace in question never exhausts the relation between same and other: "A meaningful order subsists beyond death" (236). "Violence does not stop Discourse" (239).

In other words, the violence of war does not exhaustively consume the relation to the Other. War rests on discourse, which is to say that it leaves open the possibility of a more originary relation to the Other: "This unknown that frightens, the silence of the infinite spaces that terrify, comes from the other, and this alterity, precisely as absolute, strikes me in an evil design or in a judgment of justice" (234). The time of being against death can open up another intrigue, one that is different from the struggle that postpones the fatal instant. Unlike war, peace can articulate itself in terms of what Levinas calls "being-for-the-Other" (261): "The will, already betrayal and alienation of itself but postponing this betrayal, on the way to death but a death ever future, exposed to death but not *immediately*, has time to be for the Other, and thus to recover meaning despite death" (236).

From Commerce to Peace

Work is not expressive; it attests to a will that is absent of signs and which, for this reason, finds itself exposed to the interpretation of the other as survivor. Thus the one who is there when the self is absent from what it produces, from its phenomenality, is the survivor, that is, essentially, the historiographer, the one who pronounces the verdict of history, in absentia. The Other who is in the position of the survivor regrasps the will of some subject by its works, making that absent will speak through them. The subject is powerless to prevent this treason; his or her absence means that he or she cannot defend his or her works through interlocutory speech. Insofar as he or she interprets absent wills, the Other is in fact the historiographer.

Through an interpretation that is completely exterior to our works, the self is certainly revealed as a phenomenon. But because we do not take part in this revelation, which occurs in our absence, and thus almost by accident, we are unable to come to the aid of our own revelation. We are thus immediately misunderstood within and by the historical totality that incorporates us into the universal saga of objective reason. Indeed, our revelation through our works is accomplished without us, and thus the revelation is in a way fractured and incomplete. What is revealed does not coincide with the revelator, and to the extent that the product of the will is not aided by its producer, it is left to the *Sinngebung* of the Other. The economic self as phenomenal self, falling short of expression, is thus not really there; it is visible to be sure, but without being present. Because it does not suffice to simply belong to visibility, its "reality lacks reality," insofar as it does not speak. Lacking sociality, the self is actually not present *in* its own manifestation, because it is not present *to* its own manifestation. To be present to its manifestation is *to be*, in the plainest sense of the term, or *to speak*. In other words, to be present is to break the silence of phenomenality, which is itself a road to totalization,[7] insofar as it is given over to the interpretation of the Other:

> The phenomenon is the being that appears, but remains absent. It is not
> an appearance, but a reality that lacks reality, still infinitely removed
> from its being. In the work someone's intention has been divined, but

he has been judged in absentia. Being has not come to the assistance of itself (as Plato says about written discourse); the interlocutor has not *attended* his own revelation. One has penetrated into his interior, but in his absence. He has been understood like a prehistoric man who has left hatchets and drawings but no words. (*Totality and Infinity*, 181)

Work, or infra-verbal phenomenal existence, dedicates the self to the alienation of its will, in a foreign will, in an "alien *Sinngebung*" (227). The historiographer, as the one who survives and fosters the survival of the wills of others, pronounces the "judgments of history" (247). "The surplus that language involves with respect to all the works and labors that manifest a man measures the distance between the living man and the dead—who, however, is alone recognized by history" (182).

To the "judgments of history," always pronounced in the absence of the judged, Levinas opposes "the judgment of God" (244, 46, 47), which requires the presence of the self at its own trial—which is to say that it requires that the subject speaks, that it is present to come to the defense of its works. In the "judgment of history" the accused is judged in absentia, from works that serve as the evidence for the defense. In the "judgment of God," speaking for oneself is absolutely indispensable for the trial itself to unfold: "Everything comes to pass as though the word, that word that lies and dissimulates, were absolutely indispensable for the trial, to clarify the items of a dossier and the objects constituting evidence, as though the word alone could assist the judges and render the accused present" (181).

To speak and to address the Other to whom one is correlated is to describe a world in which individuals are no longer spoken by anonymous structures, where we no longer "disappear into the totality of a coherent discourse" (243). Rather, here we speak personally, in the first person; we come to the aid of our own speech and are present at our own trials, which is to say that we are present in being: "The idea of being overflowing history makes possible *existents* both involved in being and personal, called upon to answer at their trial and consequently already adult—but, for that very reason, *existents* that can speak rather than lending their lips to an anonymous utterance of history" (23).

The apology breaks with the anonymous logos that proceeds from an impersonal objective reason, in order to produce itself as an interpersonal discourse in the first person. But if the apology breaks with the totality, it still remains exposed to the menace of death, from which it can free itself only if the will, in the apology, wills a judgment inassimilable to that of history. In other words, if it wills a judgment that does not annul the apology, which does not cause the will to dissipate within reason, but which deploys reason anew in the face to face: "Language does not only serve reason, *but is reason*" (207, emphasis added).

And yet the apology itself will not suffice on its own: "Subjectivity cannot maintain itself altogether in its apologetic position, and lays itself open to the violence of death" (242). The will must desire its judgment beyond the apology in order to exceed the horizon of ineluctable violence. The will is the bearer of its own degradation in the alienation of the Other, whether exposed to the violence of death, or appropriation by the alien *Sinngebung* of the historiographer: "It is to be emphasized that this destination of the work to a history that I cannot foresee—for I cannot see it—*is inscribed in the very essence of my power*, and does not result from the contingent presence of other persons alongside of me" (227, emphasis added). "The will essentially violable harbors treason in its own essence" (229).

In judgment, the will seeks to separate itself from the antagonism of wills that intrinsically threaten it; it seeks to find a sense and a truth beyond its own treason. That the will desires to objectivize itself within institutions means that it wishes for judgment, but to desire the judgment of history does not coincide with what Levinas calls "the truth of the will" (240, 46). The true will desires a judgment from the sensed world, which is opened by the face and within which, by the judgment that it commands, the self is maintained in the first person, in responding personally, in speaking. The world of institutions, of the objective totality and of history, represents a world that is sensed to be sure, but it is one in which interlocution has no place, in which beings are judged by their works and not for themselves: "Reason in the sense of an impersonal legality does not permit us to account for discourse, for it absorbs the plurality of the interlocutors" (207).

To the temporal being who postpones its exposure to death, institutions present themselves as a chance. Levinas thus evokes "the other chance that the will seizes upon in the time left it by its being against death: the founding of institutions in which the will ensures a meaningful, but impersonal world beyond death" (236). Further, "In the respite that the postponement of death, or time, leaves to the will it relies on institutions" (242). But the passage into the order of objective Spirit, in which reason can establish itself only by demanding the sacrifice of the first person, represents for Levinas neither the truth of reason nor the truth of the will, which must be situated elsewhere, in the call to responsibility that he refers to as "the judgment of God," or "religion"—the paradoxically true names of reason, properly understood, or what Levinas calls "the true universality of reason" (201). The latter constitutively entails the maintenance of the particular:

"Reason presupposes these singularities or particularities, not as individuals open to conceptualization, or divesting themselves of their particularity so as to find themselves to be identical, but precisely as interlocutors, irreplaceable beings, unique in their genus, faces" (252).

In the apology, "the [self] at the same time asserts itself and inclines before the transcendent" (40). And yet in the apologetic speech addressed to the Other, my freedom presents itself before the Other and finds itself thus questioned; from there, it is modified in goodness, which is to say in a freedom that is justified, and thus no longer contingent. My freedom, thus invested, becomes responsibility. The passage from the apology to goodness maintains the apologetic dimension of discourse and permits the self to attain its ultimate reality in responsibility, because "justice would not be possible without the singularity, the uniqueness of subjectivity" (246, translation amended).

In the passage from apologetic discourse to judgment properly speaking, the apologetic dimension of the self is maintained. Similarly, in the passage from arbitrary freedom to goodness, which shifts the center of gravity of the self that lives for itself to the Other, the self is never effaced by the Other. Rather, the self finds its "ultimate reality" when its egoism is thus surpassed.

The decentering of the self does not bring about its disappearance, but rather consecrates its ontological consolidation:

> The [self], which we have seen arise in enjoyment as a separated being
> having apart, in itself, the center around which its existence gravitates,
> is confirmed in its singularity by purging itself of this gravitation,
> purges itself interminably, and is confirmed precisely in this incessant
> effort to purge itself. This is termed goodness. Perhaps the possibility
> of a point of the universe where such an overflow of responsibility is
> produced ultimately defines the [self]. (244–45)

And yet this goodness is not the simple negation of the economic self. Rather, the former supposes the latter as the singular condition by which the reception of metaphysics is concretized. I cannot welcome the Other with empty hands; rather, the world of possession is the precondition of all reception, which is to say of all thematization by the speech of the possessed world, which becomes, through the intervention of discourse, an objective world.

To speak is to assume, through generosity, the transcendence of the face. To decenter oneself is not to cease to be, but to cease all return to the self—to shatter the economic circuit. This rupture does not annihilate, but rather justifies the being with which ontology itself coincides: To be in the absolute sense, is to be good. This is why goodness does not amount to the simple contrary of economy, but rather to an overcoming that is only truly "transcendent" if it is founded on the precondition of economy. The overcoming of the economic is placed in common with the goods shared between the same and the other, in "a word that, in the measure that it welcomes the Other as Other, offers or sacrifices to him a product of labor, and consequently does not play above economy" (231).

By the judgment that it desires, the will extracts itself from its own degradation, which is entailed by its exposure to death and to the will of the Other. An inversion is produced by the "judgment of God," in which "the fear of death," to which the self of the will is ineluctably exposed, is converted into a "fear of committing murder," and thus into "dreading murder more than death" (246). In other words, it is converted into a responsibility toward the Other: "Goodness consists in taking up a position in being such that the Other counts more than myself. Goodness thus involves the possibility for the [self] that is exposed to the alienation of its powers by death to not be for death" (246). In this form of responsibility, the death of the Other concerns me more than my own death.

And yet the condition of the face and of goodness, like the possibility of judgment, is situated beyond the face; it transcends the epiphany of the face, in the infinite time of fecundity. Goodness and transcendence are thinkable only if they rest on a conception of time that no longer holds anything in common with an "image of eternity" (246), or a continuous line from the present. At the root of goodness and transcendence, a conception of time is required, one that renders them possible; it is nothing other than the infinite and plural time of fecundity. The analyses of goodness and transcendence entail this infinite time of fecundity, although it has not yet become the object of an explicit analysis. Levinas proposes to engage this sense in the fourth part of *Totality and Infinity*.

The Night of Eros

In the phenomenon of love, the key terms are *ambiguity* and *equivocation*. In love, Desire and need, two experiences that *Totality and Infinity* had neatly distinguished up to this point, come to overlap. Levinas situates love "at the limit of immanence and transcendence" (254). In love, the registers of desire and need become inextricably entangled, and it is from here that the ambiguity of the phenomenon of love as paradoxical desire, a desire affected by concupiscence, emerges. Certainly, this can only mean that in love, desire regresses to need. Desire does not cease to desire, which is to say that it does not cease to maintain itself as relation to the Other, but it articulates a contradictory relation to the transcendent which affirms itself as enjoyment of the transcendent. Love does not situate itself between sensation and spiritual elevation, it is at the point of the paradoxical meeting of desire and need, wherein the desire for the transcendent, beyond need, transforms into enjoyment of the transcendent.

The essence of love falls within this ambiguity. In love, the Other appears as an object of need "while retaining its alterity," Levinas emphasizes. Love is accepted as an ambiguity, which is to say the "simultaneity of need and desire" (255), through the contradictory enjoyment of the transcendent. Love necessarily requires desire, because love is a relation to the transcendent. But, and again, it is a relation within which need is inextricably bound up, because the relation to the Other, which love articulates, is a relation of enjoyment. Love is, therefore, neither absolute need nor absolute desire. If it were absolute desire, it could not be a form of enjoyment, and if it were absolute need, it could not be a relation to the transcendent. To the extent that love is the "simultaneity of need and desire," Levinas presents the phenomenon of love as "the *equivocal* par excellence":

> The possibility of the Other appearing as an object of a need while
> retaining his alterity, or again, the possibility of enjoying the Other,
> of placing oneself at the same time beneath and beyond discourse—
> this position with regard to the interlocutor which at the same time
> reaches him and goes beyond him, this simultaneity of need and desire,
> of concupiscence and transcendence, tangency of the avowable and
> the unavowable, constitutes the originality of the erotic which, in this
> sense, is *the equivocal* par excellence. (255)

What is situated before the face is nothing other than the dimension of tenderness to which the night of erotic love, distinct from the insomniac night of the *there is*, open itself. Eros, as ambiguity, goes beyond the face, and its ambiguity is expressed in this very overcoming. Such overcoming is a form of profanation; it consists in the transgression of a limit: The erotic movement profanes that which it carries beyond the ethical presence of the Other and the face. The transcendent Other becomes the object of love and thus of enjoyment, and we thereby carry this ambiguity beyond the face toward that which is hidden. By its intrinsic ambiguity, eros transgresses the frankness of the face that deploys itself in the ethical injunction, in the prohibition against murder, and in signification. This transgression deploys a dimension that is no longer characterized by frankness but is rather fundamentally marked by equivocation.

The epiphany that is produced beyond the face is the epiphany of the beloved, which is to say of the feminine. This is because the beloved is not in fact neuter in gender, which is "the sole gender formal logic knows" (256), to which the feminine dimension is either added or not. Instead, and for this reason, the epiphany of the beloved (*l'Aimé*) as such is fundamentally the epiphany of a female beloved (*l'Aimée*), which is to say, of the feminine in general. Thus the beloved other—whoever, and whatever gender, they may be—opens up the dimension of the feminine. The characteristic mode of the epiphany of the beloved is tenderness; the beloved is tender, fragile, vulnerable.

In the regime of tenderness that characterizes her manifestation, the beloved removes herself from presence. By its fragility, that which is tender retreats from being. The tenderness of the beloved, which cannot be dissociated from the beloved, "unburdens itself" of the weight of being. That which is tender is far too fragile to accommodate itself to the full ontological presence within which the things of the world are made. Being is presence, and the tender, by its fragility, retreats from being. The ontological mode of the world, its full presence, is a regime of being far too rough for the beloved, who is marked by tenderness. The ontological mode of the tender being consists in fleeing the full ontological presence of being, of departing the field of being, and, in her evanescence, of unburdening herself of the heavy weight of being.

And yet this presence that disrobes itself of existence, which, in its evanescence, unburdens itself of the weight of being, at once evinces its own weightiness, heavier still than the very weight of being: "This extreme fragility lies also at the limit of an existence 'without ceremonies,' 'without circumlocutions,' a 'non-signifying' and raw density, an exorbitant ultramateriality" (256). This "ultramateriality" is that of nudity, the nudity of tenderness, which moves away from being, but whose retreat from being simultaneously coincides with its own extreme weightiness. This latter is heavier still than the being of existents themselves, heavier still than "the weight of the formless real" (257); it is an "exorbitant presence" (256).

This ambiguity of evanescence and ultramateriality marks the dimension of the feminine which deploys itself beyond the face. The feminine is beyond being by its fragility, delicateness, and lightness—at the same time that it is beyond being by its heaviness, by the extreme weight and ultramateriality of its nudity. This ultramateriality does not leave it destined to any form, because it is too heavy for any form; nudity is too material to be circumscribed by any form. Ultramaterial nudity exposes that which must not be shown; it is the profanation of a secret. In desire, the nudity of the beloved forces "the interdiction of a secret" (256). The nudity discovered in eros proceeds from a profanation, to which its presence attests by bringing to light what is destined to secrecy.

It is for this reason that this nudity appears in the mode of an exorbitant presence; it is shocking; it manifests the very thing that must never become manifest, and which remains essentially resistant to manifestation. Nudity is thus profane because it brings to light what must remain hidden. Being thus does not know what to do with the massive and shameless presence of nudity, because the latter is too weighty to be placed in series with other existents. Nudity reveals an exorbitant presence that exposes what must never be revealed. This shameless presence is not reabsorbed into the regime of manifestation, because what is hidden, or the secret, which is profaned by this erotic nudity, is not some thing waiting to manifest, but rather what Levinas calls the "*essentially hidden*" (256), which is, thereby, essentially nocturnal. Its profanation does not drive away the night, but rather advances itself in that night that refuses, in essence, to come to light.

What nudity therefore reveals is its own impudence; what is shown in it is not so much what is secret, as the betrayal of the secret, which is to say profanation itself: "The mode in which erotic nudity is produced (is presented and is) delineates the original phenomena of immodesty and profanation" (257). This is why "the discovered does not lose its mystery in the discovery, the hidden is not disclosed, the night is not dispersed. The profanation-discovery abides in modesty, be it under the guise of immodesty: the clandestine uncovered does not acquire the status of the disclosed" (260).[8] Something is shown that must not be seen, that does not belong, either actually or potentially, to the regime of the visible.

Profanation is thus the result of bringing to light that which is essentially clandestine. The latter is in no way accidentally hidden, but is hidden by nature. This is why erotic nudity neither discovers the clandestine nor reveals it. What is shown, rather, is the indecency of a profanation. In eros, the clandestine both shows itself and remains secret. Its secret is unlocked by the discovery, which, for that reason, is revealed in the mode of profanation. "The secret appears without appearing" (257), because what appears is the resonance of a profanation; it is not the secret itself, but the fact, and the effect, of having forced a secret to appear: "The simultaneity of the clandestine and the exposed precisely defines *profanation*" (257). What is shown thus continues to keep itself in reserve. What shows itself in erotic nudity is less something revealed as it is treason against a secret; it is the profanation of that which is essentially hidden and mysterious.

The experience of nudity does not refer to a hidden existent but to that which does not belong to the register of possible, present existents: Erotic profanation is a nocturnal event. What manifests in the erotic night is nothing less than that which, because it remains secret, beyond any presence, real or possible, unfolds itself in the mode of that which is not yet. Erotic nudity uncovers the clandestine, which refuses to give itself, and it is in this way that nudity is profanation, that is, the paradoxical coincidence of the hidden and the discovered, of the secret that remains hidden despite being discovered.

And yet if the secret ceases to be a secret in its discovery, that discovery would in fact reveal an existent destined to revelation. It is to the extent that erotic nudity maintains the coincidence of the discovered in the hidden that it is a profanation. That which is discovered in eros yet remains beyond any grasp. What reveals itself in nudity is ungraspable, because the tender body of the beloved, touched by the caress, has no ontic consistency. It reveals the fragility of the beloved whose body, in the tenderness of sensual contact, "quits the status of an existent" (258).

Profane, erotic nudity uncovers what is hidden, even as the latter remains concealed beyond any grasp; it no longer or does not yet have the status of an existent. Nudity reveals neither a real nor a possible existent, that is, real to the latent state, subjected to the light and its powers of disclosure. It is instead that which escapes to the alternative of what is either real or possible, which is to say, that which goes beyond the horizon of the powers of the self in the nocturnal. What is discovered, then, is something that is not an existent but something that maintains its secrecy in and in spite of being discovered. The erotic phenomenon falls within the equivocal, that is, within the simultaneity of discovery and hiddenness. For this reason, it is discovered as the profanation of a secret that remains secret, or the discovery of that which remains resistant to its identification as a discoverable existent.

Fragile and evanescent, the beloved does not yet have the status of an existent, because in its swooning, the beloved other withdraws into an ungraspable future. The clandestine that is uncovered is "not yet," and such "not-yet-being" (259) delimits what Levinas calls a "new category" (266). It opens that which falls "behind the gates of being" (266) to the less than nothing, which cannot be simply identified with nothingness. Less than nothingness, the erotic caress opens a future than can be neither anticipated nor actualized, an absolute future that cannot be inscribed within the register of the possible. This absolute future resonates in the erotic caress. The "not-yet-being" is not a being in waiting, or a being discoverable or anticipatable in an actualization. And the erotic caress consists in "soliciting what slips away as though it *were not yet*" (257). The caress searches for what is beyond; "it aims beyond an existent however future, which, precisely as an existent, knocks already at the gates of being" (258). The caress does not unveil; it searches, and to search is to aim at something beyond, which shields itself from discovery, to give rise to a pure future. The caress, for this reason, in groping beyond possibilities and human powers, profanes that which is not yet.

The caress thus descends into the nocturnal, and that descent is profanation. As such, the caress discovers that which remains essentially resistant to any inscription within being: the pure future that is not available in any case in the mode of a being toward the future, which is to say of a possibility. The caress leads to an adventure. It does not proceed from the exercise of a power but rather departs from a quest that revives desire, because that for which it searches "is not yet" (254, 56) an existent at all, in the sense that the "not yet" is beyond any horizon of anticipation within which it could be incorrectly understood as a future existent. The hand descends into a nocturnal adventure that transgresses the plan of the existent and its powers.

Abandoning both self and powers, the caress is neither intentionality nor comprehension. The caress "is not an intentionality of disclosure but of search" (258); it "does not act, does not grasp possibles" (259). Love, eros, "is not accomplished as a subject that fixes an object, nor as a projection, toward a possible. Its movement consists in going beyond the possible" (261). To target the tender with the caress is to target that which, by its clandestine nature, refuses to be seized. In the delight of the caress, the subject is carried beyond itself: Its intention does not aim at the sensed, which is always commensurate with its powers; it loses itself in an ungraspable beyond at the point in which the beloved other, by its fragility and characteristic tenderness, is dissolved in being, and "quits the status of existent" (258).

The caress thus breaks from the register of disclosure as *Aletheia*, which, for Levinas, still remains illuminated and powerful. The shining light obscures the dark; power reduces the future to that which is not yet present. The transgression of the horizon of possibilities, the space beyond the possible into which the caress sinks, means that the caress does not attain its goal in touching a definite being. The profanation of the caress discovers that which evades any grasp, which in turn reveals the inviolable character of the Eternal Feminine, its absolute virginity. The feminine is not something that can be grasped.

To the extent that "what the caress seeks is not situated in a perspective and in the light of the graspable" (258), it does not violate the virginity of the feminine. The erotic body, touched by the caress, "quits the status of an existent" (258). The caress does not seize an existent. By its tenderness, the beloved is touched, discovered, and profaned, but remains beyond the existent, and for that reason maintains its virginity. Its dimension is that of the "not yet," of a future that does not have the form of the possible, which is to say of the existent, but which is no longer absolute nothingness; it is "not nothingness—but what is not yet" (256). As Levinas says, "Beyond the consent or the resistance of a freedom the caress seeks what is not yet, a 'less than nothing,' closed and dormant beyond the future, consequently dormant quite otherwise than the possible, which would be open to anticipation" (258).

The caress seeks out this dimension of tenderness and vulnerability, which is to say fragility, where the Other quits being and withdraws into its own unforeseeable future. To touch is to touch a fragile being, to discover something that does not yet have the form of a thing, something that withdraws into a future beyond the possible. Indeed, the feminine withdraws just to the extent that the caress searches. The beloved evades any grasp and thus sustains pleasure through its refusal to be possessed. Reserve and decency, despite the indecency of the caress, find themselves correlated to the status of the beloved as that which is not yet a thing; she is less than nothing, held in reserve for the existent, which is to say that she escapes the powers of the self. The caress goes beyond those powers, and experiences the pleasure, that is, the insatiable and inviolable character, of the evanescent feminine.

The mode of this evanescence is that of not-yet-being, that of a being that manifests itself to being in the mode of something not yet there or, in other words, in the paradoxical mode of the clandestine. The clandestine is not without substance, it is not purely absent, but it is rather revealed as not yet having ontological substance. It remains secret within and despite being discovered: "'Being not yet' is not a this or a that; clandestineness exhausts the essence of this non-essence" (257). Tenderness announces the presence of the beloved, which is to say that the beloved is not graspable in the form of a present existent. Indeed, the presence of the beloved immediately amounts to the loss of the other as beloved. Erotic nudity manifests the feminine as that which comes to presence, without yet being present:

the pure future, or the simultaneity of the hidden and discovered, the relation to the inviolable.

The caress absorbs the self toward a future that is at once discovered
and reticent to give itself up to discovery, that is, toward a dimension situated beyond all possibility. In this way, the caress deprives the self of the
subjective position by which it illuminates the sensed object: "An amor-
phous non-[self] sweeps away the [self] into an absolute future where it
escapes itself and loses its position as a subject" (259).

Erotic nudity thus no longer coincides with the naked frankness of the
face as we have examined it. The epiphany of the face establishes signification. The transcendent being expresses itself and in so doing unravels the
form that alienates it, in order to present itself in all frankness, *kath'auto*,
from itself. To express oneself is not to delegate a sign that would refer to
a presence exterior to any manifestation, rather, it is to present oneself in
person, in manifestation, in speaking. And insofar as to speak is to come
to the aid of one's speech, to reveal oneself in all frankness, every face
presents itself in the mode of univocality. To the contrary, the feminine
face invested in eros is discovered by remaining hidden, which is to say in
refusing signification, interfering with the original frankness of the face by
remaining equivocal. By this refusal of expression—itself expressed—by
maintaining the hidden and the clandestine, which refuse all signification,
the feminine face obscures the expressive frankness of the face.

The difference between the face of the face-to-face encounter and the
face invested with eros is not a form of the distinction between expression and the refusal of expression. Rather, the feminine face is beyond the
face in that it is also a form of expression, but what it expresses is nothing less than the refusal to express. In other words, it expresses the end
of discourse. Its nudity remains clandestine, and for that reason it breaks
with the frankness of the naked face that manifests itself in the face to face
in order to renew the equivocation of the evil genius. But contrary to the
figure of the evil genius, which situates itself within reach of the face and
does not presuppose it, the feminine face, in eros, is beyond the face. In
other words, the feminine face only produces equivocation on the preliminary ground of the frankness of the face which the feminine obscures. This
is why "the [apparently] asocial relation of eros will have a reference—
be it negative—to the social" (262); and "the face, all straightforwardness
and frankness, in its feminine epiphany dissimulates allusions, innuendos"
(264). The refusal of expression is already itself expression but a confused
and inverted expression, an expression made of both light and shadow.

In love, it is not the Other that I love, but the love that the Other brings to me; my delight is evoked by his or her delight, entailing a return to oneself on the part of each of the lovers: We love ourselves through one another. My delight in the beloved is nourished by her love for me, in a paradoxical form of autoeroticism in which the transcendence of desire combines with the egoism of solitude: love as the form achieved by a paradoxical egoism, a "dual solitude" (265). However, this paradox means that having taken recourse in the love of the Other in order to love oneself, the self to which this love returns is in no way identical to the self from which it departed. That self through which two lovers find each other, but which is no longer what either of them had been before, is the child.

The future into which I project my delight is also the future in which I find myself in a kind of paradoxical return, because it comes down to finding myself beyond any projection toward the immanent possibilities of my identity. The self to which I return is a self beyond the possible. The self loses itself beyond its powers and recovers itself as self on the other side of them, but precisely as the self which it is not, as the son. The son crystallizes this return to the self mediated by the love of the other, and which, for this reason, does not refer to the self that departed, but to the self by which my possibilities and identification with those possibilities is actualized. Beyond the face, we find the child, which is to say the self of the father in the child which he is not. In this sense, fecundity constitutes the ultimate nocturnal event that consecrates the infinite becoming of being.

The Infinity of Fecundity

Eleaticism and the formal logic that follows from it prohibit the possibility that the same and the other not be bound to one another in a singular, synthetic, and continuous unity. In other words, Eleaticism would destroy the profoundly pluralistic structure of being, its transcendence. Transcendence is denied if the plurality of existence merely amounts to the synthesis of same and other—and thus to the aging of the same. But it is equally so if the existence of the same does not find itself within the other, because being would then be reduced to a unity—and thereby find itself once again reduced to aging. Plurality means that the existence of the other is not an existence separated from that of the same, though not in the totalizing sense of a unity or a pantheistic and absolute sameness, which would render the same and the other into modal variations of a singular unique substance. Plurality also means, reciprocally, that between the father and the son, it is no longer a question of two beings, which risks once again reducing being to selfhood, and to assigning each self a single exclusive being.

These two schemas represent the two variations of a singular Eleatic ontology, which reduces being to a unity and condemns the exercise of being to age. To the contrary, however, beyond the horizon of age, where the self is condemned to only be itself, imprisoned within its own powers and possibilities, fecundity reveals that the self "as subject and support of powers does not exhaust the 'concept' of the [self]" (268). For the self, to be is also, through fecundity, to be other. The father *is* his son, in the precise sense in which the father transcends the horizon of his own selfhood in the son. The selfhood of the son, in the form from which the self of the father emerges, no longer coincides with the selfhood of the departure, that of the father. In fecundity, the self is discontinuous, fragmented. This discontinuity is an ultimate event of being itself, insofar as it is social, which is to say, transcendent and plural.

In this sense, "fecundity continues history without producing old age. Infinite time does not bring an eternal life to an aging subject; it is *better* across the discontinuity of generations, punctuated by the inexhaustible youths of the child" (268). We must join Levinas in moving from the transcendence of existence so dear to the existentialists, to the transcendence of existing, which coincides with its pluralization in fecundity; to be oneself is to be, at the same time, an other being who is not oneself. To be is thus to be the same and other, though never in the sense of a totalization, which abolishes transcendence, because it denies the exteriority of the other in relation to the same. Because it is a pluralization, in fecundity the exteriority of the son is respected, even as the father *is* his son: "My child is a stranger (Isaiah 49), but a stranger who is not only mine, for he *is* me. He is me a stranger to myself" (267). It is in this sense, because the exteriority of the son is respected, because the self is discontinuous, that fecundity is introduced into being by transcendence, which is to say by plurality.

And yet according to Levinas such a transcendence of existence "is lacking in even the boldest existentialist analyses."[9] Contrary to Eleaticism, through fecundity the exercise of being finds itself divided between two ipseities, each inassimilable to the other. Here the self is not ground down into its sameness but rather transcends itself in a discontinuous existence.

The first form of transcendence, the transcendence of existence, the form with which Existentialism is so concerned, proceeds from a departure of oneself that never crosses the threshold of powers and possibilities. In it, events of being never transcend the horizon of the conscious project. It is because of this limitation that, for Levinas, the future that opens the dimension of fecundity as transcendence is not inscribed within the existential horizon of the project: "The son coveted in voluptuosity is not given to action, remains unequal to powers. No anticipation represents him nor, as is said today, projects him. The project invented or created, unwonted and new, emanates from a solitary head to illuminate and to comprehend. It dissolves into light and converts exteriority into idea" (*Totality and Infinity*, 308–9). To the contrary, Levinas emphasizes that "in fecundity the [self] transcends the world of light" (268).

The freedom of existence does not allow the self to liberate itself from the tragedy that represents the inexorable entanglement of the subject in itself. To project itself into the horizon of its own possibilities is to again fall back into itself, and to carry out a repetition in which transcendence, reduced to the freedom of the "for-itself," is modified into a destiny. Because transcendence does not exactly coincide with the freedom of the subject, the latter is condemned to repetition. It is for this reason that Levinas can speak of existential transcendence as "merely illusory and its freedom to delineate but a fate" (268); "In the new that springs from it the subject recognizes himself. He finds himself again in it, masters it. His freedom writes his history which is one; his projects delineate a fate of which he is master and slave" (275).

To the contrary, the relation to the son "resembles that which was described for the idea of infinity: I cannot account for it by myself, as I do account for the luminous world by myself" (267). Like the idea of the infinite, constituent powers, whether disclosed or transmitted, do not have an exhaustive grasp on the plural being of fecundity. The events of being that are deployed by fecundity and the idea of the infinite, insofar as they are nocturnal events, are constitutively incommensurate with such powers. As an analog to the idea of the infinite, fecundity reveals that the measure of being is not selfhood. In both cases, the event of being exceeds the powers of the subject, and the future that is thus described no longer falls within the register of possibilities attendant to the same.

The future opened up by fecundity does not correspond to the projection of the possibilities of being carried by a unique existent. The future of fecundity no longer falls under the most extreme possibilities of Dasein, because "my future does not enter into the logical essence of the possible" (267). Selfhood does not summarize being, and powers and possibilities can never exhaustively encompass the adventure of being as it is pluralized between the same and the other.

This means that being is also an existent that I am not, which does not proceed from an extension of my powers. In other words, it is a being that I am and which is not me, or, further still, a being that is "me, but not myself; it does not fall back on my past to fuse with it and delineate a fate" (271–72). To be beyond its selfhood and its power; to be, in the process of liberating itself from its assignation to the unity and uniqueness of an exhaustive existent; to be, being an existent who is not inscribed within the horizon of selfhood, in its continuation, its repetition and its aging; to be, in the mode of fecundity—all of this is to introduce into existence a multiplicity and a transcendence wherein "being is no longer Eleatic unity" (277). To exhaustively be, is to be more than myself; it is to be myself within an other and thus to rejuvenate myself in exercising being beyond my selfhood, in a rupture of continuity with my own identity, an identity to which—due to the pluralistic structure of being—I am never completely attached.

However, it seems as though we might object to Levinas, by pointing out that the influence of human powers over being appears radically, and equally, compromised by the analyses of both Heidegger and Sartre of the thrown condition of the existant, whether we refer to the latter as Dasein or the "for-itself." In Levinas's judgment, however, it is precisely in assigning the tragedy of being to thrownness that Heidegger and Sartre have underestimated the tragic significance of existence. The idea that the possibility of dominating our own condition would allow us to escape the tragic, means that the plain identification of the subject with its being would remove the tragic from thrownness. But it is precisely this kind of identification that Levinas assigns to the tragic: that of an existent fastened to itself, made to carry the burden of its own selfhood.

For Levinas, the weight of facticity is not lifted once we escape from thrownness. The tragedy of our terrestrial condition is not being-thrown, but rather our inability to liberate the exercise of being from its selfhood, our being bound to ourselves, which is to say, the fact that we are condemned to age. Within the descriptions of thrownness, the tragic character of existence is thus profoundly underestimated. This tragedy consists in an existence reduced to uniqueness, an existence bound to the permanence of selfhood: "The tragedy of subjectivity is not rooted in the finitude of my being and of my powers, but rather, and precisely, in the fact that I am a being, or a being one."[10]

Overcoming the tragic character of existence is thus not accomplished by the identification of being with powers, but in the pluralization of existence by fecundity. The terrestrial condition of human existents is experienced as thrownness only from the perspective of an extremely conservative ontology, one that binds being to a unity, which the human existent thrown into the world has lost. Thrownness can refer to the tragic condition of existants only by way of the traditional ontological assimilation of being to unity. Thrownness signifies the ontological dereliction of the existant only to the extent that it is grounded in such an ontology. But once ontology ceases to coincide with the assimilation of being to unity and is rather understood in terms of the plurality of existence, human existents cease to experience our lack of mastery over our own condition as tragic.

To the extent that Sartrean freedom describes the horizon of a fictive transcendence, which transforms into destiny and aging, the "ontological decompression" that is the "for-itself," never modifies its true distance in relation to the in-itself understood as definitive being. The definitive in being is the fate and the condition of the "for-itself" itself. It is in this sense that the distance in relation to the definitive form that fecundity accomplishes does not consist (as in Sartre) in distancing the in-itself through the advent of being defined as a project, which is to say in the mode of the possible: "*The time in which being ad infinitum is produced goes beyond the possible*" (*Totality and Infinity*, 281). The distance with regard to the definitive form, which fecundity accomplishes, "consists in a distance with regard to the present itself, which chooses its possibles" (281).

Aging intervenes at the moment that my power to place being and nothingness at a distance opens up possibilities for my freedom, but that freedom "which chooses its possibles," realizes something, ineluctably grows older from there, congeals itself in a "definitive reality" (281) in choosing given possibilities, and thus necessarily sacrificing others. The horizon of possibilities remains a horizon of powers, in which freedom falls back into the definitive form from which it has tried to wrest itself. This definitive form manifests itself as the "overwhelming responsibility" of the for-itself, which leads the latter to its destiny, a choice of possibilities for which it must accept the burden and the responsibility. In Sartre's famous formulation, "The responsibility of the for-itself is overwhelming."[11]

Responsibility, as the other side of freedom, refers to the uniqueness of the destinies to which human beings find ourselves assigned. To go beyond the possible, by way of fecundity, is to suspend the revival of the distancing from definitive being that freedom accomplishes, in a destiny that exacerbates our responsibility for our choices. Responsibility with regard to choices means that to exist in the mode of the possible ineluctably entails choosing certain possibilities to the detriment of others, which are thereby definitively lost to us. The definitive form which recaptures the for-itself, is thus translated into the responsibility that forever attests to the irreversible sacrifice of certain possibilities, the entry into a destiny that it thus returns to take up: "Memories, seeking after lost time, procure dreams, but do not restore the lost occasions" (*Totality and Infinity*, 281). As the liberation of the definitive form which would go much further than the decompression of being which the "for-itself" accomplishes, fecundity delimits "true temporality, that in which the definitive is not definitive," in which it is no longer a question of "regretting the lost occasions before the unlimited infinity of the future" (282).

Because the loss of certain choices no longer contains anything of the definitive form in the face of the infiniteness of the future, it is from responsibility, from those possibilities that tack toward given destinies, from which we liberate fecundity. Levinas directly associates the theme of responsibility with that of aging.[12] This is why *Totality and Infinity* does not give the last word to responsibility. Fecundity delimits a space beyond responsibility, which consists in the pardon. Being toward the infinite, through fecundity, is to continue in the son, who marks a discontinuity with the selfhood of the father. And yet it is precisely this discontinuity that provides a destiny and thereby liberates the self from aging: "A being capable of another fate than its own is a fecund being" (*Totality and Infinity*, 282).

Liberation is recommencement, and coincides with an existence entirely renewed and rejuvenated, which is to say absolved of what had been the irreversible sacrifice of certain possibilities. What had previously defined our choices, our decisions in being, our sacrificed possibilities, this division between possible choices and foregone choices, no longer defines an irreversible horizon for the infinite time of fecundity, because here existence can correct itself anew—that is, transcend itself—in and through a new existence. That does not mean "grasping again all that one might have been," but rather because existence begins anew, and in so doing ceases to age, in "no longer regretting . . . lost occasions" (282). There is nothing left to regret, because being rejuvenates itself in generation, starting anew such that our past choices no longer weigh on us as irreversibly determinant of our destinies.

Generation, the time of fecundity, which rests on the son's break from the father, liberates us from the definitive form; it liberates the fixation of being to a unique destiny (the fact of choosing to the detriment of other choices). The discontinuity of time lightens the burden of a past that thus no longer weighs so heavily on the fecund self, having broken with itself. Generation absolves the past of its determinative character: Our faults are no longer irreparable, but we are instead pardoned in the work of the discontinuous time of fecundity. What has been done is redeemed, repaired, and pardoned in the renewal of being, by which the self is no longer bound to its faults and choices. Renewal is thus a pardon because in liberating us from a unique destiny, in allowing the father to emerge as other in the son, fecundity repairs the irreparable, renders reversible that which had been irreversible, creates a relation to the past in which the latter is no longer definitive, where the father no longer grows older, toward a destiny to which he is irreversibly assigned.

The pardon coincides with "the reversibility of time" (283). Thanks to the pardon, by the recovery of being that the time of fecundity accomplishes, what has been done no longer weighs on the existant as a binding constraint. Fecundity effaces what had been definitive, and therefore irreparable, in the past, by renewing being in what is therefore a new existence: "The pardon refers to the instant elapsed; it permits the subject who had committed himself in a past instant to be as though that instant had not [passed] on, to be as though he had not committed himself" (283).

The discontinuity introduced by the time of generation thus allows for a relation to the past that is not one of continuation or responsibility but rather of purification and the free recovery of what was. Being is thus renewed in fecundity; it no longer ages but rather becomes infinite, renewing the past not as the burden of a fault that marks our aging but rather the return to a fact that no longer has the status of a fait accompli. In the indefinite recommencement of rejuvenation, beings continue the past but remain forever free of that past thanks to the discontinuity of time, which, in this way, is essentially the pardon itself.

In this sense, the pardon constitutes the very essence of time as the infinite temporality of being. It also means that the instances of time do not juxtapose themselves on one another in a pure discontinuity, nor do they constitute one another in the pure continuity of aging. Generation describes an infinite time that is not one of a "constant presence," which does not take the form of the mode of presence-at-hand (*Vorhandenheit*), a present continuous with an eternal soul illusorily shielded from death. Rather, generation proceeds from a being whose infiniteness mingles with an infinition, which is to say that it coincides with the discontinuity of generations that succeed one another in the infinite time of fecundity.

Death must, of course, intervene here, but unlike the being-toward-death of Dasein, here death does not constitute the absolute horizon of time. Death produces the interval of discontinuity precisely on which the infinition of being reposes. The suspension of human powers that death entails does not amount to the annihilation of being. Rather, it specifically coincides with the latter's infinite recovery—beyond its own powers—in the discontinuous, which is to say infinite, temporality that opens up the time of generations, that is, the time of fecundity.

Intentionality and Metaphysics

The inhumanity of a silent world.

—LEVINAS, "Parole et silence"

Egology and Sensibility

Against certain hasty interpretations that consider Derrida and Levinas together as the philosophers of alterity, and for that reason of the deconstruction of Western metaphysics, let us recall first and foremost that the perspective that Levinas adopts in *Totality and Infinity* is indeed a metaphysical one. We must also keep in mind that Derrida's approach to alterity aligns itself with Husserl against Levinas's critique of the latter. For Derrida, what is at stake is the return of Husserl's phenomenology to its own intuitionist principle in order to show that by its theory of writing, communication, and above all the finalism that animates its later developments, Husserlian phenomenology proves, without yet taking responsibility for it, that intuition as "principle of principles" is always already transgressed.

Certainly, on this point, we have seen that the entire thrust of Levinas's approach goes against Husserl, in attempting to detach the search for what is concrete from the noetico-noematic play of light and the adequation with which it is correlated. Here the discovery of nocturnal events is accomplished via the deductive method of rupturing the formal structures of transcendental phenomenology. In Derrida, the "principle of principles" is called into question just as much as it is for Levinas. For the former, however, this is accomplished through an exacerbation of a tension within phenomenology itself, pulled between its transcendental demands, on the one hand, and the historicist finalism of Husserl's late writings, on the other. In "Violence and Metaphysics," Derrida shows, contra Levinas, that the transgression of intuitionism is a legacy that is in fact fully Husserlian. Yet this assessment leads to conclusions that are incompatible with those of Levinas and thus to a challenge to anything like the idea of "nocturnal events."

On the question of the Other, Derrida will not criticize Husserl until much later in a rather intense discussion of Merleau-Ponty in 2000.[1] There Derrida writes:

> Husserl, on the other hand, in the name of phenomenology, and phenomenological faithfulness, prefers to betray phenomenology (the intuitionism of his principle of principles) rather than transform indirect appresentation into direct presentation, which it may never be—which would re-appropriate the alterity of the alter ego within "my Ego's" own properness.[2]

It is out of a fidelity to Husserl's fifth *Cartesian Meditation* that Derrida, in "Violence and Metaphysics," calls Levinas's views into question: "The disagreement appears definite as concerns the Other."[3] Indeed, according to Levinas, through the doctrine of appresentation, Husserl "allegedly missed the infinite alterity of the other, reducing it to the same" ("Violence and Metaphysics" [hereafter VM], 153).

Again reiterating his fidelity to the Husserlian theory of the relation to the Other as a relation that contravenes the "principle of principles," Derrida reminds us that for Husserl the Other presents itself as "originary nonpresence" (VM, 153). Indeed, contrary to Levinas, Derrida argues that "Husserl speaks . . . of the impossibility of thematizing the other in person. This is *his* problem" (VM, 154, emphasis added). Indeed, the Husserlian *alter* ego represents "the phenomenon of a certain non-phenomenality which is irreducible *for the ego*" (VM, 153, emphasis added). This means that this irreducibility requires its appearance as the appearance of something irreducible: "For it is impossible to encounter the alter ego (in the very form of the encounter described by Levinas), impossible to respect it in experience and in language, if this other, in its alterity, does not *appear for an ego* (in general)" (VM, 153–54).[4] As Derrida formulates it:

The necessary reference to analogical appresentation, far from signifying an analogical and assimilatory reduction of the other to the same,
confirms and respects separation, the unsurpassable necessity of (non-
objective) mediation. If I did not approach the other by way of analogical appresentation, if I attained to the other immediately and originally,
silently, in communion with the other's own experience, the other
would cease to be the other. (VM, 154, emphasis added)

Relating Levinas's quest to that of an experience of "the other itself as
what is most irreducibly other within it: Others" (VM, 103), Derrida asks
himself if such a quest, to the contrary of what Levinas thinks, does not
reach its final outcome in the Husserlian theory of *appresentation*. Levinas
thought, unlike Husserl, that "the Other could not be constituted as an
alter ego, as a phenomenon of the ego, by and for a monadic subject proceeding by appresentative analogy (VM, 132).

In this way, it is only by appresentation that the alter ego can appear,
precisely as the one who I am not. The analogy with my ego is thus constitutive of the possibility of my relating to another ego as other. For Derrida, far from seeing itself captured and thus reduced by the "victorious
assimilation" (VM, 155) of the "same," the alterity of the other requires
precisely what Levinas rejects, namely its constitution as intentional modification of the ego. The latter could never refer to the synthesis of the other
within "sameness" but rather makes possible an access to the other myself,
which, as such, and for this very precise reason, is not myself. In this way,
the other as alter ego refers to the other insofar as it is irreducible to my
ego; as Derrida emphasizes, "The other as alter ego signifies the other qua
other, irreducible to my ego, precisely because it is an ego, because it has
the form of the ego" (VM, 157).

As we have seen, Levinas's writings do indeed contain a problematiza-
tion of the subject understood as the point of departure—the "here"—of
the relation, irreducible at the same time that it is constitutive of its interpellation of the "here below" (*là-bas*) of transcendence (ethics). Levinas
refuses to problematize such a subject in the terms that Derrida uses, and
specifically uses against Levinas, of "transcendental violence," which for
Derrida refers to the ineliminable position of the transcendental ego for
the possibility of ethical dissymmetry as "modification" of that ego. Two
points of view thus come face to face here: For Derrida, Levinas's critique of Husserl's model of appresentation misses what must subsist within
the ego in order to open up the ethical relation to the other as alter ego,
another ego.[5] For Levinas, however, the resistance—or "egoism"—of the

subject—that part of the subject that must remain here—with regard to the ethical appeal, constitutively cannot take the form of the transcendental ego.

As I have sought to emphasize in several places throughout this text, what Levinas reproaches in Husserl's doctrine is not the prominence of the ego but rather the generality of such a form, which hinders the possibility of establishing a relation that departs from the concrete immanence, from which only the other may speak—which is to say, deploy its ethical infiniteness. Contrary to what Derrida imputes to Levinas, for the latter the Husserlian alter ego does not suffer the invasion of the same but rather the profound indetermination of the sameness from which the relation to the Other arises.

As we have seen, it is the sensible, laboring ego—and never an ego in general—that requires the idea of the infinite. The advent of ethics does not suppress sameness to the benefit of the absolutely other but rather entails that sameness as its constitutive and ineffaceable point of departure. This is because the concreteness of sameness—the sensible happiness of the ego—guarantees that the separation is maintained and thus prevents any ecstatic fusion. That the relation finds its point of departure in sameness no longer signifies the projection of its form onto the other, if and only if the ego is understood as something other than a generality. Indeed, the fundamental aim of *Totality and Infinity* is not so much to denounce the failure of philosophically traditional ontology to take into account the infinite alterity of the Other as it is to accuse that tradition of holding to a perfectly vague conception of subjectivity. And yet these two critiques converge; they constitute two aspects of the same diagnosis. For Levinas, it is not an issue of denouncing the projection of the ego onto the alter ego but rather of criticizing the subjective indetermination of the concept of the ego.

In this way, far from refusing its importance for the revelation of the Other, Levinas radicalizes the need for ethics to anchor itself in the sensible position of the self. In other words, the idea of the infinite requires the separation of the same as the constitutive point of departure for the relation to the Other. But from the moment that the ego is understood as an authentic self, the anchorage in question no longer signifies the diffusion of the self into the Other. It is not so much the idea that egoism underlies appresentation that Levinas denounces but rather the underdetermination of the egoism of the ego on which this entire theory rests. It is thus the radicalization of the egoism of the ego that allows us to understand how, moving from the same to the other, the ethical relation can no longer invest the Other with the—general—form of the ego. It is not the ego but rather egoism that is fundamentally required for the advent of a world in which one can speak.

It is true, as Derrida emphasizes, that the doctrine of appresentation *"confirms and respects the separation"* of the Other. But as I have sought to demonstrate, the problem, for Levinas, is not to deduce the irreducibility of the Other for itself but to show that the Other reveals itself by speaking—that the theory of appresentation, which misses the separated egoism of the same, necessarily forbids. The face does not address itself to an abstract ego, and for that reason the doctrine of apprehension results in a world of silence. Despite its irreducibility with regard to the ego, the alter ego does not speak, because it draws its signification from the ego that modifies it and not, *kath'auto*, from itself.

And yet if the ego cannot be found in the other—and is also irreducible to the self, whatever this alter ego is—it is that the face speaks, which is to say signifies itself. Here again it is not the irreducibility of the Other to the Ego that is at stake but the fact that this irreducibility can signify itself only if the ego from which it departs is really determined. In other words, speech—and the revelation of the world that results from it—is always grounded in the sensible fixation of being. It is from this immemorial depth that the irreducibility of the Other can come to speech, which is to say, can manifest itself.

Intentionality and Eschatology

Derrida's critique of Levinas is a defense of Husserl against a reduction of his work to a theory of "the same" and "totalization." According to Levinas's reading of phenomenology, a reading that Derrida clearly deems partial, the "truth" of intentionality in Husserl would be situated "in the value of adequation." Further, "As vision and theoretical intuition, Husserlian intentionality would be adequation. This latter would exhaust and interiorize all distance and all true alterity. 'Vision, in effect, is essentially an adequation of exteriority to interiority: exteriority is reabsorbed in the contemplating soul, and, as an adequate idea, is revealed a priori, resulting in a *Sinngebung*' (*TI*)." (VM, 148). Here Derrida deconstructs the status of absolute alterity that Levinas confers on the Other, in retranslating it within the coordinates of an intentionality grasped again from an originary moment of the transgression of limits circumscribed by the intuitionism of traditional phenomenology. For this reason, "Violence and Metaphysics" is hardly intelligible without clarification from Derrida's 1962 *Edmund*

Husserl's Origin of Geometry: An Introduction. There we see the elaboration of a paradoxical definition of intentionality, drawn beyond any intuitionism of presence, the radically historical reach of intentionality as an infinite task.[6]

Moving away from the Heideggerian concept of liberty as anticipation (*Vorlaufen*), Derrida defines the institutional intentionality of geometric ideality as an "*anticipatory* structure"[7] from which the sensible is torn and the creative target of an "*Idea in the Kantian sense*."[8] Derrida further and far from chastising phenomenological intentionality considers instead that it is a question of reapproaching the latter from the perspective of its fundamentally teleological vocation, which is to say as a structure of pure aim that the doctrine of fulfillment can only betray and destroy.[9] Thus understood, intentionality is inscribed within the horizon of a task of infinite constitution that the "metaphysics of presence" covers up.

The privilege accorded to presence results from the abdication of phenomenology in the face of the breadth of its own historical task, itself dictated by the excess of the ethico-theoretical prescription that intentionality assigns itself. Insofar as intentionality consists in the irresistible élan of an anticipation of the infinite, there are no longer objective contents present to consciousness that must be grasped otherwise than in their relativity with regard to the horizon of infinite constitution within which all intentionality is inscribed and which for that reason designates the opening up par excellence of that which remains inadequate.

Intentionality thus deploys its activity of constitution within the horizon of infinite constitution, which itself cannot be constituted. For Derrida, "the importance of the concept of horizon lies precisely in its inability to make any constitutive act into an object, and in that it opens the work of objectification to infinity" (VM, 150). Indeed, Derrida insists, contra Levinas, on this "truth" of phenomenological intentionality, that Husserl can only elucidate—and this on the other side of the "principle of principles"—his transcendental phenomenology at the very end of his oeuvre: the radical openness of intentionality to the horizons of infinite constitution that cannot themselves be constituted.[10] Levinas would therefore be incorrect to think that "Husserl finally summarized non-adequation, and reduced the infinite horizons of experience to the condition of available objects" (VM, 150).[11] Husserl, "by demonstrating the irreducibility of intentional incompleteness, and *therefore* of alterity" (VM, 148, emphasis added) would be, in the eyes of the young Derrida, the thinker of non-adequation par excellence.

It is for this reason that, against Levinas, Derrida presents intentionality grasped as such—which is to say as that epistemic form whose "proper" character entails the transgression of the "principle of principles" of phenomenology, and whose other name is "respect itself" (VM, 151).

> In the two intentional directions of which we have just spoken, *the Idea in the Kantian sense* designates the infinite overflowing of a horizon which, by reason of an absolute and essential necessity which itself is absolutely principled and irreducible, *never can* become an object itself, or be completed, *equaled*, by the intuition of an object. Even by God's intuition. The horizon itself cannot become an object because it is the unobjectifiable wellspring of every object in general. This impossibility of adequation is so radical that neither the *originality* nor the *apodicticity* of evident truths are necessarily adequations. (Cf., for example, *Ideas I*, sec. 3; *Cartesian Meditations*, sec. 9, passim.) (Of course, this does not imply that certain possibilities of adequate evident truths—particular and founded ones—are overlooked by Husserl.) The importance of the concept of horizon lies precisely in its inability *to make any constitutive act into an object*, and in that it opens the work of objectification to infinity. In phenomenology there is never a constitution of horizons, but horizons of constitution. That the infinity of the Husserlian horizon has the form of an indefinite opening, and that it offers itself without any possible end to the negativity of constitution (of the work of objectification) does this not certainly keep it from all totalization, from the illusion of the immediate presence of a plenitudinous infinity in which the other suddenly becomes unfindable? If a consciousness of infinite inadequation to the infinite (and even to the finite) distinguishes a body of thought careful to respect exteriority, it is difficult to see how Levinas can depart from Husserl, on this point at least. *Is not intentionality respect itself?* The eternal irreducibility of the other to the same, but of the other *appearing as* other for the same? For without the phenomenon of other as other no respect would be possible. The phenomenon of respect supposes the respect of phenomenality. And ethics, phenomenology. (VM, 150–51, emphasis added)

It is here that we may thus come to understand Derrida's and Levinas's radical opposition on the question of history. Levinas, for his part, defends an eschatology *"beyond the totality* or beyond history,"[12] in relation to a positive infinity. Derrida, however, in continuity with his introduction to Husserl's *Geometry*, thinks the absolute in the form of a negative transcendence: "The infinitely other would not be what it is, other, if it was a positive infinity, and if it did not maintain within itself the negativity of the indefinite, of the *apeiron*" (VM, 142). Absoluteness is not beyond history; it designates the in-definiteness—or the "negativity of constitution" (VM, 150) that is constitutive of history itself. Can we, Derrida asks, "respect the other as other, and expel negativity—labor—from transcendence, as Levinas seeks to do? . . . Infinity cannot be understood as other except in the form of the in-finite" (VM, 142).

Against any conception of the infinite as "nonnegative transcendence" (VM, 148), Derrida thinks the "other" as "that which does not come to an end, despite my interminable labor and experience" (VM, 142). Such an experience is the test of a "disquiet" toward the infinitely other, which negativity indicates and maintains as beyond and which, for that reason, can never fall within a "positive infinity"—within a presence—but rather proceeds from the "negativity of the in-definite"—which is history as the difference between totality and infinity. History is neither a finite total-ity—the view that Derrida ascribes to Levinas—nor a positive and actual-ized infinity; it is neither finite nor infinite but rather something eschato-logically beyond them both, the unfulfilled passage from one to the other: "History keeps to the difference between totality and infinity, and that history precisely is that which Levinas calls transcendence and eschatol-ogy" (VM, 153).

History thus designates the ever-unachieved work of transcendental constitution, understood as the indefiniteness of a task that is both prac-tical and excessive. In other words, history is understood as opening up to a nonpresence at the heart of phenomenality; it is neither a positive "beyond," independent of phenomenality, nor something that can be re-absorbed within phenomenality. The infinite is the infinity of a difference, an economy, which "in being history, can be at home neither in the finite totality which Levinas calls the Same nor in the positive presence of the Infinite" (VM, 146). Consequently, if "it is fitting to begin *rightfully* with transcendental phenomenology" (VM, 152), it is because the departure from violence presupposes violence, the violence of the same, "transcen-dental violence."

However, this originary and "irreducible violence of the relation to the other, is at the same time nonviolence, since it opens the relation to the other. It is an *economy*" (VM, 160). Historical violence cannot be identified with the same, but rather with the economy of the same and the other, prohibiting alterity from the moment it reveals itself as a "non-negative transcendence," as a face, simultaneously entailing both war and the hori-zon of peace—which has no sense but for the horizon of war: "Eschatology is not possible, except through violence" (VM, 162). But in Derrida's view, contrary to that of Levinas, war does not have the last word on history, if it is an economy of same and other, the game of difference between totality and infinity.

For Derrida, transcendence—or eschatology—lies in history as the movement of overflowing the closure of finite sameness. It is the other overflowing the same, understood for this reason as the *in*-finite, which is to say, again, as "that which does not come to an end, despite my interminable labor and experience" (VM, 142). For Levinas, the concept of the infinite is eschatological in that it entails a suspension of the teleology of constitution—however indefinite it may be. Here the advent of eschatology suspends history, not only in that the transcendent passage from finite totality to the positivity of the infinite happens through it, but also in that eschatology suspends any recourse to our constituent powers to deduce the event of the revelation of the infinite.

Alterity cannot proceed from the same, however indefinite and irreducible to any parousiastic grasping of the inscription of eschatology within historical violence may be. Intentionality, properly understood, by the excessiveness of the historically infinite task to which it responds, contravenes any metaphysics of presence; it remains the norm from which it becomes possible to conceive the alterity of a horizon that is itself inconstitutable. Intentionality, in the historicity of its infinite task, remains a negative determinant principle, which confirms an inconstitutable nonpresence at the heart of constituted presence, the difference between the same and the other, of the other from the same. Such alterity thus stands in opposition to Levinas's conception of a positive infinity.

Eschatology does not refer to the illusory presence of a teleologically saturated sense, but to the suspense of teleology by the advent of an irreducible presence that originates with the same. This includes Derrida's negative deduction of alterity, which is to say again in light of the maintenance of intentionality as ultimate principle following Husserl. The refusal of the Other in war paradoxically attests to the insurmountable presence of the Other, the undecided and undecidable evidence of the presence of the Other: "Society is the presence of being."[13]

The deduction of nocturnal events of being through the rupture of the structures constituted by transcendental phenomenology does not in any way amount to a contestation of theoretical intentionality, but of the actual conditions of its application. When Levinas reproaches phenomenology for reducing the other to the same, for attempting to enclose the alterity of the Other within phenomenological intuition, it is not a question of merely confirming the insufficiency of intuition with regard to an infinite Other always in excess of the grasp of intentionality, but to denounce a categorical error. To reach for the things themselves by intuition presupposes being taught, without which the primacy of teaching, however it is understood, would be reducible to the light of intuition—not even to a conception in which teaching overflows the latter—because teaching is the foundation of intuition.

We can only apply an intentional framework to the Other through a circular reasoning in which intentional thematization already presupposes the acquisition of that which it targets. But this acquisition does not belong to the register of thematization in principle. It supposes the presence of an asymmetrical idea that no positive or negative thematization can measure. To speak *of* the Other in thematizing already necessarily presupposes speaking *to* the Other. But this second register—that of sociality—cannot be reduced to the first. If the transcendence of the face is defined by the fact that it overflows intentionality, the face would certainly also overflow my powers, though without calling them into question. The ethical calling into question of my powers refers to a situation that suspends the reference to powers as a positive or negative standard. This suspension is called ethics, or society.

All thematization, including that of the Other, ipso facto entails addressing the Other, receiving the idea of the infinite, the sociality and teaching that are not situated on the same plane as that of thematization:

> The knowledge that absorbs the Other is forthwith situated within the discourse I address to him. . . . In discourse the divergence that inevitably opens between the Other as my theme and the Other as my interlocutor, emancipated from the theme that seemed a moment to hold him, forthwith contests the meaning I ascribe to my interlocutor.[14]

We therefore cannot posit thematization as somehow prior to being in a social relation with the Other, because the latter is the originary event without which thought is not thematized. Indeed, we find the very same error, on the level of principle, in describing the alterity of the Other as an excess with regard to intentionality: that of quite simply measuring negatively, that is, in the light of intentionality, measuring that which cannot in principle be measured. However, and again, this is not because the transcendence of the Other would be negative, which is to say negatively relative to the powers of constitution, but because we cannot see how that which conditions the deployment of intentionality would be indebted to any level of intentionality that it renders possible.

Indeed, when Levinas reproaches Heidegger for having sought to reduce the infiniteness of the existent to a third term—the being of the existent (*l'être de l'étant*)—in rendering it commensurable with Dasein's powers of comprehension, he is denouncing precisely the same circularity—that is, not the irrelevancy of the question of the sense of being—its overflow in any infinitism of absolute alterity in which the presence of the existent would resist comprehension and thus define itself by this resistance to integration—but the deduction based on the comprehension that, rendering it possible, is in no way commensurable with it: nocturnal events of being. Any question that bears on the sense of being is addressed first: All comprehension supposes something other than comprehension, namely nothing other than sociality itself, the nonnegotiable fact of being in a social relation with the Other, which is in no way evident, not even negatively. It is only from this encounter with the existent, which is irreducible to the being of the existent, that the question of being itself can draw its intelligibility: "We affirm the priority of the existent with regard to being, which is to say the necessity of having encountered the existent in order to even post the problem of being."[15]

It is thus not a question for Levinas of opposing existing phenomenologies with a new object of intentionality or comprehension, which would be defined by its ungraspable excess. Rather, it is an issue of criticizing the consistent categorical confusion that loses sight of the dissymmetry of the idea of the infinite with regard to those general human powers of intellection that originate from subjectivity or its avatars. The social relation to the Other is not, therefore, in opposition to either intentionality or comprehension; this relation does not consist in marking the work of constitution or comprehension with an unfathomable and ever-unfulfilled negativity. Rather, it consists in uncovering those elements that undergird intuition and are for that reason invisible to the light of intuition.

The categorical error of the ontology of knowledge lies in the confusion that consists in attempting to deduce what undergirds and constitutes events from the visibility of the light of those events themselves. To revive these constitutive factors demands an original deductive method. From here emerges the nocturnal character of a phenomenology as research into the concrete, which aims to redirect us toward originary events of being by rupturing those structures constituted by phenomenology. However, the deduction of the other by the same—and the domination of the other by the same, entailed by that deduction—is inevitable for philosophy as long as ontology merely amounts to the diurnal events of intellection, of absolute knowledge or ontico-ontological comprehension. This is what allows us to understand the sense in which *Totality and Infinity* is an eschatology of messianic peace. In responding to a new situation within being, in the context of an ontology that circumscribes being within the powers of intellection or comprehension, Levinas's work inscribes within being events that do not fall within the light of intellection and which, for that reason, have never had a place within ontology—until now.

In deducing the ontological productivity of metaphysical events, *Totality and Infinity* leads to a—nocturnal—enlargement of ontology and thus announces the advent, within being, of the human sociality beyond war and empire. Eschatology therefore consists in decoupling being from totalization, in deposing an exclusive understanding of being and establishing ethics as an event of being—the absolute becoming of being—beyond the totality of knowledge. But exceeding knowledge in this way also opens up another horizon, within which the concrete recovery of intelligibility is rooted in the situation of interlocution, which is to say of ethics.

We do not have ethics first and then knowledge. The ethical consists in speaking, which is to say to discover the world in its signification through the open field of questions and answers. A world that is disclosed is a world in which one speaks, that is a world in which the ethical injunction resonates within the self, whether or not we desire it. The objectivity of the world attests to the idea of the infinite within me—the very fact of sociality. It is in this way that there is nothing artificial about the return to nocturnal events within phenomenological intuition. The fact of recovering concreteness below the luminosity of intellection, through the rupture of its formal structures, or in other words of describing events taken in isolation and articulated in relation to one another by a deduction or concretization—even if Levinas recognizes that the actual subject already possesses the idea of the infinite—has an eschatological meaning.

It is a question, then, of enlarging ontology beyond the intellective limits of intuition that have up to this point circumscribed the plane, the framework, of ontology, in discovering a nocturnal ontology that undergirds the very work of such diurnal intellection. This inscription within ontology of nonintuitive events, which until now did not pertain to it, is the eschatological mark of Levinas's work. Ethics is thus no longer an illusory projection onto being, but is revealed not merely as an event of being itself, but its ultimate event. The theoretical dissociation of the plan of being from the ontology of knowledge announces the coming within being—until now dominated by history and war—of ethics as the advent of messianic peace between human beings. It further consecrates the advent of a world in which human beings speak and wherein speech will recover its originally ethical signification. Because the social work of speech is to break down the barriers that exist within the world, as a world in common held within the interval between questions and responses, totalization cannot open up the world.

Further, and again contra the traditional interpretation, in gauging the ontological project of *Totality and Infinity*, we can now see that it consists in nothing less than the discovery of a de-totalized communism.[16] Totalization, the work of war and politics, cannot open up the world which is either common or not. But this alternative remains unintelligible without the enlargement of ontology which eschatology entails. That enlargement announces a de-totalized sociality which brings about the truth of being as a multiplicity, and thus the world as a world essentially shared between those who dwell within it, insofar as they are all essentially interlocutors.

Totalization, the absoluteness of politics, suppresses the communalization of the world, its "becoming common," or what I have called de-totalized communism, which is to say the world becoming world. This future, this becoming, coincides with the equally radical form of becoming of being in the absolute sense, beyond the totality of absolute knowledge or any absolute politics that always mark the repression of the multiple and infinite deployment of being—the transcendence of being which human sociality concretely produces. The absolute development of being—justice, in other words—brings with it the de-totalization of the real. In its ultimate deployment, being is multiple as sociality and by fecundity. But this power of de-totalization rests on the eschatological enlargement of ontology—the "becoming nocturnal" of being in its ultimate events. The absolute regime of being is thus paroxysmal. This full ontological regime is accomplished as peace, as the nocturnal de-totalization of being in its becoming the world.

1. See Lingis's note in Emmanuel Levinas, *Totality and Infinity: An Essay on Exteriority*, trans. Alphonso Lingis (Pittsburgh: Duquesne University Press, 1969), 24n.

2. See ibid., 23n.

FOREWORD: THE PRESENCE OF THE INFINITE
1. And it is a point of argumentation for Levinas, perhaps even the final one, that to even deny presence—as in the case of murder—is again to admit its reality.

PREFACE: THE NOCTURNAL FACE OF BEING
1. "The ontological language in *Totality and Infinity* is not at all a definitive language. The language in *Totality and Infinity* is ontological because it wants above all not to be psychological. But in reality, it is already a search for what I call 'the beyond being,' the tearing of this equality to self which is always being—the *Sein*—whatever the attempts to separate it from the present" (Emmanuel Levinas, "Questions and Answers," in *Of God Who Comes to Mind* [Stanford, Calif.: Stanford University Press, 1998], 82). For a detailed analysis of the passage that leads Levinas from ontology to that which is "otherwise than being," see the invaluable article of Rodolphe Calin, "La métaphore absolue, le faux sépart vers l'autrement qu'être," *Les cahiers de philosophie de l'Université de Caen*, no. 49 (2012).

2. This is also what allows me to measure the extent of Levinas's philosophical renovations following *Totality and Infinity*—even if my perspective here does not ultimately align with them, precisely because of the restrictions they implicitly place on ontology, which return to and modify the prodigious innovations of perspective opened up by the elucidation of those "nocturnal events" that are events of being.

1. MESSIANIC ESCHATOLOGY, OR THE PRODUCTION
OF ULTIMATE EVENTS OF BEING

1. Emmanuel Levinas, *Totality and Infinity: An Essay on Exteriority*, trans. Alphonso Lingis (Pittsburgh: Duquesne University Press, 1969), 21. Further references to this title will be by page number within parentheses in the text.

2. "*There are absolutely no moral facts.*" Friedrich Wilhelm Nietzsche, *Twilight of the Idols*, in *The Anti-Christ, Ecce Homo, Twilight of the Idols, and Other Writings* (Cambridge: Cambridge University Press, 2005), "Improving Humanity," §1, 182.

3. Ibid., §1, 183.

4. "*Not* contentedness, but more power; *not* peace, but war; *not* virtue, but prowess (virtue in the style of the Renaissance, *virtù*, moraline-free virtue" (Friedrich Nietzsche, *The Anti-Christ*, in *The Anti-Christ, Ecce Homo, Twilight of the Idols, and Other Writings* [Cambridge: Cambridge University Press, 2005], §2, 4; see also §6, 6).

5. See Martin Heidegger, *Introduction to Metaphysics*, trans. Gregory Fried and Richard Polt (New Haven, Conn.: Yale University Press, 2014), 67; [47] in the original.

6. "War is the father of all and the king of all." Heraclitus, Fragment 53, quoted in Heidegger, *Introduction to Metaphysics*, 67n4.

7. Friedrich Wilhelm Nietzsche, *Daybreak: Thoughts on the Prejudices of Morality* (Cambridge: Cambridge University Press, 1997), §103, 60.

8. See *Totality and Infinity*, 26, for Levinas's discussion of "production" as a technical term.

9. Translator's note: As noted in my prefatory comments, throughout the present work we will follow Lingis in translating *étant* as "existent," *être* as "being," *éxistant* as "existant," and *l'éxister* as either "existence" or "existing," depending on context (see *Totality and Infinity*, 23n). From here, the French terms will appear in brackets only when further emphasis, clarification, or comparison is required. —DW.

10. Translator's note: Moati uses the term "c'est-à-dire," or "that is," here in the technical sense specified by Levinas in the preface, in terms of having deduction and concretization: "In our exposition it is indicated by expressions such as 'that is,' or 'precisely,' or 'this accomplishes that,' or 'this is produced as that'" (ibid., 28). The present work follows the Lingis translation in rendering "c'est-à-dire" as "that is," "that is to say," "which is to say," etc., as appropriate. —DW.

11. Transcendent being reveals itself from the moment it speaks and is thus in no need of placing itself in the position of the signified in its own speech. The intelligibility of this speech must not be reduced to the signified content that it articulates. It reveals to the same extent that, as *discourse*, all

speech reveals the presence of the interlocutor, which Levinas calls, turning away from the Structuralist lexicon, the *signifier*, understood as *the one who signifies*.

12. Ibid., 21. Translation amended. At the author's request, the French *face* here will be rendered as "side" throughout, in order to avoid confusion with the technical term *visage*, which will always appear as "face," in reference to the "face of the other." —DW.

13. Emmanuel Levinas, *Otherwise Than Being, or Beyond Essence* (Pittsburgh: Duquesne University Press, 1998), 3.

14. As we will see, it is the *social relation* that concretely deploys the idea of the infinite: To have the idea of the infinite is to be in relation with the Other.

15. Emmanuel Levinas, "Parole et silence," in *Oeuvres 2, Parole et silence* (Paris: Grasset-Imec, 2009), 80. Translator's note: As specified in my prefatory comments, original translations of all references from the collection *Oeuvres 2, Parole et silence* (specifically "L'écrit et l'oral," "Pouvoirs et origines," and "Parole et silence") by Daniel Wyche.

16. Levinas, "Pouvoirs et origines," 134.

17. I employ the term "drama" here, even though Levinas, for his part, is far more reserved in using it. In a note concerning events of being that are accomplished beyond the face, he emphasizes that "they are conjunctures in being for which perhaps the term 'drama' would be most suitable, in the sense that Nietzsche would have liked to use it when, at the end of *The Case of Wagner*, he regrets that it has always been wrongly translated by action." Following Nietzsche, Levinas specifies that "it is because of the resulting equivocation that we forgo this term" (*Totality and Infinity*, 28n2). It is, indeed, a lexical equivocation, which would lead us to confuse the nocturnal drama with the very thing from which we seek to liberate this category—namely, an action that is understood as an active intervention in the realization of a project.

18. At the end of the preface, Levinas reclaims—as the scare quotes will attest—in displacing it, the late Heideggerian theme of "letting be," understood by Heidegger as *Geschehenlassen der Welt* (see Martin Heidegger, *The Essence of Reasons*, trans. Terrence Malik [Evanston, Ill.: Northwestern University Press, 1969]), and later as *Gelassenheit* ("releasement," "calm composure," or "serenity"): "The aspiration to radical exteriority, thus called metaphysical, the respect for this metaphysical exteriority which, above all, we must 'let be,' constitutes truth" (Levinas, *Totality and Infinity*, 29). For all of the reasons that I have developed here, such a thematic could only take on its true sense for Levinas from the Face—that is, from ontology understood as metaphysical in its ultimate events—rather than the primordial revelation of the world.

19. Translator's note: I have replaced Lingis's awkward use of the verb "equaling" with the more common "equating." —DW.

20. Didier Franck points out that Heidegger twice emphasizes (in §42 and §49 of *Being and Time*) that existential structures present the "generality," the "emptiness," and the "formality" that characterize all ontological determination: "This is to say those ontic situations *par excellence* which manifest these structures do not have any ontological significance themselves, and that existentials are fully comprehensible without reference to the situations which they constitute *a priori*. The phenomenological intelligibility of a concept is indissociable from the examples and situations out of which it is formed; concepts cannot and must not be separated from phenomena. Thus the 'formality' of the existential analytic which does not furnish any indication of the formation of its own concepts, represents a fatal flaw in phenomenology which Levinas methodically struggles to overcome." Didier Franck, *Dramatique des phénomènes* (Paris: PUF, 2001), 154–55 (original translation by Daniel Wyche).

2. TO RECEIVE THE IDEA OF THE INFINITE

1. See Translator's Note in the front of the book. Throughout the text, we have followed Lingis in translating *autrui* by the capitalized Other, and *autre* with the lowercased other, although we have departed from his standardizations by translating *le moi* as "the self."—DW.

2. Translator's note: The French *jouissance* will be translated throughout as "enjoyment," whereas *bonheur* will appear alternately as either "happiness" or "contentment." —DW.

3. Emmanuel Levinas, *Totality and Infinity: An Essay on Exteriority*, trans. Alphonso Lingis (Pittsburgh: Duquesne University Press, 1969), 23 Further references to this title will be by page number within parentheses in the text.

4. Levinas insists on the fact that the description of the solitary enjoyment of the ego "assuredly does not render the concrete man," who indeed "has already the idea of infinity, that is, lives in society and represents things to himself" (ibid., 139).

5. I must insist that in absolutely no case do the analyses of the egoistic separation seek to give an account of the effective existence of a moment of exclusively solitary experience. It is never a question of leaving the ethical horizon within which human beings already possess the idea of the infinite. That which signifies the exhaustive elucidation of the ethical as a relation that is separated demands the deformalization of the formal notion of "separation." This deformalization coincides with the production of events wherein separation concretely elucidates itself as the atheist enjoyment of the self. It is in this sense that *Totality and Infinity* is not a treatise of phenomenological

constitution—proceeding by steps and layers of constitution—but rather of deformalization as a renewal of the phenomenological method. It is not a question of abandoning rigor for obscurity, but rather of deducing, by way of deformalization concrete occurrences of structures constituted by being. Regarding concretization, see chapter 1.

6. It is in this sense, again, that Levinas does not in any way rehabilitate some kind of altruistic "moraline," if by "altruist" one means the opposite of "egoist." The philosophy developed by Levinas in *Totality and Infinity* unreservedly endorses the Nietzschean assessment according to which "an 'altruistic' morality, a morality in which selfishness *fades away*—, is always a bad sign" (Friedrich Wilhelm Nietzsche, *Twilight of the Idols*, in *The Anti-Christ, Ecce Homo, Twilight of the Idols, and Other Writings* [Cambridge: Cambridge University Press, 2005], §35, 209).

7. Cf. Jean-Paul Sartre, "Intentionality: A Fundamental Idea of Husserl's Phenomenology," in *Critical Essays (Situations I)* (New York: Seagull Books, 2010).

8. Levinas borrows the notion of "trans-ascendance" from Jean Wahl in order to designate the movement of metaphysical ascension.

9. "To the myth of Ulysses returning to Ithaca, we wish to oppose the story of Abraham who leaves his fatherland forever for a yet unknown land, and forbids his servant to even bring back his son to the point of departure" (Emmanuel Levinas, "The Trace of the Other," in *Deconstruction in Context*, ed. Mark C. Taylor [Chicago: University of Chicago Press, 1986], 348).

10. See chapter 4 below.

11. Translator's note: Following Lingis, the French *demeure* is translated throughout as *dwelling*, and *maison*, which appears below, as *home*. —DW.

12. It is not insignificant that Levinas himself contributed to the translation of Husserl's *Meditations* into French.

13. Edmund Husserl, *Cartesian Meditations*, trans. Dorion Cairns (The Hague: Martinus Nijhoff, 1960), Meditation V, §53, 116–17.

14. Translator's note: In the Lingis translation of *Totality and Infinity* this passage reads "the metaphysician and the other can not be totalized," whereas I have rendered the original French *se totaliser* here as "do not totalize one another," which the author and I take to be more accurate to both the spirit and the letter of the text. —DW.

15. "We propose to call 'religion' the bond that is established between the Same and the Other without constituting a totality" (*Totality and Infinity*, 40).

16. This is a notion to which I return below.

17. In this respect it is fundamental that the opening of the separation does not replace the category of the correlation by which it would see itself returned and reduced, that is, denied the "the reciprocal of the transcendence

of the other with regard to me" (*Totality and Infinity*, 53). What Levinas calls the "metaphysical asymmetry" of the other with regard to the self implies a relation of the same to the other incapable of constituting a totalization of the one and the other.

18. If separation is required by the idea of the infinite, the atheism that it engenders is characterized by its closure to any horizon of transcendence. With atheism, the self lives without the other, and yet the absence of the thought of a separated self oriented toward that being outside of which it lives, again disallows the assignment of the status of infinite to this exterior being that is ignored by the self. In order to produce itself in being, the infinite requires the desire or the thought of the self from which it is separated, in that the content of the infinite coincides with its infinition.

19. "La sensation demolit tout système" (Emmanuel Levinas, *Totalité et infini: Essai sur l'exteriorité* (Paris: Livre de Poche, 1990), 53).

20. Levinas refers here to the Aristotelian thesis according to which a substance is "in virtue of itself" (*kath'auto*), in that it "has no cause other than itself" (Aristotle, *Metaphysics*, in *The Basic Works of Aristotle*, ed. Richard McKeon [New York: Random House, 1941], Delta, 18, 1022a32–33; 771).

3. THE SENSIBLE DEPTH OF BEING

1. In this respect, the "rupture of participation" represents a form of rewriting of the phenomenological *epoché*, ("bracketing," or "putting out of action") but without appealing to a transcendental ego, as it is sensation— as act of withdrawal—that suspends participation. Such a suspension thus coincides with the affirmation of a concrete self.

2. We will return to the significance of Levinas's assimilation of the historiographer to the status of survivor below; the time of the historiographer is the time of the death of the will, the time in which the individual's sense of being is drawn from a source external to one's own will.

3. Emmanuel Levinas, *Totality and Infinity: An Essay on Exteriority*, trans. Alphonso Lingis (Pittsburgh: Duquesne University Press, 1969), 57. Further references to this title will be by page number within parentheses in the text.

4. Translator's note: We have decided to use "worldly" in this context for *intramondain*, rather than "inner-worldly," which has been used in some translations of Levinas (and indeed Heidegger). In both cases, the phrase denotes "this-worldly" life, the daily, quotidian lives of human beings in the world. "Worldly" more readily, and clearly, references this meaning in English.—DW.

5. Emmanuel Levinas, *Time and the Other, and Additional Essays*, trans. Richard A. Cohen (Pittsburgh: Duquesne University Press, 1987), 63.

6. Contrary to certain (far too syncretic) readings, I must insist on all that so radically distinguishes Levinas's thought from that of Lacan on this point. Precisely because, for Lacan, by way of a topological deformation, the object-goal (*Aim*) of enjoyment—the object *petit a*—paradoxically represents an *obstacle* to the realization of enjoyment (*Goal*). The formal modification of intentionality in Lacan maintains a dissociation of the *goal* of enjoyment from its *object-goal*. For Levinas, the problematic of enjoyment implies the existence of a substantial subjectivity correlative with this enjoyment. Whereas for Lacan, it implies the nonsubstantial, lacking subject—Lacan's barred subject (S)—in the sense that here desire *lacks its object*, and wherein enjoyment deliberately misses this very object. For a complete development of this thesis, see Raoul Moati, "De l'intentionalité à la pulsionalité, la subjectivation du *Todestrieb*," *Studia Phenomenologia* X (2010).

7. Levinas, *Time and the Other*, 63.

8. It is important to clearly distinguish *enjoyment* from *disposition*, in the ontological sense of *Befindlichkeit*. If it is true that the comprehension of *Dasein* is never without an affective counterpart, the fact remains that such a counterpart supports the inscription of Dasein within the ontological horizon. To the contrary, it is because sensation as enjoyment undermines any participation in the regime of ontology that Levinas maintains that enjoyment "does not express (as Heidegger would have it) the mode of my implantation—my disposition—in being, the tonus of my bearing" (*Totality and Infinity*, 113).

9. Translator's note: In French, *jouir de* can mean both "to enjoy" something and "to have or possess" (as it can to a lesser extent in English). Moati invokes this homonym here. —DW.

10. As we will see, the category of "thing" does not include that of the object, as the former precedes the work on the element, where the object as correlate of representation supposes the departure from the economic register, that is to say, the thematization of things possessed by *language*. In thematizing them, language *objectifies* things. Thematization alters the boundaries of economic possession, and this renders possible the representation of things in objects.

11. Cf. the following section.

12. Regarding this point, cf. the following section as well.

13. Cf. Emmanuel Levinas, *Existence and Existents*, trans. Alphonso Lingis (Pittsburgh: Duquesne University Press, 2001).

14. Translator's note: At the request of the author, the French *face* is consistently rendered here as *side*, so as to avoid any confusion with the French *visage*, which will always appear as "face," capitalized. —DW.

15. "Readiness-to-hand," for the reasons elucidated above.

16. Cf. Emmanuel Levinas, "The Ruin of Representation (1959)," in *Discovering Existence with Husserl* (Evanston, Ill.: Northwestern University Press, 1998), 111–21. Further references to this title will be by page number preceded by the abbreviation RR within parentheses in the text.

17. This aspect has been highlighted by Jocelyn Benoist in an interview with Danielle Cohen-Levinas. See "Quelque chose qui ne se voit pas, mais qui parle: Entretien avec Jocelyn Benoist," in *Lire Totalité et infini d'Emmanuel Levinas: Etudes et interprétations*, ed. Danielle Cohen-Levinas (Paris: Editions Hermann, 2011).

18. Cf. Emmanuel Levinas, *Discovering Existence with Husserl* (Evanston, IL: Northwestern University Press, 1998).

19. Cf. Jean-Paul Sartre, "Intentionality: A Fundamental Idea of Husserl's Phenomenology: Intentionality," in *Critical Essays (Situations I)* (New York: Seagull Books, 2010.

20. On this point, cf. "The Work of Edmund Husserl (1940)," in *Discovering Existence with Husserl* (Evanston, Ill.: Northwestern University Press, 1998

21. In this respect, the "intentionality of enjoyment" as the nourishment of the world, contests each step of the Sartrean interpretation of intentionality as a way to "to tear oneself out of the moist gastric intimacy, veering out there beyond oneself." For Sartre, intentionality allows us to reject "the illusion common to both realism and idealism, that to know is to eat" ("Intentionality: A Fundamental Idea of Husserl's Phenomenology." It is just such a conception of intentionality that Levinas opposes in his reflections on "the intentionality of enjoyment," as Jean-François Courtine has so well shown in "L'ontologie fondamentale d'Emmanuel Levinas," in *Emmanuel Levinas et les territoires de la pensée*, ed. D. Cohen-Levinas and B. Clément (Paris: PUF, 2007).

22. It should be further noted that these analyses distinguish themselves from those of Merleau-Ponty, accused by Levinas, but without blaming him, of reducing the register of the transcendental constitution of consciousness to the level of the body proper: "The structure of constitutive consciousness recovers all its rights after the mediation of the body that speaks or writes" (*Totality and Infinity*, 206).

23. Levinas is referring to §36 of *Being and Time*, specifically the following passage: "The remarkable priority of 'seeing' was noticed particularly by Augustine, in connection with his Interpretation of *concupiscentia*. . . . But we even use this word 'seeing' for the other senses when we devote them to cognizing. . . . For we do not say 'Hear how it glows,' or 'Smell how it glistens,' or 'Taste how it shines,' or 'Feel how it flashes;' but we say of each, 'See'; we say that all this is seen. Therefore, the experience of the senses in general is designated as the 'lust of the eyes'; for when the issue is one of knowing

something, the other senses, by a certain resemblance, take to themselves the function of seeing—a function in which the eyes have priority" (Martin Heidegger, *Being and Time*, trans. John Macquarrie and Edward Robinson [Oxford: Blackwell, 2001], 171, Eng. trans., 215–16).

4. THE TERRESTRIAL CONDITION

1. Emmanuel Levinas, *The Theory of Intuition in Husserl's Phenomenology* (Evanston, Ill: Northwestern University Press, 1995), lv.

2. Ibid., lvii.

3. Emmanuel Levinas, "Martin Heidegger and Ontology," *Diacritics* 26, no. 1 (1996): 19. Translator's Note: The phrase *étroitement liée* in the original French appears simply as "closely involved with" in the English version of this paper; I have translated it with the more literal, and accurate, "directly tied." —DW.

4. Levinas, *Theory of Intuition in Husserl's Phenomenology*, 24.

5. Ibid., 92.

6. On this point, see Jacques Taminiaux, "Un autre lecture de l'histoire de la philosophie," in *Sillages phénoménologiques, auditeurs et lectures de Heidegger* (Brussels: Ousia, 2002), 227–52.

7. Emmanuel Levinas, "The Work of Edmund Husserl (1940)," in *Discovering Existence with Husserl*, by Emmanuel Levinas (Evanston, Ill.: Northwestern University Press, 1998), 70–71.

8. Ibid., 78.

9. Ibid., 70.

10. Levinas, *Theory of Intuition in Husserl's Phenomenology*, 157.

11. Levinas, "Work of Edmund Husserl," 84.

12. Martin Heidegger, *Being and Time*, trans. John Macquarrie and Edward Robinson (Oxford: Blackwell, 2001), 285, Eng. trans. 330

13. Levinas, "Work of Edmund Husserl," 85.

14. Ibid., 87.

15. Ibid., 61.

16. Ibid., 84.

17. Note that in *Totality and Infinity*, the contestation of the sovereignty of representation entails a critique of the very history that Levinas valorizes in these early phenomenological works.

18. Emmanuel Levinas, "Pouvoirs et origines," in *Oeuvres 2, Parole et silence* (Paris: Grasset-Imec, 2009), 115.

19. Emmanuel Levinas, *Totality and Infinity: An Essay on Exteriority*, trans. Alphonso Lingis (Pittsburgh: Duquesne University Press, 1969), 144. Further references to this title will be by page number within parentheses in the text.

20. Levinas, "Pouvoirs et origines," 109–10.

21. Ibid., 133–34.

22. Regarding Sartre's reprisal of the Heideggerian theme of "facticity," see the section titled "The Facticity of the For-Itself," in Jean-Paul Sartre, *Being and Nothingness*, trans. Hazel E. Barnes (New York: Philosophical Library 1956), 121.

23. Levinas, "Pouvoirs et origines," 136.

24. Emmanuel Levinas, "Parole et silence," in *Oeuvres 2, Parole et silence* (Paris: Grasset-Imec, 2009), 87.

25. Ibid., 88.

26. Levinas, "Pouvoirs et origines," 151.

27. Ibid., 89.

28. Levinas, "Parole et silence," 88.

29. Ibid., 89.

30. Ibid., 94.

31. Levinas, "Pouvoirs et origines," 134.

32. Ibid., 136.

33. Regarding the question of the irreducible *hiccéité*, the fact of being-here, of the subject to any form of ethical summons, cf. Jocelyn Benoist, "Le cogito levinassien: Levinas et Descartes," in *Positivité et transcendance, suivi de "Lévinas et la phénoménologie,"* ed. Jean-Luc Marion (Paris: PUF, 2000).

34. Levinas, "Parole et silence," 102.

35. Ibid., 88.

36. Levinas, "Pouvoirs et origines," 135.

37. Ibid.

38. Ibid., 137.

39. Ibid.

40. Ibid., 140.

41. Levinas, "Parole et silence," 98.

42. Levinas, "Pouvoirs et origines," 138.

43. Levinas, "Parole et silence," 99.

44. Cf. chapter 7, "Being toward Infinity," for a further elaboration of this point.

45. Levinas, "Pouvoirs et origines," 140.

5. THE UTOPIA OF THE DWELLING

1. Several important debates regarding the status of the feminine in Levinas's work appeared following the publication of *Totality and Infinity*. As an entire volume could be devoted solely to this question, I will try, in a way that is both preparatory and insufficient, to provide certain points of clarification regarding Levinas's exact language on this question, which seem to have been overlooked by many commentators. It must be emphasized that

Levinas is indeed the thinker of sexual difference par excellence. Liberated from the primacy of the neuter (which is nothing other than the imposition of an unconfessed phallocentric perspective), philosophy may speak from a determinate—masculine—position, from which the other—thus the feminine in relation to the author—reveals herself. It may be asked then, having liberated itself from the neuter, if *Totality and Infinity* does not thereby authorize its own rewriting from the other's perspective—in this case, the feminine perspective. It seems as though this possibility is entailed by the remarks—to be found in both the preparatory conferences and in *Totality and Infinity* itself—that the feminine relation should be explicitly understood as the accomplishment of the relation to the other qua other par excellence. "It is not another liberty which is given in the face-to-face, *but rather the mystery of the Other, the feminine within it*; it is not something which escapes our power, but which essentially hides itself, which is to say that it does not exist within the element of light, and finds itself beyond power and non-power. *The sexuality which we have drawn closer to time itself, appears to us to accomplish the social relation*" (Emmanuel Levinas, "Parole et silence " in *Oeuvres 2, Parole et silence* [Paris: Grasset-Imec, 2009], 85, emphasis added). Thus for Levinas, it is constitutive of the other that by its formal status as the other it always reveals itself as an epiphany of the feminine, regardless of whether or not a given other is empirically masculine or feminine. In other words, there is necessarily something of the feminine in the other, insofar as he or she is other.

2. As we have shown above in chapter 1, the dwelling place concretizes recollection.

3. Emmanuel Levinas, *Totality and Infinity: An Essay on Exteriority*, trans. Alphonso Lingis (Pittsburgh: Duquesne University Press, 1969), 150, emphasis added. Further references to this title will be by page number within parentheses in the text.

4. See Martin Heidegger, *Being and Time*, trans. John Macquarrie and Edward Robinson (Oxford: Blackwell, 2001), ¶40, 188–93, Eng. trans. 233–35. For a detailed explication of Heidegger's position after *Being and Time*, see Françoise Dastur, "Espace, lieu, habitation," in *Heidegger et la pensée à venir* (Paris: Vrin, 2011), 45–58.

5. At the same time, Levinas presents familiarity as "an accomplishment, an en-ergy of separation" (*Totality and Infinity*, 155).

6. Lingis writes in his note: "'Les choses meubles'—The thing (*chose*) will be defined as a '*meuble*'—being related to the home by the possessive grasp it is a 'movable,' a 'furnishing'" (157n).

7. For a detailed analysis of this independence within Levinas's full oeuvre, see Rodolphe Calin, *Levinas et l'exception du soi* (Paris: PUF, 2005), 129–35.

8. Levinas refers here to the scene of the gaze in Sartre; for more on this point, see chapter 6 below.

9. See Lingis's footnotes in *Totality and Infinity*, 131n, 157n, and note 6 above.

10. See again ibid., 131n, 157n, and note 6 above.

11. Translator's note: Lingis translates *corps propre* as "lived body," which I have retained here for the sake of consistency; cf. ibid., 164. —DW.

12. Note that Levinas here refers to Husserl's distinction between *Leib* and *Körper*, in the fifth *Cartesian Meditation*.

13. This paradox is excellently clarified by in Calin, *Levinas et l'exception du soi*, 147–48.

14. Translator's note: This term, "acte manqué," translates the Freudian term "parapraxis," or the more colloquially familiar "Freudian slip"; although Lingis translates it "abortive act," we have used "parapraxis" in order to maintain the Freudian connotations; see *Totality and Infinity*, 88, 176, and 228. —DW.

15. Again, "abortive" here refers to parapraxis in the Freudian sense.

16. According to an analogy with the Sartrean schema of the "for-other," which will be developed below.

17. For an elaboration of this paradox, see the first paragraph of chapter 6.

18. Stéphane Mosès, "Rosenzweig et Levinas: Au-dèla de la guerre," *Rue Descartes, Emmanuel Levinas*, no. 19 (1998): 85–98.

19. It is important to recall here that Kierkegaard, Schopenhauer, and Nietzsche represent for Rosenzweig the philosophical of the "new thought," which contests the Hegelian primacy of the "all thinkable." For an illuminating elaboration of this question, see Sophie Nordmann, *Philosophie et Judaïsme*, Philosophies (Paris: PUF, 2008).

20. For a more detailed commentary on this passage, see again Mosès, "Rosenzweig et Levinas."

21. In the Kabbalah of Luria, *tsimtsum* refers to the self-limiting of God, which allows for the existence of the created world.

22. The processual intrigue that leads from enjoyment to ethics may give the impression that the passage from one to the other entails the simple negation of enjoyment within ethics. In reality, such a description has no other virtue than to clarify the irreducibility of desire to need. However, each step that Levinas describes proceeds from an elucidation of a concrete man who already possesses the idea of the infinite. If it is indeed the case that desire does not have the structure of need, the desiring human being—possessing the idea of the infinite—characterizes himself or herself by the fact that he or she lives—thanks to the idea of the infinite, as we have seen—from the satisfaction of his or her needs through his or her labors. There is no descrip-

tive step within *Totality and Infinity* that does not ultimately lead back to the sociality of human beings: The world is for-another only insofar as it is also enjoyed, labored on, and possessed to a certain extent. The world is only for-another by means of separation, which is to say by the detour of the egoistic life that is rendered possible by ethics, because the former is indispensable to the development of the latter. It is indeed fundamental to the development of social life that not everything about human beings be social. We must not, therefore, be in any way deceived in terms of the expositional orientation of *Totality and Infinity*: there is no case in which the human being does not already possess the idea of the infinite. All of the stages described by Levinas bring us back, in multiple constitutive dimensions, to social life itself.

23. Even if, as we have seen, Levinas does not forget to recall that it is the Other who gives our needs the time required to differentiate their materiality in labor.

6. THE METAPHYSICAL CONTEXT OF INTENTIONALITY

1. "This guiding activity of taking a look at Being arises from the average understanding of being in which we always operate and *which in the end belongs to the essential constitution of Dasein itself*" (Martin Heidegger, *Being and Time*, trans. John Macquarrie and Edward Robinson [Oxford: Blackwell, 2001], 27–28, ¶2).

2. Emmanuel Levinas, *Otherwise Than Being, or Beyond Essence* (Pittsburgh: Duquesne University Press, 1998), 24. Franck also devotes several important passages to this question in *L'un-pour-l'autre*, in which he says, "Need we really add here that the if the question of being must be raised in full transparency, it would become impossible to consider the *concrete circumstances* of its exposition insignificant, the *situation* within which its power of interpellation is deployed? That we are giving, for example, a course delivered to students, and presented week by week? Or a treatise that the reader interprets, page by page?" (Didier Franck, *L'un-pour-l'autre* [Paris: PUF, 2008], 17, emphasis added; original translation by Daniel Wyche).

3. Emmanuel Levinas, "The Proximity of the Other," in *Alterity and Transcendence* (New York: Columbia University Press, 1999), 97. See also Franck, *L'un-pour-l'autre*, 17–18.

4. Emmanuel Levinas, *Totality and Infinity: An Essay on Exteriority*, trans. Alphonso Lingis (Pittsburgh: Duquesne University Press, 1969), 96. Further references to this title will be by page number within parentheses in the text.

5. Levinas, *Otherwise Than Being*, 25.

6. Emmanuel Levinas, "L'écrit et l'oral," in *Oeuvres 2, Parole et silence* (Paris: Grasset-Imec, 2009), 218

7. Ibid., 223.

8. Ibid., 222.

9. "*Being and Time* has argued perhaps but one sole thesis: Being is inseparable from the comprehension of Being (which unfolds as time); Being is already an appeal to subjectivity" (*Totality and Infinity*, 45).

10. Levinas, "L'écrit et l'oral," 217.

11. Ibid., 221.

12. Plato, *Phaedrus*, in *Plato: The Complete Works*, ed. John M. Cooper (Indianapolis: Hackett, 1997), (275e), p. 552.

13. Levinas, L'écrit et l'oral," 213.

14. Ibid., 217, emphasis added.

15. Emmanuel Levinas, "Pouvoirs et origines," in *Oeuvres 2, Parole et silence* (Paris: Grasset-Imec, 2009),146, emphasis added.

16. On this point, see chapter 1 above.

17. Emmanuel Levinas, "Parole et silence," in *Oeuvres 2, Parole et silence* (Paris: Grasset-Imec, 2009), 82–83, emphasis added.

18. Levinas, "Pouvoirs et origines," 148.

19. Ibid., 148, emphasis added.

20. See Heidegger, *Being and Time*, 105–6, 47.

21. For a detailed explication of this point, see again chapter 1 of the present work.

22. As we have seen, the circulation of the goods of the world, from the One to the Other, can never be understood on the model of an exchange between merchants, because money—as "universal equivalence"—attests to the relativity of the world—always understood within the horizon of possession—namely a world in which speech carries no ethical—that is, thematizing—weight, in which things still lack substance. A world in which social crystallization is reduced to economic exchanges is a world in which the idea of the infinite is completely repressed. Universality, the becoming in-themselves of things, presupposes the full realization of society as the abolition of possessive exclusivism by the eschatological development—announced by *Totality and Infinity*—of ultimate events of being. Things draw their substance from their thematization in language. At the same time, the thematizing power of language ipso facto coincides with its ethical ability to question the possessive self.

23. For example, among several other sequences, "The subject is 'for itself'" (Levinas, *Totality and Infinity*, 87). For Levinas, the concretization of the self, its material and sensible life, do not only bear witness to the insignificant and contingent facticity of the for-itself, but the concrete dimensions from which subjective life finds the material and substantial signification without which, according to Levinas, the transcendental movement of the subject would remain unintelligible. The Levinasian self is thus a for-itself

concretely understood as hunger and egoism but also as a laboring body inhabiting a dwelling: Its "presence 'at home with oneself' exceeds the apparent simplicity the abstract analysis of the 'for itself' finds in it" (ibid., 157).

24. Recall, however, that such a passage is at work from the second to the third section of *Totality and Infinity*. In the first section of the book, Levinas takes as his point of departure the evidence of the situation of interlocution within which we always already find ourselves.

25. "What the *cogito* reveals to us here is just factual necessity: it is found—and this is indisputable—that our being along with its being-for-itself is also for-others; the being which is revealed to the reflective consciousness is for-itself-for-others" (Jean-Paul Sartre, *Being and Nothingness*, trans. Hazel E. Barnes [New York: Philosophical Library, 1956], 282).

26. Note that for Sartre, unlike Levinas, the Other cannot in any way be equated with the for-itself.

27. As we have seen, Levinas's analyses proceed by way of deduction—not by a reduction—that is, through the rupture of the constitutive structures of transcendental phenomenology, in order to bring forward interlocution as the ultimate event of ontology, which undergirds every structure of light, all objective knowledge.

28. Sartre, *Being and Nothingness*, 270.

29. Ibid., 250. Derrida remarks on this point as well, in a critical note addressed as much to Sartre as to Levinas; see Jacques Derrida, "Violence and Metaphysics: An Essay on the Thought of Emmanuel Levinas," in *Writing and Difference* (London: Routledge, 2001), 154n44.

30. Sartre, *Being and Nothingness*, 271–72, emphasis added.

31. Ibid., 250.

32. Ibid., 275.

33. Ibid.

34. Ibid.

35. Ibid., 268.

36. Ibid., 256.

37. Ibid., 263.

38. I will refer to this, in a very preliminary way, as "de-totalized communism."

39. Translator's note: Lingis translates *autrui*, one of two terms that denote the Other in Levinas's work, as "the face" here, which appears in French as *le visage*; I have included the original term in brackets for the sake of clarity. —DW.

40. This explains why, as we have seen, the idea of the infinite provides the time required by labor to organize and thus consolidate the enjoyment of the self. The concrete person possesses the idea of the infinite, which is

to say that he or she labors and is possessed by it. However, "by it" here also means that it is within the horizon of the Other that the world is oriented. In this sense, through language, possession never goes so far as to close itself off within a possessive exclusivism.

41. Here Levinas quotes "Rabbi Johanan in the name of Rabbi Jose b. Kisma (Sanhedrin 103b)," in Emmanuel Levinas, *Difficult Freedom: Essays on Judaism*, trans. Seán Hand (Baltimore: Johns Hopkins University Press, 1990), xiv.

42. Sartre, *Being and Nothingness*, 260.

43. In this regard, the totalization that denies any form of being to the eschatology of peace—by relegating it to the level of opinion and thus lacking ontological consistency—participates in this repression. In proposing an expanded ontology, *Totality and Infinity* announces an inscription within being of events that, up to the present, have not had a place in ontology—that is, have not been understood as events of being.

44. "The evidence of the *cogito*—where knowledge and the known coincide without knowledge having had to be already in operation, where knowledge thus involves no commitment prior to its present commitment, is at each instant at the beginning, is not in *situation* (which, moreover, is what is proper to all *evidence*, a pure experience of the present without condition or past)—cannot satisfy the critical exigency, for the commencement of the *cogito* remains antecedent to it" (*Totality and Infinity*, 85–86).

45. "Desire is a lack of being. It is haunted in its inmost being by the being of which it is desire" (Sartre, *Being and Nothingness*, 88).

46. If what is desired were assimilated or assimilable, desire would run aground on its own metaphysical aspirations. Unlike a need, whose goal is to fill some kind of lack, desire nourishes itself on that which the desired produces beyond desire. Desire maintained in a state of desire engenders neither frustration nor lack because desire is not need. Contra the latter, desire comes to be desired more and more intensely. Such a relation confirms a relation to the desired insofar as the latter coincides not with fulfillment but rather with the increase of the distance that separates the desired from the one who desires—which is to say is accomplished in the nonadequation in which the Other produces itself as transcendent, which is to say speaks, has a face, and stands facing me.

47. It is for this reason that Levinas's analyses of labor do not break with the Hegelian paradigm, but rather reach their fullest expression within the limits of economic immanence.

48. Alexandre Kojève, *Introduction to the Reading of Hegel*, trans. James H. Nichols (New York: Basic Books, 1969), 25.

49. Ibid., 215n15, emphasis added.

50. "The for-itself, as the foundation of itself, is the upsurge of the negation. The for-itself founds itself in so far as it denies in relation to *itself* a certain being or a mode of being. What it denies or nihilates, as we know, is being-in-itself" (Sartre, *Being and Nothingness*, 88).

51. Ibid., 90.

52. Alexandre Koyré, "Hegel à Iena," in *Études d'histoire de la pensée philosophique* (Paris: Gallimard, 1971), 161 (original translation by Daniel Wyche).

7. BEING TOWARD INFINITY

1. Emmanuel Levinas, *Totality and Infinity; An Essay on Exteriority*, trans. Alphonso Lingis (Pittsburgh: Duquesne University Press, 1969), 196. Further references to this title will be by page number within parentheses in the text.

2. See the section titled "Being in Itself: From Silence to Speech," in chapter 5, regarding Rosenzweig.

3. The Hegelian infinite has historically and philosophically "sublated" (*aufheben*) that of Descartes. For that reason, the Cartesian discovery could no longer deploy a genuinely eschatological force of rupture with regard to totalization. The ontological situation to which such a discovery belongs is no longer favorable to a development of being that hinders its speculative recapturing and retranslation as Absolute Spirit.

4. It is here that the analyses of the section titled "The Ethical Relation and Time" distinguish themselves from those of the preface. The goals of these two sections are not the same.

5. Note that Levinas replaces "anxiety" [*angoisse*] with "fear" [*peur*], concepts that, it must be kept in mind, are in no way equivalent in Heidegger.

6. For the deduction of time from alterity, which takes advantage of the preliminaries established in Levinas's investigations here, see "Time and the Other," in *Time and the Other, and Additional Essays*, trans. Richard A. Cohen (Pittsburgh: Duquesne University Press, 1987).

7. "The visible forms, or tends to form, a totality" (*Totality and Infinity*, 243).

8. Translator's Note: Lingis includes the following footnote keyed to the word "discovered": "Throughout this section *découvrir* and its cognates suggest that we understand 'discovering' as an 'uncovering.'"

9. Levinas, *Time and the Other*, 91.

10. Emmanuel Levinas, "Parole et silence," in *Oeuvres 2, Parole et silence* (Paris: Grasset-Imec, 2009), 97.

11. Jean-Paul Sartre, *Being and Nothingness*, trans. Hazel E. Barnes (New York: Philosophical Library 1956), 553.

12. It would be incorrect here to see only an implicit reference to responsibility in the exclusive sense elaborated by Sartre. This association very

much refers us to the Levinasian horizon of responsibility for the Other. To be responsible is to grow old, just as Levinas so clearly affirms in *Otherwise Than Being*: "Subjectivity in ageing is unique, irreplaceable, me and not another; it is despite itself in an obedience where there is no desertion, but where revolt is brewing. These traits exclude one another, but they are resolved in responsibility for another, older than any commitment" (Emmanuel Levinas, *Otherwise Than Being, or Beyond Essence* [Pittsburgh: Duquesne University Press, 1998], 52).

CONCLUSION: INTENTIONALITY AND METAPHYSICS

1. In §9, Tangent III of *On Touching—Jean-Luc Nancy*, Derrida makes the following remarks: "If I have often spoken of pre-originary mourning on this subject [what Derrida calls, following Nancy, "Being Singular Plural"], and tied this motif to that of expropriation, it has been in order to mark that interiorization, in this mourning before death, and even introjection, which we often take for granted in normal mourning, cannot and must not be achieved. Mourning as im-possible mourning—and moreover, ahuman, more than human, prehumen, different from the human "in" the human of humanualism [*l'humainisme*]. Well, despite all the differences separating the discursive way in which I am holding forth at this moment from a discourse in Husserl's style, and probably as well from the great massifs of phenomenology, I do not find this way to have more affinities with the discourse that Husserl obstinately upholds on the subject of appresentation (which I am tempted to extend and radicalize, while paying the price of the necessary displacements—but this is not the place to insist on this) than with the one of a *certain* Merleau-Ponty" (Jacques Derrida, *On Touching—Jean-Luc Nancy*, trans. Christine Irizarry [Stanford, Calif.: Stanford University Press, 2005], 192). In an interview that same year, Derrida could claim that "Husserl must have recognized that in the experience of time and in the experience of the other, his principle of principles, intuitive access to the thing itself, 'in person,' was held in check. Access to an alter ego, for instance, does not offer itself to any originary intuition, only to an analogy, to what is called an analogical 'appresentation.' We are never on the side of the other, of his originary here-and-now; never inside his head, if you like. This is an essential breach in philosophy" ("Others Are Secret because They Are Other," in *Paper Machine* [Stanford, Calif.: Stanford University Press, 2005], 145).

2. Derrida, *On Touching—Jean-Luc Nancy*, 192.

3. Jacques Derrida, "Violence and Metaphysics: An Essay on the Thought of Emmanuel Levinas," in *Writing and Difference* (London: Routledge, 2001), 153. Further references to this title will be by page number preceded by VM within parentheses in the text.

4. Regarding the gesture of the rupture with the totality, Derrida takes issue with the fact that the latter opens up a metaphysics, one of "positive infinity" and "nonnegative transcendence" (VM, 142, 48), there where Derrida maintains a thought of the "other" as "that which does not come to an end, despite my interminable labor and experience" (VM, 142). That experience is always the test of a "disquiet"—which is Difference—toward the infinitely other, which negativity reveals and maintains as beyond, and which, for that reason, can never replace a "positive infinity," and which proceeds from the "negativity of the in-definite"—which is history. In the words with which Derrida concludes his 1961 introduction to Husserl's *Origin of Geometry*, which is inscribed within the same continuity as "Violence and Metaphysics": "The pure and interminable disquietude of thought striving to 'reduce' Difference by going beyond factual infinity toward the infinity of its sense and value, i.e., while maintaining Difference—that disquietude would be transcendental" (*Edmund Husserl's Origin of Geometry: An Introduction*, trans. John P. Leavey [Lincoln: University of Nebraska Press, 1989], 153).

5. For Derrida, following Husserl and contra Levinas, access to the alterity of the Other must pass by the alterity of the ego, which is to say by finitude and history, which entail a "transcendental violence." And yet the relation to alterity—and therefore nonviolence—is imaginable only through the latter: "There is a transcendental and pre-ethical violence, a (general) dissymmetry whose archia is the same, and which eventually permits the inverse dissymmetry, that is, the ethical nonviolence of which Levinas speaks. In effect, either there is only the same, which can no longer even appear and be said, nor even exercise violence (pure infinity or finitude); or indeed there is the same and the other, and then the other cannot be the other—of the same—except by being the same (as itself: ego), and the same cannot be the same (as itself: ego) except by being the other's other: alter ego. That I am also essentially the other's other, and that I know I am, is the evidence of a strange symmetry whose trace appears nowhere in Levinas's descriptions. Without this evidence, I could not desire (or) respect the other in ethical dissymmetry. This transcendental violence, which does not spring from an ethical resolution or freedom, or from a certain way of encountering or exceeding the other, originally institutes the relationship between two finite ipseities. . . . For this transcendental origin, as the irreducible violence of the relation to the other, is at the same time nonviolence, since it opens the relation to the other. It is an economy. And it is this economy which, by this opening, will permit access to the other to be determined, in ethical freedom, as moral violence or nonviolence" (VM, 160).

In other words, we cannot exit the cordon of the finitude of the ego, as it is from these that it becomes possible to think the Other as alter ego.

This recognition thus entails the irreducibility of violence, which is to say the irreducibility of history and the finitude of the ego (which is called, following Husserl, a thought of responsibility). The relation of violence and nonviolence is thus an economy of the same and the other; ethics does not proceed from the latter overwhelming the former in a peace that is "beyond history." In other words, peace only has a sense within the horizon of infinite history. But the latter is not outside of the in-definite game of differ*a*nce, which entails the impossible eschatological suppression of violence within messianic peace, namely a relation to the other liberated from the primacy of the ego, which is to say the violence and/or of responsibility. In effect, "The 'messianic triumph' 'armed against evil's revenge' would have to have been ushered in. This messianic triumph, which is the horizon of Levinas's book, but which 'overflows its framework' (*TI*), could abolish violence only by suspending the difference (conjunction or opposition) between the same and the other, that is, by suspending the *idea* of peace. But here and now (in a present in general), this horizon cannot be stated, an end cannot be stated, eschatology is not possible, except through violence. This infinite passage through violence is what is called history" (VM, 162 [*TI* is the abbreviation used for *Totality and Infinity* in VM]).

It is upon the foundation of this primary violence, that of the ego, that the theme of finitude and therefore that of "infinite responsibility" for history can bring to light, and in so doing render possible, the overture to the other as another ego. Here Derrida defends the Idea of peace as an infinite idea in the Kantian sense, which is to say as an injunction to an infinite responsibility for an indefinite history, without which (responsibility), "the horizon of peace would disappear into the night (worst violence as previolence)" (VM, 162). Further, "To overlook the irreducibility of this last violence, is to revert— within the order of philosophical discourse which one cannot seek to reject, except by risking the worst violence—to an infinitist dogmatism in pre-Kantian style, one which does not pose the question of responsibility for its own finite philosophical discourse. It is true that the delegation of this responsibility to God is not an abdication, God not being a finite third party: thus conceived, divine responsibility neither excludes nor diminishes the integrity of my own responsibility, the responsibility of the finite philosopher. On the contrary, divine responsibility requires and calls for this latter responsibility, as its *telos* or its origin. But the fact of the inadequation of these two responsibilities, or of this unique responsibility for itself—this history or anxiety of the infinite—is not yet" (VM, 162–63).

It is thus its anchorage in the finitude of the ego (which entails the irreducibility of violence) which conditions the possibility of a historical responsibility that would permit the ego to open itself to the alterity of the other insofar as it emerges as alter ego, which is to say that it never puts a stop to indefinite history as economy or differ*a*nce of the same and the other. Derrida thus assumes a completely Husserlian position in this text, to the point of recognizing something primordial in the theme of finitude in its relation to history and thus as the establishment of a possible relation to originary violence: "Nothing can appear outside the appurtenance to 'my world' for 'I am'" (VM, 164). Derrida then immediately cites Husserl's *Formal and Transcendental Logic*: "Whether it is suitable or not, whether it appears to me monstrous (due to whatever prejudices) or not, I must stand firm before the primordial fact (*die Urtatsache, der ich standhalten muss*), from which I cannot turn my glance for an instant, as a philosopher" (Husserl, *Formal and Transcendental Logic* [1969], 237, cited in VM). Further on, Derrida continues this meditation: "Let us note in passing that the "subjective a priori" recognized by transcendental phenomenology is the only possible way to check the totalitarianism of the neutral, the impersonal 'absolute Logic,' that is, eschatology without dialogue and everything classed under the conventional—quite conventional—rubric of Hegelianism" (VM, 164–65).

    6. For an elaboration of this point, see Raoul Moati, *Derrida et le langage ordinaire* (Paris: Hermann, 2014).

    7. Derrida, *Edmund Husserl's Origin of Geometry*, 134.

    8. Ibid., 135.

    9. This is what will justify, for Derrida, the deconstruction of the aspects of phenomenology most resistant to its teleology.

    10. As we have seen in chapter 3, this already constituted the leitmotif of Levinas's interpretation in "The Ruin of Representation (1959)," in *Discovering Existence with Husserl* (Evanston, Ill.: Northwestern University Press, 1998).

    11. Derrida is here referring to the preface of *Totality and Infinity*, in which Levinas asks, "What does it matter if in the Husserlian phenomenology taken literally these unsuspected horizons are in their turn interpreted as thoughts aiming at objects!" (Emmanuel Levinas, *Totality and Infinity: An Essay on Exteriority*, trans. Alphonso Lingis [Pittsburgh: Duquesne University Press, 1969], 28). I have, for my part, attempted to show in the body of the present work that there is a certain injustice in not considering the extent to which Levinas's "intentionality of enjoyment" is grounded in the overcoming of intention by itself, from which the nocturnal exceeding of representation by the sensible results. There is no doubt that this is the passage Derrida is referring to when he asks, "Who better than Levinas first gave us to understand these Husserlian themes?" (VM, 150).

    12. Levinas, *Totality and Infinity*, 22.

    13. Ibid., 181.

14. Ibid., 195.

15. Emmanuel Levinas, "Parole et silence," in *Oeuvres 2, Parole et silence* (Paris: Grasset-Imec, 2009), 78.

16. Considerations such as these will doubtlessly carry us beyond Levinas, beyond the letter of his text at least, even if the latter does not omit to insist, contra the ontological idealism of Hegel and Heidegger, on the importance of those material conditions without which the advent of sociality—of social life—would remain perfectly hollow.

Aristotle. *Metaphysics*. In *The Basic Works of Aristotle*, edited by Richard McKeon. New York: Random House, 1941.

Benoist, Jocelyn. "Le cogito levinassien: Levinas et Descartes." In *Positivité et transcendance, suivi de "Lévinas et la phénoménologie,"* edited by Jean-Luc Marion, 105–22. Paris: PUF, 2000.

Calin, Rodolphe. "La métaphore absolue, le faux départ vers l'autrement qu'être." *Les cahiers de philosophie de l'Université de Caen*, no. 49 (2012).

———. *Levinas et l'exception du soi*. Paris: PUF, 2005.

Char, René. *Furor and Mystery and Other Writings*. Translated by Mary Ann Caws and Nancy Kline. Boston: Black Widow Press, 2010.

Courtine, Jean-François. "L'ontologie fondamentale d'Emmanuel Levinas." In *Emmanuel Levinas et les territoires de la pensée*, edited by D. Cohen-Levinas and B. Clément. Paris: PUF, 2007.

Dastur, Françoise. "Espace, lieu, habitation." In *Heidegger et la pensée à venir*. Paris: Vrin, 2011.

Derrida, Jacques. *Edmund Husserl's Origin of Geometry: An Introduction*. Translated by John P. Leavey. Lincoln: University of Nebraska Press, 1989.

———. *On Touching—Jean-Luc Nancy*. Translated by Christine Irizarry. Stanford, Calif.: Stanford University Press, 2005.

———. "Others Are Secret because They Are Other." In *Paper Machine*, 136–63. Stanford, Calif.: Stanford University Press, 2005.

———. "Violence and Metaphysics: An Essay on the Thought of Emmanuel Levinas." In *Writing and Difference*, 97–192. London: Routledge, 2001.

Franck, Didier. *Dramatique des phénomènes*. Paris: PUF, 2001.

———. *L'un-pour-l'autre*. Paris: PUF, 2008.

Heidegger, Martin. *Being and Time*. Translated by John Macquarrie and Edward Robinson. Oxford: Blackwell, 2001.

———. *The Essence of Reasons*. Translated by Terrence Malik. Evanston, Ill.: Northwestern University Press, 1969.

———. *Introduction to Metaphysics*. Translated by Gregory Fried and Richard Polt. New Haven, Conn.: Yale University Press, 2014.

———. *On the Way to Language.* Translated by Peter D. Hertz. New York: Harper and Row, 1971.

Husserl, Edmund. *Cartesian Meditations.* Translated by Dorion Cairns. The Hague: Martinus Nijhoff, 1960.

———. *Formal and Transcendental Logic.* Translated by Dorion Cairns. The Hague: Martinus Nijhoff, 1969.

Kojève, Alexandre. *Introduction to the Reading of Hegel.* Translated by James H. Nichols. New York: Basic Books, 1969.

Koyré, Alexandre. "Hegel à Iena." In *Études d'histoire de la pensée philosophique.* Paris: Gallimard, 1971.

Levinas, Emmanuel. *Difficult Freedom: Essays on Judaism.* Translated by Seán Hand. Baltimore: Johns Hopkins University Press, 1990.

———. *Discovering Existence with Husserl.* Evanston, Ill.: Northwestern University Press, 1998.

———. *Existence and Existents.* Translated by Alphonso Lingis. Pittsburgh: Duquesne University Press, 2001.

———. "L'écrit et l'oral." In *Oeuvres 2, Parole et silence.* Paris: Grasset-Imec, 2009.

———. "Martin Heidegger and Ontology." *Diacritics* 26, no. 1 (1996): 11–32.

———. *Otherwise Than Being, or Beyond Essence.* Pittsburgh: Duquesne University Press, 1998.

———. "Parole et silence." In *Oeuvres 2, Parole et silence.* Paris: Grasset-Imec, 2009.

———. "Pouvoirs et origines." In *Oeuvres 2, Parole et silence.* Paris: Grasset-Imec, 2009.

———. "The Proximity of the Other." Translated by Michael F. Smith. In *Alterity and Transcendence.* New York: Columbia University Press, 1999.

———. "Questions and Answers." Translated by Bettina Bergo. In *Of God Who Comes to Mind.* Stanford, Calif.: Stanford University Press, 1998.

———. "The Ruin of Representation (1959)." In *Discovering Existence with Husserl,* 111–21. Evanston, Ill.: Northwestern University Press, 1998.

———. *The Theory of Intuition in Husserl's Phenomenology.* Evanston, Ill.: Northwestern University Press, 1995.

———. *Time and the Other, and Additional Essays.* Translated by Richard A. Cohen. Pittsburgh: Duquesne University Press, 1987.

———. *Totalité et infini: Essai sur l'extériorité.* Paris: Livre de Poche, 1990.

———. *Totality and Infinity: An Essay on Exteriority.* Translated by Alphonso Lingis. Duquesne Studies, Philosophical Series. Pittsburgh: Duquesne University Press, 1969.

———. "The Trace of the Other." In *Deconstruction in Context,* edited by Mark C. Taylor. Chicago: University of Chicago Press, 1986.

―――. "The Work of Edmund Husserl (1940)." In *Discovering Existence with Husserl*. Evanston, Ill.: Northwestern University Press, 1998.

Moati, Raoul. "De l'intentionalité à la pulsionalité, la subjectivation du *Todestrieb*." *Studia Phenomenologia* X (2010).

―――. *Derrida et le langage ordinaire*. Paris: Hermann, 2014.

―――. *Événements nocturnes: Essai sur Totalité et infini*. Paris: Hermann, 2012.

Mosès, Stéphane. "Rosenzweig et Levinas: Au-dèla de la guerre." *Rue Descartes, Emmanuel Levinas*, no. 19 (1998): 85–98.

Nietzsche, Friedrich Wilhelm. *The Anti-Christ*. In *The Anti-Christ, Ecce Homo, Twilight of the Idols, and Other Writings*. Cambridge: Cambridge University Press, 2005.

―――. *Daybreak: Thoughts on the Prejudices of Morality*. Cambridge: Cambridge University Press, 1997.

―――. *Twilight of the Idols*. In *The Anti-Christ, Ecce Homo, Twilight of the Idols, and Other Writings*. Cambridge: Cambridge University Press, 2005.

Nordmann, Sophie. *Philosophie et Judaïsme*. Philosophies. Paris: PUF, 2008.

Plato. *Phaedrus*. In *Plato: The Complete Works*, edited by John M. Cooper. Indianapolis: Hackett, 1997.

"Quelque chose qui ne se voit pas, mais qui parle: Entretien avec Jocelyn Benoist." In *Lire Totalité et infini d'Emmanuel Levinas: Etudes et interprétations*, edited by Danielle Cohen-Levinas. Paris: Editions Hermann, 2011.

Sartre, Jean-Paul. *Being and Nothingness*. Translated by Hazel E. Barnes. New York: Philosophical Library 1956.

―――. "Intentionality: A Fundamental Idea of Husserl's Phenomenology." Translated by Chris Turner. In *Critical Essays (Situations I)*. New York: Seagull Books, 2010.

Taminiaux, Jacques. "Un autre lecture de l'histoire de la philosophie." In *Sillages phénoménologiques, auditeurs et lectures de Heidegger*, 227–52. Brussels: Ousia, 2002.

Valéry, Paul. *Variety*. Translated by Malcolm Cowley. New York: Harcourt, Brace, 1927.

CPSIA information can be obtained
at www.ICGtesting.com
Printed in the USA
BVOW00s2207071216
470023BV00001B/26/P

9 780823 273201